Dan Ge Performance

Dan Ge Performance

MASKS AND MUSIC IN CONTEMPORARY CÔTE D'IVOIRE

Daniel B. Reed

INDIANA
University Press
Bloomington & Indianapolis

Publication of this book is made possible in part with the assistance of a Challenge Grant from the National Endowment for the Humanities, a federal agency that supports research, education, and public programming in the humanities.

This book is a publication of
Indiana University Press
601 North Morton Street
Bloomington, IN 47404-3797 USA

http://iupress.indiana.edu

Telephone orders 800-842-6796
Fax orders 812-855-7931
Orders by e-mail iuporder@indiana.edu

The paper used in this publication meets the minimum requirements of American National Standard for Information Sciences—Permanence of Paper for Printed Library Materials, ANSI Z39.48-1984.

Manufactured in the United States of America

Library of Congress Cataloging-in-Publication Data

Reed, Daniel B. (Daniel Boyce), date
    Dan Ge performance : masks and music in contemporary
Côte d'Ivoire / Daniel B. Reed.
        p. cm.—(African expressive cultures)
Includes bibliographical references and index.
    ISBN 0-253-34270-8 (alk. paper)—ISBN 0-253-21612-5
(pbk. : alk. paper)
    1. Dan (African people)—Rites and ceremonies.   2. Dance—
Anthropological aspects—Côte d'Ivoire.   3. Dan (African
people)—Music.   I. Title.   II. Series.
    DT545.45.D34 R44 2003
    793.3'196668—dc21
                                                            2002154305

1 2 3 4 5 08 07 06 05 04 03

Dedicated to the revival
of the spirit of peace,
unity,
and tolerance in Côte d'Ivoire

Contents

PREFACE AND ACKNOWLEDGMENTS

All ethnographic research for this book was conducted prior to 1999, when the first coup in Ivorian history brought to an end the long period during which Côte d'Ivoire was known as a haven of peace, stability, tolerance, and relative prosperity in the West African region. In September 2002, as this book was in press, another coup attempt was made which quickly descended into a civil war that has divided the country. At the time of this writing, a fragile cease-fire is holding, but the conflict is far from resolved. Worst of all, the ethnic, religious, and regional tensions that are central to this conflict, and which have worsened considerably since the death of Félix Houphet-Boigny in 1993, have in the context of this conflict reached the level of a humanitarian crisis. Muslims and northern immigrants, once drawn to Côte d'Ivoire because of its economic opportunity and openness to foreigners, are either hiding out in mosques or fleeing the government-held areas of the country following weeks of harassment and violent attacks. Meanwhile, tens of thousands are fleeing the rebel-held north in search of food and shelter. At the time of publication, where this crisis is headed is unknown, but what is clear is that the cosmopolitan Côte d'Ivoire described in this book is now history, having been replaced by a country torn apart by tensions that for nearly four decades were transcended for the common good.

As a result of this crisis, communication with my consultants has been even more difficult than usual. I have received word from only a few of my consultants and colleagues, via e-mail; at time of press, I do not know how most of the people central to this book are faring in this time of crisis. Thus I begin this book with a declaration of hope not only that my consultants and colleagues all are safe and well but that, somehow, a peaceful solution can be found that will guide the country out of this morass and back to the kind of tolerance and stability that formerly characterized Côte d'Ivoire.

This book results from the collective efforts of many people to whom I owe gratitude, especially my dear consultants and colleagues in Côte d'Ivoire. First and foremost I thank my primary consultants Biemi Gba Jacques, Gueu Gbe Gonga Alphonse, Goueu Tia Jean-Claude, Gba Ernest, Gba Gama, Oulai Théodore, Mameri Tia Thomas, and Amso Edomtchi. To these primary consultants and to the many other Ivorians who were so generous with their time, I offer profound thanks, particularly for their permission to use the results of our interactions in publication. I also thank everyone at L'Institut National Superieur des Arts et de l'Action Culturelle, especially my mentors and friends Paul Dagri and Adépo Yapo. The staff at Centre Culturel Americain I thank for their support and help. Thanks as well to Biemi Alain for his eleventh-hour e-mail translation assistance. For their friendship and hospitality during stints in Abidjan, I thank the Dagri and Yapo families and fellow Fulbrighters Susanna DeBusk and Melissa Martin. I express deep appreciation to the Biemi family in Biélé and the Mameri family in Déoulé for their generous hospitality during our periodic stays in their compounds. My friends Emmanuel and Nana Fremah Yankey of Yamoussoukro deserve special thanks not only for their hospitality but also for nursing me back to health in 1994. Finally, I thank my first research assistant Tiemoko Guillaume and his family for putting me up, putting up with me, and introducing me to Dan life during the summer of 1994.

I also have many people on the western side of the Atlantic to thank for this book's outcome. To many people I owe thanks for their repeated and careful readings of early drafts of this work, for their helpful discussions and debates, and for their inspiration, guidance, and concern. Ruth M. Stone has been a mentor in every sense of the word. She has consistently encouraged and nurtured my work, even and especially when I felt like I was going out on a limb, and for this I thank her profoundly. Thanks to Patrick McNaughton for his inspired view of art and his ever-present sense of humor. Sue Tuohy I thank for reminding me to write from my passion and to stay in touch with why ethnomusicology matters. I thank Roger Janelli for his kind yet critical feedback and John W. Johnson for his enthusiasm and encouragement. Thanks also to Bill Siegmann and an anonymous reader who offered insightful comments that were particularly instrumental in determining the book's final form.

Many others have offered ideas, challenges, practical advice, and vital training. I thank Kassim Koné, Emmanuel Yankey, Patrick O'Meara, Brian Winchester, Henry Glassie, John McDowell, Dorothy Lee, Beverly Stoeltje, Michael Jackson, Paula Girshick, Lester Monts, and the late Ronald Smith for all they have contributed to my development as a scholar. To Ruth Aten, Camille Rice, Velma Carmichael, Jan Thoms, and Susan Harris I offer sincere thanks for their patience and support. I thank Hande Birkalan and Susan Oehler for spirited conversation and for reading early dissertation chapter drafts. John and Erica Lindamood I thank for their insightful readings of paper drafts and proposals over the years. Thanks to my brother Tim Reed for helping with the challenging Zaouli transcription, and to Alan Burdette at the SAVAIL Lab at I.U. for helping me stretch Finale in order to render this transcription on computer. Rob Grossman, thanks for the fabulous photo. Thanks to my cohorts in Monkey Puzzle Nils Fredland, Nicole Serena Kousaleos, Jerry McIlvain, and Dan Schumacher for keeping me laughing through the many stressful years of research and writing.

I thank my parents, in-laws, and brothers for taking care of finances and pets and storing belongings during our time abroad and for their support of my work and their love, which I return a millionfold.

To Dee Mortensen and Jane Lyle at Indiana University Press and copy editor Kate Babbitt, I offer thanks for helping me fine-tune and improve this book. I have especially valued my relationship with Dee, whose support and constructive criticism over the past three years have made this a better book. Dee, *i nwe baara mun* (thank you for the work).

Two people deserve not only my deepest gratitude but also direct and substantial credit for this project's outcome. These are the members of our 1997 "research team" Biemi Gba Jacques and Nicole Serena Kousaleos. Jacques was much more than a research assistant; he was also a friend, a roommate, and a consultant. Our conversations sparked many important breakthroughs in my research. His spirit occupies these pages.

My wife Nicole Serena Kousaleos put her own studies on hold to travel with me in 1997. I cannot imagine this book without her. In the field, she nursed me through many illnesses, coached me through culture shock and the psychological trials of fieldwork, offered methodological and theoretical advice at critical junctures, and repeatedly helped me to see the big picture when I was drowning in a sea of ethnographic detail. Her insight and intuition helped guide this research toward its present focus. Back in the United States, she read and reread drafts of chapters and reminded me to write from experience. At every step of the way she has been generous with her support of my research. Her belief in my ability and in the value of this endeavor has sustained me through frequent bouts of doubt. Nicole, my partner and inspiration, a thousand *barika*s could not express the depth of my love and appreciation.

Finally, I thank my children Zoë Jade and Adrian Sian, who bring indescribable joy to my life.

Fieldwork upon which this book is based was funded by a Fulbright scholarship from the Institute for International Education (1997), a Richard M. Dorson Dissertation Research Grant from the Indiana University Folklore Institute (1997), and a Pre-Dissertation Travel Grant from the Indiana University African Studies Program (1994). Translations of works from German into English were funded by a New Faculty Grant from the University of North Carolina at Greensboro Office of Research Services (1999). All field recordings (video, DAT, and analog cassettes) upon which this book is based are deposited in the Indiana University Archives of Traditional Music (Accession number 98-005-F).

Much of this book is a revision of my dissertation (Reed 1999), while portions of the narrative about the PDCI party, and the associated analysis, are also found in an article in *Africa Today* (Reed 2001).

A Web site featuring excerpts of audio and video field recordings and additional photographs relevant to this text can be found at http://iupress.indiana.edu/reed/.

NOTES ON LANGUAGE

Research for this book was conducted in French, Dan, and Jula. Biemi Gba Jacques helped me to translate most Dan materials into French. I alone am responsible for translation of materials from French and Jula into English, including French-language publications. To avoid encumbering the flow of the text, I generally reproduce in this book only the English translations, with the exception of song texts and some spoken texts from performances, which appear both in the original language and English. Rather than constantly repeating translation credits, I offer credit and profound thanks to Jacques here. Jacques' translating work is but one of his many contributions without which this book would not have been possible.

Although I recognize the value of criticisms against using colonial-language spellings (see Conrad and Frank 1995, ix; and Charry 1996), I use French spellings for people and place names, because Ivorians do. In other words, town and city names are as they can be found on most maps, and spellings of peoples' names are as they would themselves write them (with the minor exception that Ivorians tend to capitalize all letters of family names). Most Ivorian names begin with the family name and end with the given name, as in "Biemi (family name) Gba (middle name, also a family name) Jacques (given name)." I have chosen not to reverse this custom (and place given names first as is common in the United States) in order to identify and represent people as they would in their home context.

With some misgivings, I have chosen to use the ethnic group name "Dan." The history of naming these people and of them naming themselves is long and complex (see, for example, Holsoe and Lauer 1976). Scholars use the term "Dan" to refer to the large cluster of peoples who straddle the Ivorian/Liberian border. On the Liberian side, they are generally called "Gio," while Dan living in Côte d'Ivoire are usually called "Yakuba."[1] In my experience, Ivorian Dan identified themselves with a variety of terms according to context, affirming the idea that identity, and especially ethnic identity, is situational. In French-speaking circles and when identifying themselves to the outside world, my consultants usually identified themselves as "Yakuba." Certain of my consultants, however, interchanged "Yakuba" and "Dan" in these contexts. When speaking Dan, though,

---

1. The origins of this term are disputed, though many attribute it to a communication mishap in a colonial encounter; as the story goes, French colonial officers, when they first encountered Dan people, asked them what they call themselves. The Dan, of course, did not understand French, and speaking among themselves, kept repeating "*ya pö nin ɓa*" or "he said," which somehow was badly transliterated as "Yakuba" and misconstrued as a response identifying their ethnicity (Holsoe and Lauer 1976).

several different terms were common. In Dan, younger people tended to call themselves "Yaba" (which, according to Biemi Gba Jacques, is a "French-influenced" word, meaning a Dan-ized version of the French invention "Yakuba"), while older people preferred "Danwopömɛn" (person who speaks Dan). Meanwhile, nearly all scholars, including Dan scholars, use the term "Dan" in their publications. I was very tempted to use the term "Yakuba," despite its reputed colonialist origins, because it is the term my consultants most often used to identify themselves to the outside, but "Dan" is the term that will be recognized both by my consultants and the academic community.

No less challenging is writing the Dan language. The previous literature on the Dan presents a variety of orthographic approaches. As is the case with studies of all historically oral languages, orthography is affected by the way the person writing hears the language, which is influenced by this person's native language. As far as I know, only scholars at the Société Internationale de Linguistique (SIL) in Abidjan have attempted to standardize Dan orthography (Baba, Deli, Bolli, and Flik 1994). SIL scholars have made excellent efforts toward creating a single set of orthographic characters for use in all sixty Ivorian languages, and they write Dan with those characters. I have borrowed certain elements of their work here and combine them with my own background in northern Mande languages to create what I hope is a system that will be comfortable for English speakers. Dan is a tonal language, with between three to five distinct tones, depending on regional dialect. I have chosen not to include tone marks here, both to encourage legibility for readers of English and because my linguistic training is insufficient to handle this difficult matter well.

Following is the orthography I have used for writing the Dan language. Consonants are as in English with the following exceptions:

Sound	Description	Dan example	English meaning
ɓ	implosive "b"; imagine beginning with an "m" and moving toward a "b," all in one sound	*ɓaa*	drum
ɗ	implosive "d"; imagine beginning with an "n" and moving toward a "d," all in one sound	*ɗe*	mother
gb	"g" and "b" together in one sound	*gbin*	heavy
kp	"k" and "p" together in one sound	*kpɛɛ*	dry
ŋ	"ng" as in English "so<u>ng</u>"	*gbuŋ*	iron pellet

Vowels are as follows:

Sound	English Approximate	Dan example	English meaning
a	f*a*ther	*da*	enter
e	b*a*te	*we*	nothing
ɛ	b*e*t	*kwɛwo*	sound of hand-claps
ë	b*u*t	*dë*	father
i	b*ea*t	*yi*	water
o	b*oa*t	*do*	know
ɔ	b*ou*ght	*kɔ*	hand
ö	somewhat like w*ou*ld in English, more like p*eu* in French	*pö*	say
u	b*oo*t	*gu*	within

Some vowels can also occur in long form, doubling the length of the vowel, as in "*gblɛɛn*" (long, tall). Vowels may also occur in nasalized form, as in the name of the city, "Man," or the ethnic group "Dan." In these cases, the /n/ should not be pronounced more than is needed to connote nasalization. Thus, "Man" is *not* pronounced like the opposite of "woman" in English, but more like "ma" of "mama" with a more nasalized ending. This sound is more familiar to French speakers, as in "*blanc.*" Lastly, the plural is formed in Dan by the addition of the suffix "*nu,*" as in "*ɓaanu*" (drums) or "*genu.*"

CAST OF CHARACTERS

In contrast to most previous studies of Dan *genu,* my focus here is on people and the roles and meanings of this performance complex in their lives. It was my goal to understand Ge from multiple perspectives, and many people contributed significantly to this research. I learned a lot from those individuals, too numerous to name here, who perform regularly as part of the Gedro and Gegbadë groups; many of them appear in the pages of this book, either in narratives or quotes. But of the many people who have taught me about Ge, several are especially central to this book, and I would like to introduce them here.

No one is more important to this book than Biemi Gba Jacques. Jacques played many roles in this research. I hired him to work with me as a research assistant, to help me make contacts, navigate unfamiliar cultural territory, interpret events and recordings, document events, and translate recorded materials. He did all these well and went far beyond mere "assistance," frequently suggesting important directions in the research and taking initiative to explore certain areas on his own accord, which provided me with useful information I might otherwise have lacked. And yet, being an initiated Dan man, Jacques also served as one of my most important consultants, teaching me a great deal about Ge and his interpretations of Dan life.

Jacques was uniquely well positioned to help me in this research. The eldest son of a university professor and a secondary school teacher, Jacques was born in France while his father was attending graduate school. Jacques did not, however, grow up abroad; rather, shortly after his birth his parents shipped him back to his mother's family in the small village of Biélé, north of Man. There Jacques spent the first five years of his life, living in the compound of his grandfather (the village chief), his three wives, and their many children. When his parents returned to Côte d'Ivoire for teaching positions, Jacques rejoined them in the nation's largest city of Abidjan, where he has lived from the age of 5 until today. Throughout his youth, however, Jacques returned to Biélé for summers.

Because of this personal history, Jacques is an interesting combination of insider and outsider with regard to his family's home village and his identity as a Dan person. Though he is considered and considers himself a native son of Biélé, his friends and family who have spent their lives there jokingly call him "our foreigner." Jacques is deeply rooted in Dan tradition and is worldly. This combination made him an excellent research collaborator, as he understood equally the traditions of Ge and of academe. An enthusiastic learner, Jacques viewed his participation in my research as a continuation of his initiation. Village-initiated and city smart, gregarious yet pensive, playful yet methodical, Jacques' spirit occupies this book, which would not have been possible without him.

Much of my basic introduction to the philosophy of Ge came from my conversations with a charismatic elder with a gift for oratory named Gueu Gbe Gonga Alphonse. Monsieur Gueu Gbe has been called "the sage of sages" by

Man mayor Bouys Philippe.[1] Gueu Gbe earned this reputation by working for years in local politics; he is today retired from his position as director of the Man office of the federal Direction of Tourism. Widely revered in the Man region for his cultural acumen, Gueu Gbe even in his retirement is frequently consulted by local politicians regarding cultural affairs. Gueu Gbe, Biemi Gba Jacques said, is like an elder guardian of a metaphorical sacred house of Dan tradition in the contemporary urban setting of Man.

My music teachers not only taught me how to sing and drum but also provided me with some of my richest material on the workings and meanings of Ge in their lives. I learned about drumming in Ge performance, and much, much more, from a brash and brilliant young man named Goueu Tia Jean-Claude. Jean-Claude was unique in that he had earned the role of master drummer in Ge performances when only in his early 20s. A true prodigy, Jean-Claude is quick-witted and intense, and these qualities are as present in his drumming as in his general demeanor. I studied singing and song texts with farmer and Ge performer Gba Ernest. An elder who is recognized in the Man region for his dazzling singing and masterful and creative drumming, Gba Ernest was a kind and patient teacher. His laughter and benedictions still ring in my ears.

Gba Gama, bar owner and youth president in Petit Gbapleu (Man), is the point man for the cultural revival that has occurred in his neighborhood. Though not himself a Ge performer, Gba Gama's organizational skill and belief in the value of Ge has enabled him to attract many young people to "the tradition." He applied these same skills to help me in my research, and I learned much about entertainment *genu,* among other things, thanks to his assistance. Oulai Théodore, head of the sacred house in Grand Gbapleu where Gegbadë resides, invited me into the world of more highly sacred *genu.* An intellectual in his mid-30s, Théodore is known throughout the Man region and beyond as a leading expert in the arts of healing and solving sorcery-related conflicts. Finally, I thank Mameri Tia Thomas for arranging for me to learn about the Yam Festival and life in his beautiful and troubled village of Déoulé. Tia lives in two worlds at once, working both as a traditional healer and for the Man office of the Bureau of Agricultural Development. Charismatic, comedic, and complicated, Tia is like a trickster figure, and every day with him and/or in his village was as unpredictable as the wind. But through him, I learned much about Ge spirituality and conflict, which, for better or worse, is an important aspect of the world of Ge.

Of the many nonperformers who contributed to my understanding of Ge, probably none was more important than Madame Amso Edomtchi.[2] A powerful, outspoken woman of Dida ethnicity, Edomtchi's struggles with violent sorcery-related conflict in her family led her to call upon Gegbadë for help. In so doing, Edomtchi expanded her Christian beliefs and problem-solving strategies, syncretically incorporating Ge into her life and her understanding of the world. Despite the tragedy engulfing Edomtchi and her family, her interactions with me

---

1. Mayor Bouys made this comment in his opening remarks at the first annual Gueheva Festival in Man on March 28, 1997.

2. Throughout this book, I generally use peoples' real names in order to accord personal agency and give credit where credit is due. I have chosen, however, to use pseudonyms for Amso Edomtchi and her family, whose real names I am protecting as per their request because of the gravity of their situation.

were always filled with humor and a deep sense of commitment to hope. That this fast-talking charismatic woman welcomed me to study her profound struggles and life-altering decisions meant a great deal to me and is a testament to her indomitable spirit.

Dan Ge Performance

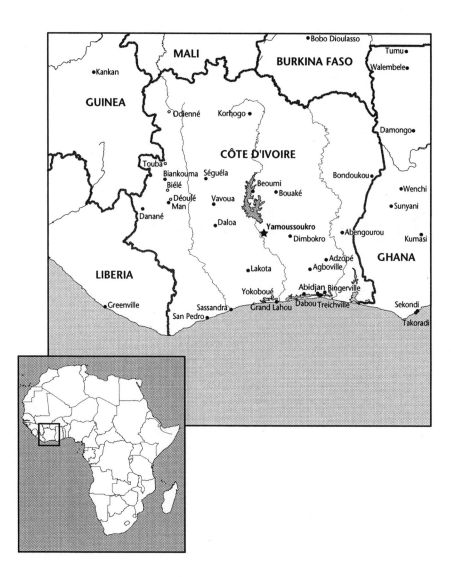

I would prefer if when you begin your book that you
remember that in the Dan region, the thing that you people
call "mask" is called "*ge*" . . . and that in the Dan region,
people who speak French refuse for "*ge*" to be called "mask."

—GUEU GBE GONGA ALPHONSE, SEPTEMBER 1, 1997,
MAN, CÔTE D'IVOIRE

INTRODUCTION

Talking about Ge

The subject of this book is the performance of a multifaceted religious and artistic
phenomenon that the Dan people of western Côte d'Ivoire call Ge. Ge, which in
scholarly literature has been translated as "mask," appears among humans as a
dancing and musical embodiment of Dan social ideals and beliefs. *Genu* (plural)
are most fundamentally part of a pantheon of spirit intermediaries between people
and God. Most of my Dan consultants agree that the spirits who manifest as *genu*
originate in the wilderness, in certain mountains, trees, or streams of the forest
environment that surrounds human settlements in the Dan homeland region. Each
ge manifests in a particular way in performance in the world of humans. Most
but not all *ge* manifestations include a masked dancer and specific music sound.
Many *genu* dance to an ensemble of three to four drums, a gourd rattle, and a
mixed chorus. Each *ge* manifests for particular reasons. There are *genu* for rejoicing and entertainment, *genu* who direct initiation, *genu* who enforce fire reg-
ulations during the dry season, and *genu* who act as judges to settle conflicts, to
cite just a few examples. Ge is furthermore the spiritual base of the experiential
education taught during initiation, which includes a philosophy of social ideals,
values, and ethics involving proper behavior for adults in Dan society. As such,
for many Dan who continue to practice what they often call "the tradition," or
"the religion of our ancestors," Ge is at the root of Dan identity, of what it means
to be Dan.[1]

During the colonial and postcolonial eras, Dan have experienced dramatic
changes that have had direct implications for Ge and Ge performance. Postcolonial life in the city of Man features increasing religious and ethnic diversity, a
complex diversified economy, increased mobility, mass media and mass communications, and a nation-state governmental infrastructure, all of which affect
the practice of Ge. In Ge performance, people draw upon an old performance
complex, with its inherent mutability, flexibility, and efficacy, to employ communicative strategies that enable them to accomplish goals in relationship to an
increasingly pluralistic world.

Participants in Ge performance create both community and conflict, negotiating multiple, multifaceted identities in the process. My consultants use Ge performance to maintain connection to the ancestors and spirits central to their notions of Dan religious and ethnic identity while simultaneously positioning themselves vis-à-vis the new realities—peoples, institutions, and ways of life— of their world.[2] Through Ge performance, people are entertained, and performers generate income for themselves and for their struggling local and national bureaus of tourism. Through Ge performance, people solve disputes and create dissention. Through Ge performance, my Dan consultants enact and legitimate their own power relationships. Governmental officials use Ge performance to validate their own power and importance. People accomplish these and other goals by manipulating pathways of communication, some older (e.g., numerous intermediaries between human and spirit worlds), some newer (e.g., mass media, mass communications, and ethnographic researchers), but most involving music in some way.

Music, the fuel that drives Ge performance, has received little attention in the literature on Dan *genu;* I will emphasize the centrality of sound to the performance of Ge. In Ge music (*getan*), performers find aesthetic resources that they manipulate to realize tasks at hand. This is true for both of the *genu* most central to this book: Gegbadë and Gedro. Gegbadë (lit., father of Gba [a family name] *ge*) performers use music to attract the spiritual power that enables them to solve sorcery conflicts and heal, manifesting Dan spiritual powers in collaboration with the Ivorian judiciary to combat socially destructive spiritual behaviors. Gedro (lit., frog *ge*) performs to manifest excellence in dance, incorporating popular-music references to make the enactment of Dan ethnic and religious identity relevant in the ethnically and religiously diverse context of 1990s Man. In performances of both Gedro and Gegbadë, *ge* music serves as the primary means through which participants accomplish their goals.

Ge performance exists in the world, and the world is present in Ge performance. During Ge manifestations, performers invoke other Dan *genu* and spirits, they reference Allah and Jesus, they incorporate songs and rhythms from other genres of Dan music and mass-mediated popular music, they sing and speak in numerous languages, they make reference to technology such as telephones and televisions, and they weave these and many other intertextual references together, creating a complex pastiche of sound, words, and images.[3] The inherently intertextual process of Ge performance creation bears a great deal of resemblance to the processes of African popular-music creation as described by numerous researchers (Barber and Waterman 1995; Collins and Richards 1982; Turino 2000; Waterman 1990a, 1990b; Wondji 1983). Collins and Richards observe that "an important part of the appeal of 'popular' music in West Africa is the range of references upon which it is based, and the delight an audience takes in decoding these influences and quotations" (1982, 131, in Barber and Waterman 1995, 257). Like their pop-musician counterparts, Ge performers cull influences (both aesthetic and spiritual) from a wide variety of sources and recontextualize them in Ge performances, inscribing them with new meanings in the process. That these processes are evident in this "traditional" (as defined by the performers themselves) performance intrigued me, as genre-mixing and the unmooring of signs from their original contexts are features typically associated with postmodernism and "creolized" popular artistic forms (cf. Barber and Waterman 1995). Interethnic, interreligious, in interaction with everything from forest spirits to federal officials, Ge performance is a pathway of communication through which my consultants relate to their world and get things done.

This book explores how and why a traditional performance complex can hold relevance for people in a cosmopolitan contemporary West African setting. For Ge performers, the decision to embrace "the tradition" in response to competing forces (e.g., Islam or popular music) does not represent a step backward toward a static practice from a purer time. Rather, Ge is a dynamic, vibrant phenomenon that is as complex, as cosmopolitan, and as modern as are the performers themselves. Performers and other practitioners view their decision to embrace Ge as a step forward, using resources from the past that they strategically reshape to help them deal with their contemporary lives. This book shows that contemporary Africans can express fully modern identities through what they define as a traditional expressive form.

WHY "GE?"

Some of my consultants requested that I use the term "Ge," and not "mask," in my publications. I am more than happy to honor their requests. Even a cursory glance at the first paragraph will reveal that Ge is far more than a "mask."[4] Using the term "Ge" is ethnographically sound, since no appropriate translation for the word exists, and ethically responsible, since it was the request of some of my most important consultants. I use the capitalized word "Ge" as a proper noun to refer to the philosophy, the education, and the institutional aspects of this phenomenon, and the lowercase "*ge*" to refer to individual spirits who appear in performance. In so doing, I am following the suggestion of my research assistant, collaborator, and friend Biemi Gba Jacques, who explained that this is analogous to the distinction made in French between "*Eglise*" (Church) to refer to the institution, and "*église*" (church) to refer to individual buildings of worship.

When speaking French, however, my consultants themselves frequently used the word "*masque.*" Thus, since I conducted many interviews in French, the reader will find scattered throughout this book direct quotations in which the English translation "mask" appears. This brings up the issue that this book is, to a great extent, my attempt to represent what my consultants *wanted* me to represent about Ge. Always, when I first met people, I introduced myself and my research by explaining that I was not there to learn and expose to the world secret knowledge that is the exclusive province of initiates. I told them that I was there to learn what anyone and everyone on the street in Man was permitted to know about Ge performance. I wanted to know what *they wanted me to know*. I am therefore representing, to the best of my ability, what my consultants wanted me to represent, with few exceptions. It is not my goal in this ethnography to represent the capital "T" Truth about Ge performance in 1990s Ivorian life. Rather, I aim to portray what happened in a fieldwork encounter, during which an American ethnomusicologist spent time studying an African performance practice. This book is my attempt to piece together some kind of a story—at least a "partial truth" (Clifford 1986)—out of this experience of cross-cultural interaction.

Despite initial announcements of my research intentions, I nevertheless ended up learning a great deal of "secret" information. As my consultants and I grew more comfortable with one another, and, I like to think, they became convinced of my sincerity and trustworthiness, they became less guarded about certain aspects of Ge. As a result, I unwittingly became privy to information that consultants did not share with the general public. Occasionally, I had to ask whether this, that, or the other thing someone had just told me was something I could share with others, and if so, with whom and in what form. Some things I learned I cannot write about in this book.

For example, I, like any Dan person, cannot publicly identify an individual who performed a *ge*. This presents an odd predicament for someone concerned with issues of agency, as I am. In some regions of Africa, masked dancers can be identified by name. Zoë Strother freely identifies masked dancers among the Pende of central Africa (1998). Even among the Gouro, who, like the Dan, are a southern Mande group who live in Côte d'Ivoire, a masked dancer can lift the mask off his face as he makes his way to a performance space. Not so for the Dan. Yet everyone save the youngest of children knows that there is a person "behind the mask" (*gewëd̈ë*—"face of the *ge*")[5] and beneath the clothing of a dancing *ge*. Many people even know who that person is, even though they cannot speak this knowledge in a public setting. People deliberately talk around the issue, finding creative ways to discuss the subject of Ge performance without naming names. An intentional ambiguity surrounds this issue: it is okay to know but not okay to say that there is a person beneath the dancing figure. Taking my consultants literally, Ge performance cannot be considered spirit mediumship, because a dancing *ge* is not a person embodying a spirit, but rather *the ge is the spirit itself.* Ge performance does not represent; it *is.* An analogy, which may be familiar to many readers, is the notion of transubstantiation. Catholics who participate in communion know that someone went to the store and bought wafers and wine. But during communion, Catholic doctrine holds that those foodstuffs are transformed into the body and blood of Christ. Likewise, the fact that people knew that there was a person beneath a *ge*'s outfit did not make the presence of the spirit any less real.

And yet, there was a kind of "wink wink, nudge nudge" quality to discussions in which everyone present knew, but could not speak, the name of a *ge* performer. This frequently occurred during interviews, in which everyone, including me, knew which person in the room had "accompanied" the *ge* that we were discussing. I have chosen to write about this issue with this same sense of deliberate ambiguity. I will not, of course, name anyone who "accompanied" or was "behind" any *ge*. Yet just as people did in the Man region, readers eventually might figure out, or at least have some good guesses for, who these people are. And that is perfectly acceptable. I will not identify people, but it is fine if readers *infer* who they are. I have chosen this tactic both to adhere to my ethical obligations regarding this matter and to attempt to represent, in the way I write about the issue, the way Dan people talked with me about it.[6]

The Dan language has no one standard word or phrase for describing a *ge*'s presence among people, but my consultants did tend to describe this in one of two ways. One was *"ge dua gu"* which literally translates as "The *ge* is in the raffia." This phrase refers to the fact that most *genu* who manifest visually wear sacred raffia skirts. *"Ge dua gu"* draws on that metaphor to state that a *ge* has taken on a corporeal form. My consultants also said, *"ge kpin,"* which translates as "the *ge* is outside," this referring to the *gunkɔ,* or sacred house, where *ge* paraphernalia is kept—the village home of *genu.* Since *genu* are usually "inside" the sacred house, saying they are "outside" means they are manifest in performance in the world of humans.

In French, my consultants often described a *ge*'s presence similarly, using the words *"dehors"* (outside) and *"sortir"* (to go out).[7] Consultants very commonly used the verb *"manifester"* and the noun *"manifestation"* to describe *ge* performance events. *"Manifester"* has several meanings in French, including the English cognate "manifest," "appear," "show," and "display clearly." Ivorians use *"manifestation"* to describe many types of gatherings of people, from political protests to performances. I have chosen to use the words "manifest" and "manifestation" interchangeably with "perform" and "performance," as they are the best options in English for expressing the nuances and connotations of the ways my consultants described the presence of *genu* among humans.

METHODS

I have been studying Ge performance since 1993 and have lived in the city of Man, Côte d'Ivoire, conducting field research for nearly twelve months, including part of the summer of 1994 and more than ten months of 1997. All of my Dan consultants come from the northern Dan region and live either in Man itself or in the region between Man and Biankouma. In 1994, I worked with a Dan research assistant named Tiemoko Guillaume and Ivorian ethnomusicologist Adépo Yapo. We lived in the Tiemoko family compound in Man, which we used as a home base while conducting research in surrounding villages. In 1997, my wife Nicole Kousaleos and I lived and worked with a Dan man named Biemi Gba Jacques, the three of us forming what we affectionately called our "research team."

In 1997, Nicole was a doctoral candidate in folklore. Having received similar training to mine, Nicole was able to advise me and help me navigate through many theoretical and methodological uncertainties. Not only did I benefit from

Figure Intro.1. Biemi Gba Jacques being mock-interviewed by a comedic *ge*. Photograph by Daniel B. Reed.

Figure Intro.2. Nicole Kousaleos taking a break from videotaping.
Photograph by Daniel B. Reed.

having the emotional support of my partner during most of my time abroad, I also profited from having a trained folklorist to consult. Jacques played many roles in my research, including research assistant, consultant, language coach, and friend. Jacques was critical to this project's outcome. A bright, conscientious young man, Jacques had been a student at an Ivorian university. The year Nicole and I arrived, however, Jacques was in transition, having dropped out of school due to frustration over recurrent strike-related university closings. Ethnographic literature is rife with tales of troubles with research assistants (Gottlieb and Graham 1993; Spindel 1989; Stoller and Olkes 1987). Often marginal characters—people without ties and responsibilities—are the ones available for such temporary positions. Jacques, in contrast, was an extraordinary worker and a caring friend. My relationship with Jacques was also beneficial because of his familial connections in the Man region. We conducted nearly all of our research with members of Jacques' family (in the extended Ivorian sense of the word) and friends and acquaintances of his family. Working with Jacques, I gained access to and trust from *ge* performers that would have been nearly impossible to elicit on my own.

To effectively explore the many facets of Ge performance and to attempt to grasp its many meanings, I designed a field methodology with many different components and strategies. I participated in numerous ways in Ge performances: as a conspicuous audience member; as a documenter through Hi-8 videotaping, DAT recording, and photographing (which Nicole, Jacques, and I handled as a team); and, on rare occasions, as a drummer and singer. After I prepared detailed indexes of the DATs and videos, Jacques and I used them for text translation and for developing research questions. We then conducted feedback interviews (Stone and Stone 1981) with event participants. As we watched and listened to these recordings, consultants and I interpreted and analyzed the events together, a process that enabled me to better approach their perspectives and understandings of the meanings and uses of *genu* in their lives. We also held interviews with a range of local people, including, but not limited to, the *ge* performers themselves. The result is more than 120 hours of taped discussions, including oral histories. I fleshed out the historical aspect of my study with research in several archives in Abidjan. I collected additional material, including videos shot by others of Ge performance events, newspaper and magazine articles pertinent to my research, and cassettes of popular music that *ge* performers sometimes incorporate. I spent time with people, casually talking. In the informal interactions that took place as a result of living in Man, I learned a great deal about how my consultants lived their daily lives, which helped me to understand the roles music and *genu* played in their lives. I wrote volumes of field notes, in which I began initial analyses and interpretations.

Last, but far from least, I studied music with master drummer Goueu Tia Jean-Claude and vocalist/drummer Gba Ernest. I honestly did not have a clear idea of what I was looking for when I began studying the drumming and singing aspects of Ge performance. I simply knew that I had read enough ethnomusicological ethnographies in which learning how to play had been an extremely effective method toward understanding peoples' ideas about and uses of their music. I am a person who loves to play music, so I was also following my heart. It was Dan music, in part, that had drawn me to western Côte d'Ivoire in the first place; in its fascinating array of timbres and complex polyrhythms, Dan music seemed to concentrate and intensify some of my favorite characteristics of West African music. So I dove in, unaware of how important this method would eventually prove to be. In these lessons, I learned that music sound is the spiritually activating force in Ge performance. Certain techniques and aesthetic principles are used to mediate between the worlds of spirit and humans. Specifically, the interactions between the master drummer and the dancing *ge* proved to be *the* most important place to look for communicative strategies and the generation of meanings. Only by learning how to perform this music was I able to understand how this communication works and its importance not just to the spiritual and technical workings of Ge performance but also to my consultants' lives. While the sonic aspect of Ge is discussed throughout this book, in Chapters 5 and 6 I spotlight singing and drumming in order to demonstrate the centrality of music to the concept and process of Ge.

My regular music lessons also helped me to develop deeper relationships with certain people who became not just consultants but teachers and, to some extent, friends. These lessons, usually held at our house, were at first very formal and stiff. Gradually, as I got to know my teachers better and they became more comfortable in our home, the lessons became much less formal, sometimes filled as much with jokes and laughter as with the sounds of drums and singing. The transition from a formal lesson/interview context to an informal feeling of "hanging out" was crucial to the building of relationships and the deepening of my ethnographic experience; from these lessons came my richest material.

The deepening of my relationships with Jean-Claude, Gba Ernest, and the friends who would frequently accompany them to our house for lessons had repercussions far beyond the lessons themselves. When I first arrived in 1994 and for the first few months of my stay in 1997, I (through the intermediary of my research assistants Tiemoko Guillaume in 1994 and Biemi Gba Jacques in 1997) was usually the one to initiate contact with *ge* performers, asking permission to study their performances and their lives. Slowly but surely, this became less necessary as I began receiving regular invitations to events. By June of 1997, I was receiving so many such invitations that I actually could not keep up and was occasionally forced to decline.

This is of course just a cursory description of what happened in "the field." As several of the authors of the edited text *Shadows in the Field* so convincingly argue, we create a false division between the field experience and preparations for, and analysis and write-up of that experience (see especially Barz 1997). I, like all ethnomusicologists, spent years preparing for "the field," studying French and Bamanankan,[8] reading previous literature, discussing ideas with colleagues and mentors, developing research questions, writing grant proposals. And in a certain sense, my field experience continues up to today, as I continue to interact with my consultants both literally (through the mail and phone) and figuratively (through the various field media) as I write. Fieldwork is, in reality, just living— albeit a specially framed and focused kind of living—that does not end when we return from some metaphoric "field." I prefer to think of fieldwork not as a particular spatially or temporally bound experience (see Babiracki 1997 and Rice 1997). Rather, fieldwork is, as Michelle Kisliuk writes (though she prefers the term "field research"), "a broad conceptual zone united by a chain of inquiry" (1997, 29).

Another factor that cannot be overemphasized is the extent to which fieldwork is a reciprocal, interactive process (Drewal 1992; Jackson 1989; Roseman 1991). Anthropologist Michael Jackson asserts that "the radically empirical method *includes* the experience of the observer and defines the experimental field as one of interactions and intersubjectivity" (1989, 4). Understood in this way, ethnography is less a matter of a subject viewing an object than of an interaction, a meeting of subjects, or agents, in space and time.

On what may appear to be (but in fact is not) a crude level, my research was reciprocal in that there were monetary exchanges involved nearly every step of the way. Doing research on the subject of Ge is not a cheap endeavor. Gba Daouda, a Dan anthropologist who conducted dissertation research about Ge—some of it with members of his own family—writes of his own research experience, "In the Dan region, in keeping respect for the Mask tradition, one must each time offer a kola, drink, and/or chickens to the ancestors before engaging in discussion or interviews" (1984, 26). The "kola" Daouda mentions can sometimes literally be an offering of kola nuts (a traditional gift as a sign of respect for authority), but it is more frequently a metaphor for a monetary gift. Offering of a kola is considered to be standard protocol when dealing with any aspect of Ge, from arranging a performance to seeking a private consultation. For practitioners of Ge, the gift of a kola is viewed as a sacred gesture to the ancestors, accepted on their behalf by elders in the sacred house, to demonstrate respect for "the tradition." Thus Gba Daouda and I both were required to participate in this system in order to learn about Ge. Payment in this context should not be viewed as something that "cheapens" what we ethnographers have learned, nor does it render profane the tradition of Ge. Payment is rather an integral part of that tradition. I had come to them asking for teachers and information; they in turn made certain demands of me. This transaction was just one of many ways in which my fieldwork was a two-way street.[9]

As will become clear, Ge performance is a business for some, a way of making money. We need not look to Africa for examples of people whose work is simultaneously sacred and profitable. Priests, ministers, and rabbis are just a few examples of people who earn their livelihoods through sacred practices. At times, performers were blatant in their attempts to establish relationships with me that they knew could prove to be financially profitable. Consultants valued relationships with our research team for other reasons as well. Much has been written about the importance in Dan culture of being known as being good at something (see, for example, Johnson 1986). Some consultants told me that they were flattered that I had come all the way from North America to study what they did and inferred that our relationship would add to their local renown. As word of our presence in Man spread, some *ge* performers began seeking us out, inviting us to film, photograph, and record their performances. Since providing copies of all media was a part of every agreement that I made with potential consultants, they also saw our association as a way to obtain such documents of their performances. While I was filming, recording, and photographing performers, shaping them into images, sounds, and words that I could bring home to share with people in the United States, consultants were taking the opportunity to meet their own interests, shaping our interactions into something useful for themselves. In sum, I became a pathway of communication for my consultants to use to accomplish goals through Ge performance. Consultants told me that they wanted to use the publication of my research to attain goals such as informing otherwise inaccessible people about Ge and increasing their own renown. In fact, this book, like Ge, is an intersubjective creation, based upon agents (my consultants and, of course, me) crafting reality and identity to meet particular goals.

The deeper my relationships with people became, the more reciprocal the process became. With no one was this more true than Biemi Gba Jacques. Jacques viewed his participation in this research project as a way of continuing his initiation into things Dan, of extending his knowledge about specific aspects of his culture, and thus as deepening his sense of his ethnic identity. On a more personal note, by living and working together, we developed an intimacy that remains to this day.

INTERSUBJECTIVITY AND INDIGENOUS THEORY

Here, I am building on intellectual trends which, taken as a whole, represent a paradigmatic shift from what Mark Johnson calls an "Objectivist" worldview to what he terms "empirical phenomenology" (1987, xxxvii). Johnson describes the Objectivist worldview as disembodied or transcendent, grounding his argument in the Cartesian mind/body split, which describes meaning as objectively pure, existing prior to human experience. In this view, meaning originates in the universal transcendent realm of reason and operates by a single set of universal rules of logic. Epistemologically, the Objectivist stance allows for a " 'God's eye' point of view, that is, a perspective that transcends all human limitation and constitutes a universally valid reflective stance" (xxiii).[10]

Clearly, all ethnographic pursuits have historical roots in this Objectivist worldview. Many early anthropologists, folklorists, and ethnomusicologists represented worlds in which their only presence was as a distanced, voice of authority from a "bird's-eye perspective" (Erlmann 1996, 11). This kind of objective distance was considered imperative for accurate description of cultural phenomena. In contrast, the phenomenological notion of intersubjectivity describes a reality which consists neither of a singular notion of transcendent objective truth nor of subjective viewpoints of isolated individuals; rather, meaning is formed in human interaction—in the interaction of subjectivities, or *inter*subjectivity. Subjectivity is not denied; rather, subjectivity is seen as socially constructed (Jackson 1996, 27). Each individual's viewpoint is understood to be developed through social interaction. Since Ge performance is a public event, its various meanings are clearly socially constructed and contested. Ge performance exemplifies the idea that meanings are constructed through the intersubjective interaction of agents in social space. By utilizing descriptive narrative in this text, I am attempting to explore the intersubjective and social creation of meaning in peoples' experience of, and discourse about, Ge.

Phenomenological ethnography thus decenters meaning and, to some extent, authority. Veit Erlmann notes that ethnographers must attend to multiple and shifting vantage points (1996, 11). In this book, I explore the meanings Ge performance generates from multiple perspectives—those of performers and organizers of events; elders and the young; Christians, Muslims, and practitioners of Dan religion; people of various ethnic groups; and politicians, judges, and journalists. Through both my theoretical approach and my representational style, I attempt to recognize the multiple voices of meaning-creation in such a way as to highlight the authority of these voices. Yet I do not wish to suggest that my approach completely does away with the authority located in the ethnographer's voice. I am, after all, the one writing this text, despite my attempts to foreground the polyvocal process that has resulted in this ethnography. My approach is one that attempts to *lessen* the centering of authority and meaning in the voice of the scholar, both in the ethnographic process and in the creation of text. But attempting to do away with scholarly authority entirely would be denial; ethnographers assume a certain authority, without which this type of work would not be possible (Reed 1993, 83).

I recognize the authority of my consultants by attempting to understand their own theories about what they do. Johannes Fabian calls for moving beyond asymmetrical theory/method relationships ("subject here, object there; theory and method on our side, reality and facts on theirs" [1990, xv]). Some of my consultants theorized their own lives with an enviable sophistication and poetic flair. Throughout the book, I include extensive first-person quotations so the reader can "hear" my consultants, in their own words, describe their experience with Ge and theorize its meanings.[11] Ge was, for some people, both theory and practice. Consultants and I discussed theory about religion, proper behavior, aesthetics, identity, and many other facets of the multifaceted concept of Ge; these conversations inform the entire book but are especially central to the detailed exploration of the concept of Ge that makes up Chapter 4.

Some of my consultants' ideas about and uses of the term "tradition" deserve special attention. French-speaking consultants often called Dan religion "the tradition" and regularly made use of the term "modernity" (and derivatives thereof) as well. As I show in Chapter 3, their use of these terms indicates notions of tradition and modernity that are nuanced and complex. For them, "tradition" was held as a separate category from things "modern" and "popular" and from religious ideas from other sources such as Islam and Christianity. Yet the boundaries between these separate categories, as my consultants represented them to me, were fluid, permeable, and historically contingent. "The tradition" was adaptable; it was timeless yet of the moment. This book will demonstrate ways that performers make this old performance complex relevant to their world, both in theory and in practice. Though they call Ge "the tradition," self-consciously according it the weight and authority associated with this term, the creative process of Ge

performers echoes that of African popular musicians and artists, a process scholars such as Ulf Hannerz, Christopher Waterman, and Karin Barber have called
"creolization." By exploring consultants' ideas about tradition, I am responding
to Henry Glassie's call to listen to our consultants' ideas about this controversial
word, to see how they are defining and using this term (1995). Certain academics
(including this one—Reed 1996) expound what tradition *should* mean; here, I
decenter the term's definition to explore what it *does* mean to some of my consultants.[12]

I thus re-engage the terms "tradition" and "modernity" from an experiential
perspective. While I recognize that these words are problematic and can be read
in dualistic or binary terms, I deliberately embrace them because my consultants
themselves use them to interpret their actions and understand their worlds. I furthermore recognize that these terms have roots in an ideologically driven, evolutionary discourse (Comaroff and Comaroff 1993, xii) and that their overuse has
"given them a spurious solidity" (Barber 1997a, 1). Yet I find ethnographic value
in exploring the ways Africans themselves are using these epistemological categories "to describe and understand the cultural universe within which they operate" (ibid., 1). When I counterpose concepts such as tradition and modern,
tradition and popular, Dan religion and Islam, I am not pursuing a Levi-Straussian
binary structuralism but rather am attempting to represent these concepts the way
consultants viewed them, the ways they lived them in their experience of their
world. Categories such as "tradition" and "modernity" are important signposts
for my consultants as they navigate their world.[13]

BEYOND BOUNDED COMMUNITIES

The world that my consultants inhabit is fluid, multilayered, and dynamic, and I
make deliberate effort here to portray Ge performance within that context. In his
study of the music of Peruvian highlanders and migration, Thomas Turino writes,
"Given the mobility of twentieth-century Peruvian life, bounded, rural ethnographies are no longer practical" (1993, 6). The same can be said of late twentieth-
century Côte d'Ivoire. As Turino argues, many fine ethnomusicological ethnographies in the 1970s and 1980s, influenced by structuralism, presented "elegant
depictions of the tight coherence of cultural practices, aesthetics, and ethics across
various realms of social life in small-scale settings" (ibid., 9). Yet, he continues:

> Typically, however, these studies do not stress individual subject positions
> within the depiction of specific groups, nor do they emphasize the more discrete
> levels of disagreement, contradiction and conflict. They also tend to isolate the
> specific social setting from its broader regional, national, international, and
> historical contexts. (ibid.)

As Turino advocates, in this ethnography I stress the voices, thoughts, and
opinions of individuals—including instances of conflict and contradiction as well
as cooperation and agreement—within a broad historical and cultural context. In
so doing, I build on the strengths of previous studies while extending them in
certain key ways. I imagine that few ethnomusicologists have had the fortune of
conducting fieldwork in a region about which so much excellent ethnography has
already been published. Hugo Zemp's *Musique Dan* (1971) stands the test of time
as an outstanding example of the study of indigenous concepts about and uses of
music. Unlike many ethnographies of its time, *Musique Dan* does not represent

the Dan as a homogeneous musical/cultural monolith. Rather, Zemp discusses regional diversity in everything from religious ideas to musical concepts to instruments. He includes extensive first-person quotations of Dan individuals. All in all, I could not have asked for a more solid ground base upon which to build my own work than I found in Zemp's comprehensive study of the musical life and ideas of Dan peoples. Yet *Musique Dan,* like most ethnomusicological monographs of its time, tends to represent the Dan in seeming isolation from their larger cultural and geographical context. My own study extends Zemp's work by attempting a more microlevel study (dealing with a single genre of performance and working more intensively with fewer people) placed within a more macrolevel context, both in historical and cultural terms.

MASK PERFORMANCE, CREATIVE PROCESS, AND IDENTITY

Grasping the role of Ge in identity negotiation requires not just placing Ge and Dan people in a broad social and historical context but also understanding Ge as a creative process. In focusing on process, I am building on performance-oriented approaches that have taken hold in several fields. Art historian Sidney Kasfir notes that through most of the past century, research of African masks was generally bifurcated into that of art historians, who looked at the mask as a physical artifact expressing aesthetic values, and that of anthropologists, who viewed masks solely as sociocultural symbols. In so doing, scholars divided up the study of masks in a way that bore no relation to the perceptions of the performers themselves (Kasfir 1988, 2). Kasfir cites the importance of art historian Robert Farris Thompson's work, which overturned these past trends of scholarship by opening up new ways of looking at art in Africa. Thompson suggested the possibility of viewing art as a verb in his monumental work *African Art in Motion: Icon and Act* (1974). As the title suggests, Thompson called for redefining what constitutes a work of visual art by expanding the physical artifact to include the *enactment* of the artifact. In isolating the mask from its role in performance, previous art historians divorced the artifact from its context; in integrating the mask and its performance, Thompson and others have attempted to understand the meanings and uses of masks as they are conceived of in specific African settings.[14]

Contemporary scholars of African masks with whom I feel affinity react against previous tendencies merely to identify "tribal styles" of single cultural groups in implicit isolation from the rest of the world. Select studies conducted during the past two decades show masks and mask performances as dynamic expressive arts created by agents who generate meaning for themselves in relationship to local, regional, and even global contexts and influences (Arnoldi 1995; Bravmann 1983; Drewal and Drewal 1983; Drewal 1992; El-Dabh and Proschan 1979; Fischer and Homberger 1986; Gba Daouda 1982; Harding 1990; Imperato 1980; Johnson 1986; McCluskey 1987; McNaughton 1993; Nunley 1987; Strother 1995, 1998; Wooten 2000a, 2000b). In this literature we find masks dancing in contexts such as political rallies, contemporary theatrical productions, regional competitions, and sacred rituals; we see carvers whose influences range from dream spirits to international sports stars; we see masks whose physical forms reference everything from colonial dress to airplanes.

Mask performance is a means through which West Africans interact with the world around them; in the process, they negotiate identities (cf. Wooten 2000a). Let me pause for a moment to describe what I mean by the word "negotiate." Inherent in my use of this word is the idea of a *process of interaction* between parties. Something must be settled; thus, there is the implication of *conflict,* in the sense of the central drama that any good novel presents, which seeks resolution. When negotiating, people are up against something that they must move through, around, or over, possibly an obstacle or a boundary.

My consultants negotiate various boundaries through Ge performance. They negotiate their relationships to their natural environment and their ancestors and their relationships between themselves and God. They negotiate their relationships to other religious traditions and other ethnic groups and their relationships to one another. They negotiate relationships between local, regional, and national power bases and between systems of justice of differing origins. They negotiate boundaries between the religious and the secular, which include the relationship between what they define as traditional and popular music and dance. Overall, my consultants negotiate boundaries between various forces in their lives and Ge and in the end create meanings for themselves in the complex, heterogeneous, and fluid setting of 1990s Côte d'Ivoire. These boundaries are not unanimously agreed upon; they are continually contested and, as a result, shift and change. In this book, I will recount numerous instances of the contestation of the boundaries of Ge and Ge performance, including conflicts over how Ge performance should be conducted, what music should be included/excluded, and where performances should be held. Through these and other ways, my consultants negotiate the place and meaning of Ge in their lives.

Mask performance is one means through which West Africans express and generate notions of community identity. Though West Africans have been highly mobile for centuries, mobility increased dramatically in the twentieth century. As a result of this mobility and mass media (among other factors) people increasingly encounter and are confronted by difference in their daily lives. Identity issues increasingly come to the fore in such contexts, and people use their arts to establish commonality and difference. Underlying this process is the idea that people express identity in *relationship* to others, through performance (Bauman 1971). Ge performance is particularly well suited for this process, as it is not only a form of artistic expression but also a public enactment of Dan religious ideas; beyond that, many Dan identified Ge as the very thing that undergirded the idea of Danness. This expression of religious and ethnic identity is taking place in contexts in which increasingly more people of other ethnic and religious identities are present.[15] Overall, then, Ge performance exemplifies the Comaroffs' characterization of ritual performance as a means for people to "empower themselves" by asserting "a measure of control over worlds often perceived to be rapidly changing" (Comaroff and Comaroff 1993, xiv).

STRUCTURE AND STYLE

Over the past several decades, many ethnographers have made effective use of narrative forms of representation. The contemporary use of narrative in ethnographic writing grew out of the reflexive movement which blossomed in the 1980s, in which ethnographers challenged "objective" perspectives and authoritative representational styles seemingly removed from the field experiences with individuals upon which ethnographic writing is based (see Clifford and Marcus 1986; Crapanzano 1980; Jackson 1989). In more recent years, many ethnographers have attempted to foreground experience by incorporating narrative forms of representation into their written accounts (see, for example, Abu-Lughod 1993; Arnoldi 1995; Kamara 1992; Kisliuk 1998; and Lawless 1993).[16] Others have explicitly adopted literary conventions, very effectively bringing to life stories of field experiences and the people in those stories (Gottlieb and Graham 1993; Stoller and Olkes 1987; Stoller 1989). In these and other examples, the degree to which narrative becomes the primary mode of representation varies. Jackson has extended this idea to the point of writing an ethnographic novel (1986). In this book, I interweave two primary representational styles—one which is analytical and another which is narrative. I include narrative to emphasize the contingency of ethnographic research; that is, to keep this book—including its theory and analysis—grounded in empirical data: my experiences with particular people in particular contexts.

I have structured this book somewhat unconventionally, with my field experience while studying Ge performance in mind.[17] Neither Ge performance nor fieldwork are neat and tidily packaged like ethnographies tend to be (Barz 1997). Rather, both the subject of this book and the process by which I learned about it were unpredictable and full of surprises. Similarly, narratives appear at irregular intervals throughout this text, sometimes at the beginning of chapters, other times within chapters, while three chapters (1, 7, and 8), consist almost exclusively of narratives. Like Ge performance, this book does not follow a linear or a chronological sense of time. This book makes use of the metaphor of a road—a common metaphor in West Africa (Stone 2000; Drewal 1992)—which has no real beginning or end but rather links points in time, people, and events in a fluid path. Roads or paths may connect the village to the city, the world of spirit to the world of humans, communities to other communities—just as the social actors who are a part of the complex phenomenon that is Ge negotiate many pathways and create new connections in performing their tradition. In traveling these many pathways of communication, these many roads, contemporary Dan make meaning in a complex and changing world.

A particular and perhaps surprising twist in the road occurs in Chapters 7 and 8, where the reader will encounter narratives that include excerpts of actual field notes from my field journals (cf. Barz 1997; Stone 2000). My goal of creating a representational style that matches my ethnographic experience finds its furthest point of development in these chapters. These chapters *feel* more like my field experience in Côte d'Ivoire—unpredictable and improvised. The field notes in these chapters include many details and thoughts that are not directly relevant to my arguments in this ethnography. Yet I have let some of this detail be to invite the reader more deeply and directly into my field experience itself, in which so much more occurred than what I am choosing to highlight in this book. To a greater extent than in the narratives sprinkled elsewhere throughout the book, in Chapters 7 and 8 I provide greater context for the necessarily narrowly constructed argument of a book. Additionally, including field notes permits a more direct view into the field experience and the research process, allowing readers "to experience our individual processes of knowing, those paths we took to arrive at understanding, interpretation, or analysis" (Barz 1997, 46).

While, to some extent, I deconstruct the ethnographic process with Chapters 7 and 8, laying bare a part of the process of the creation of this text, these chapters do not merely leave the reader at random points on the road without a map as a guide. Much material is present in these chapters that illustrates and supports the main themes of this book, and both chapters include interpretation and concluding analysis. Still, although I offer some analysis throughout and at the end of each chapter, by including field notes I invite the reader to explore additional themes and alternative interpretations. With these chapters, I invite the reader one step closer to a direct view of how I know what I know about Ge performance.

ROAD MAP

In order to immerse the reader immediately in the feeling and flow of Ge performance, Chapter 1 features a lengthy narrative of a Ge performance. This narrative, which recounts my first experience with Gegbadë, serves as an introduction to how Ge performance works, in a spiritual and technical sense. Many aspects of Ge performance that are introduced in Chapter 1 are further elaborated in later chapters. The narrative in Chapter 1 also shows how this book's central themes play out in performance. Just as for young uninitiated Dan in Man, in this book the road to understanding Ge begins in the experience of a performance event.

Chapter 2 portrays the social and religious context in which I conducted this research. I draw upon my ethnographic experience, including oral histories, along with archival data and previous literature to discuss certain social and religious changes of the colonial and postcolonial periods and their implications for Ge performance. Following this general discussion of the history and contemporary setting of Man, Chapter 3 presents an in-depth look at a particular *ge* (Gedro) in a particular community (the Man neighborhood of Petit Gbapleu). This specific case exemplifies the pluralistic setting of contemporary Man and the roles and meanings of Ge performance within that setting. At the center of conflicts about Petit Gbapleu community identity is a youthful anti-Islamic Ge revival whose performers adapt their performance to their contemporary context, incorporating popular-music references that appeal to the diverse populace that makes up audiences in contemporary Man. This chapter highlights these performers' own interpretations of what they do, in particular their ideas about tradition and modernity and the relationship between Ge performance and their identities as Dan people in the modern world.

The title of Chapter 4, "What Is Ge?" seems to suggest that a definition follows, but this chapter does not define so much as it describes in more detail this multifaceted, rich, and complex concept. Although this Introduction opens with a cryptic, one-paragraph summary description of Ge and this summary is elaborated upon in the first three chapters, Chapter 4 provides a deeper and more nuanced treatment of this term, especially with regard to its religious dimension. Ge has four components: the notion of a forest spirit, that spirit in performance, the foundation of the traditional education that takes place in initiation, and the enactment of that education or, in other words, ideal behavior for adults in Dan society. Chapter 4 is like a path through the sacred forest—an initiation of sorts into the profundity and complexity of Ge—for which the first four chapters serve as preparation.

Having delved deeply into the conceptual world of Ge, this book then turns to one of the most central aspects of Ge performance: music sound. Chapters 5 and 6 are dedicated to an analytical discussion of the sonic aspect of the manifestation of Ge, an aspect that has been underemphasized in previous scholarly literature. Through *getan,* or the music/dance of Ge, much communication takes place, between humans and the spirit world, between performers and audience members, and between performers themselves. As such, an analysis of *getan* is essential to understanding what happens in Ge performance and why. These two chapters explore in detail the power of words, drums, and other sounds in manifesting Ge and the subtle connection between musical aesthetics and communicative strategy that is central to Ge performance.

In Chapters 7 and 8, I return to narrative voice and invite the reader to stop along the road and experience some particularly fascinating performances: a Gedro performance in a festival at the Man soccer stadium (Chapter 7), and a Gegbadë performance to solve a sorcery problem in south-central Côte d'Ivoire (Chapter 8). These two chapters make use of narratives constructed partially of field notes, in order to bring the reader as close as possible to the ethnographic experiences that inform this book.

Chapter 9 concludes this book by focusing on the idea of Ge as a pathway of communication, through which performers, the people who hire them, and others meet needs and find meanings. All of these people contribute to the intersubjective construction of meanings surrounding Ge and Ge performance. In Chapter 9, I offer brief summaries of the transformative power of Ge in the lives of several of my consultants and of the ways studying Ge transformed my own perspective about the potential roles and meanings of a traditional performance complex in a contemporary pluralistic setting.

ONE

On the Road to Man

On a hot dusty January day in the small city of Man, Nicole, Jacques, and I were looking for a place to live. The harmattan—the dust that blows south from the Sahara—had arrived late this dry season. People walking the streets and riding in taxis covered their mouths and noses with handkerchiefs to block the ubiquitous dust swirling in the wind. The three of us, along with several other friends, were walking along Rue de Lycée, one of the many major dirt-road arteries in Man, choking on the heavy dust being kicked up by passing taxis, anxious to find shade.

Suddenly, I heard a sound—a repeating rhythm—approaching from the opposite direction. Through the dusty air, a form appeared—someone playing a gourd rattle and singing. As he came closer, I saw he wore a tall curved leather hat in colors of red and cream, covered with cowrie shells. Then, as we continued toward him and he toward us, it became clear that he was a *ge*—the first I had seen during this trip to Côte d'Ivoire, which had begun just a couple of weeks earlier. Noticing our interest, he stopped before us, dancing and singing. His blue-and-cream–striped Dan clothing and light raffia skirt swayed with his body's movements. His dark wooden face featured thin slit eyes outlined in white and delicate cheekbones descending into protruding red lips. His muted voice buzzed and growled as he sang through his wooden face, "*Ɓa nin a Kpaclöclö*" (I am Kpaclöclö). With a gourd rattle in his hands and the ankle bells on his dancing feet, he created complex layered rhythms to accompany his song. His feet moved side to side and back and forth in quick rhythmic steps, while his torso remained upright and stiff, jerking occasionally along with the rhythm. He stopped for a moment, then shook my hand before dancing and singing for a few minutes more. I dug some coins out of my pocket and gave him a gift. Then we continued on our separate ways.

I was thrilled and immediately began firing questions at Jacques, my pocket notebook and pen in hand. This was a *trukë ge,* a kind of *ge* who travels around from family to family, entertaining people with song, dance, and humorous stories. In this context, the *trukë ge* was something like a cross between an American street performer and an Irish mummer (Glassie 1975), though also, like all *genu,* a sacred phenomenon. What most surprised me was that we had experienced this *ge* on a busy city street. Nothing I had read or experienced during my initial visit to this area in 1994 had led me to expect that Ge performance could occur outside of village settings. Previous literature on the subject of Dan masks portrayed them exclusively in village contexts as a part of the functional workings of village life. During my first trip to Côte d'Ivoire in 1994, although I had slept most nights in Man at the compound of my research assistant Tiemoko Guillaume, we had done all of our "research" in nearby villages. Without asking, Guillaume had assumed that I would want to go to villages to learn about *genu*. It had never occurred to me to ask him whether *genu* ever appeared in Man. Only at this moment did I realize that amid the streets lined with shops and bustling with traffic, against the backdrop of the Islamic calls to prayer, among the diverse multiethnic populace in which the Dan likely are a minority, *genu* perform.

AN INVITATION TO A GEGBADË PERFORMANCE

The reason Jacques, Nicole, and I were walking the streets of Man in the first place was that I had changed my mind about where I wanted to locate my study. When planning my 1997 trip, I had proposed a field location a bit farther north, near Touba, in the ethnic borderlands between the Dan and Mau peoples. My goal had been to study mask performance as an arena for interethnic interaction. But when I arrived in Touba in 1997, I learned that in the Touba region, nearly all active mask performances were those concerned with sorcery conflicts. The thought of studying something so serious and conflict-ridden did not appeal to me. Fieldwork of dance and entertainment *genu* was challenging enough. I doubted whether people working out sorcery accusations would welcome the intrusion of a team of researchers. I had been telling myself that I wanted to study only things that people were excited about, that they wanted to share with me. The potential ethical and practical difficulties involved in researching situations in which people were being accused of killing one another seemed like something to avoid. So we happily returned to Man, where *genu* of many types were abundant.

Back in Man, Jacques, Nicole, and I eventually found a place to live, in a house owned by Jacques' uncle that was perched on the side of a steep hill overlooking Man and the lush green mountains that encircle the city. I focused my research on entertainment *genu,* and in particular on a dance *ge* (*tankë ge*) based in Man named Gedro. Sparked by that initial meeting on the road in Man, I had become intrigued by entertainment *genu,* who, being lower in the sacred hierarchy of Ge, could wander the streets and perform widely in this multiethnic, polyreligious city. Studying these more accessible and public *genu* seemed an ideal way to learn about what Ge means for people in the diversifying context of Man today and how this old performance complex relates to their contemporary lives. But five months into our stay, I received an invitation that would alter my course and broaden the research beyond what I had initially imagined.

During this period I began drum lessons with the master drummer for Gedro, a young man by the name of Goueu Tia Jean-Claude. One rainy-season day in June, Jean-Claude arrived unexpectedly at our house. "You are invited to a manifestation," he announced, "of a powerful *ge* for whom I drum. His name is Gegbadë." Far more sacred than Gedro, Gegbadë was a *zu ge*—a type of *ge* who heals, offers divinations and blessings, and solves problems of sorcery. I had fled Touba to avoid sorcery *genu,* and here I was again encountering this discomfiting phenomenon. Again I had to confront my feelings about it all. I was apprehensive, even a little frightened at the prospect. Frankly, it did not sound like much fun. I could easily decline, especially since there were so many choices. *Genu* were everywhere in Man. I was not lacking in research opportunities. And was this really something that people would want to have studied?

But I had been *invited* to study this *ge*. The leaders (*gedëmεn;* lit., "fathers of the *ge*")[1] of this sacred house had sent Jean-Claude as an envoy directly to me, asking me to attend and record this event. Everything I had done up to that point had been with entertainment *genu;* I knew little about more sacred *genu*. It was an offer I could not refuse.

On the day of Gegbadë's manifestation, Jean-Claude led Jacques and a still somewhat reluctant me to Grand Gbapleu, a village on the edge of the city of Man. Grand Gbapleu has effectively become a neighborhood of Man, having made this transition in just the past ten to fifteen years as the city has grown outward, following the valleys between its steep craggy hills and mountains. We exited a taxi on the relatively recently paved road heading east out of Man and walked downhill on a dirt road, past mud-brick and concrete-block houses. We passed women pounding grain with 6-foot-long wooden pestles in large goblet-shaped mortars, children playing chasing games, elder men seated on benches watching the afternoon fade. Finally we arrived at the compound of Oulai Théodore, the man in charge of the sacred house of Gegbadë. Jean-Claude greeted us warmly and instructed us to sit on a wooden bench in a courtyard between several buildings. As we sat, we noticed that the door of the building behind us was concealed by a wall made of woven dried raffia—the unequivocal marker of a sacred house.

The performance to which we had been invited was ostensibly being held for two reasons. First, Gegbadë was to provide a consultation, or divination, to a man of Mau ethnicity (a northern Mande group just to the north of the Dan) named Djomande. Djomande, who like nearly all Mau was Muslim, had traveled from his home in the Touba region, about 100 kilometers north of Man, because his wife was afflicted with an illness that he did not understand. Aware of Gegbadë's reputation, he had come seeking advice about what to do. Second, Gegbadë was performing to announce the imminent departure of his group. A local governmental official had come to Théodore, asking him to take his *ge* to the village of Bofesso—about twenty-five kilometers north—to solve a sorcery conflict. In such a situation, the *ge* and his group cannot just pack up and head out of town. Rather, Gegbadë must announce to the village chief and other powerful elders his intention to leave. So the second stated purpose for this performance was for Gegbadë to tour Grand Gbapleu, visiting the chief and elders to deliver this news. As on many days in Theodore's compound, however, other people had come as well, seeking help. Theodore's compound was regularly full of people waiting their turn to discuss with him their problems and their requests for his services. On this day, parties from two other nearby villages—Zagoué and Glongouin—were also present, seeking help from the renowned healer (*zumi*) Théodore and his *zu ge*.

As we waited for the performance to begin, Jacques, Jean-Claude, and I chatted. Gradually others joined us on the benches in the courtyard before Théodore's sacred house. Gegbadë performances do not begin at fixed moments in clock time but rather follow a negotiated sense of time.[2] Only when the necessary people have arrived and the required spiritual preparations are completed does

Figure 1.1. Musicians building energy for Gegbadë to manifest.
Photograph by Daniel B. Reed.

the first stage begin: playing music to call the spirits (*yinannu;* sing., *yinan*) who accompany the *ge* from the spiritual realm. The manifestation of the *ge* occurs not at a fixed time but when the spiritual energy has reached a necessary peak.

Time passed, and people came and went. Théodore and other initiated members of his group wandered in and out of the sacred house, each time removing their shoes before they entered, just as Muslims do when they enter a mosque. Shoes, Théodore later instructed me, must be removed prior to entering any sacred space to respect and maintain the boundary between the pure and sacred and the earthly, the human, the everyday. "[Shoes] go everywhere," Théodore instructed. "They are dirty, so they are not worn when a *ge* is doing serious business" (Oulai 1997a).[3] The ban on shoes is just one of several "totems" (*tiyin*) or rules that performers and audience members must follow before and during Gegbadë performances. All such rules are followed in order to create an environment that maximizes the potential spiritual efficacy of the performance.

Various people arrived, among them a jovial elder man named Gonëti. Wearing a navy blue suit, a T-shirt, and bright blue plastic shoes, Gonëti would serve as principal singer (*geatanɓomɛn*) for the event. Shortly thereafter, Jean-Claude, assuming the role of master drummer (*ɓaakpizëmɛn* or *ɓaadezëmɛn*), began playing the master drum (*ɓaade*), accompanied by two apprentices playing the accompanying drums (*zikri* and *ɓaanëyakwade*) and by the elder Gonëti playing the gourd rattle (*gle*).

Gradually, while still playing, the musicians moved toward a space near the door of the sacred house, and the energy of the performance began intensifying. The elder Gonëti began singing, as did some of the drummers and others who were being drawn to the performance site by the sound of the music. As the rhythms and melodies of *getan*—the musical and dance aspects of *ge*—began floating through the air, bouncing off the concrete and mud-brick homes of Grand Gbapleu, people began gathering in the courtyard, some watching, many joining in by singing, clapping, and dancing. For many Dan, older songs such as those typically performed at a Gegbadë manifestation evoke a profound sense of Danness; these songs get people up and inspire them to participate. Eventually, a crowd of roughly fifty people had gathered, forming a large semicircle, which had the effect of enclosing the courtyard, creating a bounded performance space. In the part of the semicircle nearest the door of the sacred house, where the drummers had first gathered, a "performing nucleus"[4] of about fifteen people gathered. Along with the drummers and the elder lead vocalist, this core group consisted of several young men, five or six young women, and as many young girls who sang the responsorial chorus while they danced and punctuated the repeating rhythmic patterns with artfully placed clapping accents.

As the crowd gathered, the music became more and more joyful and intense, as *getan* generally is. Volume raised, tempo increased, and vocal and percussion improvisations became more frequent and innovative. The performance, which had begun so casually, developed more focus. Many of the performers smiled often and had rapt expressions on their faces. When moved to do so, a man or woman left the group to enter into the center of the semicircle to dance, bending at the waist, turning the shoulders, moving across the ground with subtle quick turns of the feet. Sweat began dancing off people's bodies. Gradually, several people whom I would later meet and befriend began appearing in the performance space. *Gekia* (assistant to the *ge;* pl. *gekianu*)[5] Louan Dominique emerged from the sacred house, followed a few minutes later by ritual specialist Seri, a Bété[6] man who had become an important initiate in this sacred house. The norm is that Ge is a family affair, with only family members participating in performances of *genu* who come from their own family's sacred house (and only select families in any Dan settlement have a sacred house). Théodore himself, however, has left his natal village and his immediate family; thus, he has been required to attract people with the necessary skills to produce his *ge* performances. Even many of the Dan members of Gegbadë's group come from communities other than Grand Gbapleu. The diverse origins of the members of Théodore's sacred house reflect the mobility of so many Ivorians.[7]

Seri and Jean-Claude both wore mud-brown *bubus* (Dan shirts) that had been dipped in yet another medicinal wash to make them resistant to attacks of negative sorcery (*duyaa*). One of Seri's primary responsibilities was to oversee Gegbadë performance events, to keep people in line. He included Jacques and me in his purview, at one point chasing curious children away from the camcorder. Then Seri began playing the bells called *dɔɔga*, occasionally giving them to a young man named Patrice when he was needed back in the sacred house. The penetrating sound of the *dɔɔga* raises above even the volume of the drums, in order, Théodore later explained to me, to let everyone present know that a powerful *ge* is arriving. The elder lead singer Gonëti danced and sang joyfully, all the while playing the *gle,* tastefully embellishing the standard patterns, which inspired me to offer him a monetary gift. Between songs, he made a brief speech, thanking me. Seri and Dominique continued going in and out of the sacred house, occasionally delivering messages to Jean-Claude.

After ten or fifteen minutes, Seri stepped out of the sacred hut with a large plastic pitcher of palm wine. The elder Gonëti shouted for joy, causing laughter to break out in the crowd. Patrice began ritually pouring gourd-cupfuls of palm wine for the performers to drink. Holding the pitcher in his left hand and pouring into the gourd held by his right hand, Patrice tasted a sip to ensure it was not poisoned, then offered the gourd properly, with his right hand, to Jean-Claude. More than once, Jean-Claude sipped the gourd cup with his right hand while he continued drumming with his left. When he handed the gourd back, he drummed a signal of thanks: "*Barika barika! I gwë gu, i gwë gu*" (Thank you! May you live long). Palm wine is always present at Ge performances, usually in great quantities, which, my consultants explained to me, helps sustain the vast amounts of energy required to perform at this level of intensity for long periods of time.

Despite the obvious building of energy, I initially misinterpreted this stage of the event as mere warming up while they waited for the *ge* to appear. I would later learn in music lessons and interviews that this was far from a warm-up jam session. Rather, *getan* at this stage of a performance plays a crucial role: it attracts the *yinannu* who accompany and animate the *ge*. The fervor and intensity I was witnessing in the musicians' performance serves this purpose. It is thus imperative that the performance begins with this level of what my consultants frequently called "*animation*." Only then can the *ge* exit the sacred house and enter the world of humans. Without music, in other words, a *ge* such as Gegbadë cannot appear among people. And it cannot be just any music; it must be *getan,* performed with such energy and skill that the *yinannu* who accompany the *ge* from the mystical realm (*geɓɔ*) are inspired to arrive. Between songs, performers kept the energy high by singing short musical interludes called *tankwi.*

The musicians played for about twenty minutes before the *ge* manifested. Increasingly, Jean-Claude's attention was directed toward the raffia wall shielding the sacred house. He began frequently drumming in a particular manner which creates, in sound, the translucent boundary between the worlds through which the *yinannu* arrive. A woman in the chorus initiated the song "*zɔngo wa dɛ, ge nin nu ba*" (The ge has arrived.) Finally, during a break between songs, sounds began emanating from behind the raffia wall that shielded the door to the sacred house. Gegbadë had indeed arrived.

After the long wait and buildup, this moment was thrilling. Performers who were outside began interacting with the *ge,* who sang and spoke using a wide variety of voices. At one moment his voice sounded muffled, the next it buzzed and screeched like no human voice can.[8] The timbral range of the *ge*'s voice was captivating. From my perspective, and that of everyone present except the core group of musicians, Gegbadë was not visible for some minutes after his presence had become audibly known. I could follow the voice of the *ge,* emerging from within the walls of the sacred house, proceeding slowly through the space enclosed by the raffia wall. But I could not see him. From time to time, some of his *gekianu* became visible as they backed out of the raffia enclosure, shouting cries of encouragement to the *ge.*

At this point, the *ge* himself began directing the music. He started and then stopped the music frequently, allowing musical segments to last only thirty seconds to a minute. In the spaces between the music, he spoke or sang, often in proverbs. Following the Dan custom of "passing the word" from figures of authority to the public through intermediaries, and to ensure that everyone presnt could understand, the *gewoɗiöyɔrɔmɛn* ("person who transmits the words of the *ge*") repeated each phrase of the *ge*'s muffled proclamations in a loud, clear voice:

Gedëmɛn,	Fathers of the *ge* [initiates],
Geazumikpi,	Powerful *zu* of the *ge,*
Gonëti,	(Proper name of the elder singer),
We ö zusënnu wo bɔ kpinɗö-ɓa,	The palm wine that the *zu* apprentices have brought outside here,
A do kɔ ö ɗö,	The manner of offering the palm wine,
A ɗo kɔ ö ɗö—	The manner of comportment—
Ye ɓi nin i ɓa won ka.	These things are your responsibilities

Gonëti, the elder singer, responded:

N ziö,	My ancestor,
Barika barika barika!	Thank you!

Gegbadë then said, "*Ya kë ɗu*" (Therefore), and intoned a song, "*Ka do ɗu we/ de ɗo ziö n ke*" (You have arrived for nothing—who is going to follow me?). The musicians responded, singing and playing for a few moments until a *gekia* gestured for them to stop.

Time flowed like this for the remainder of the performance in short segments.[9] Gegbadë directed this event by weaving together small segments—a short speech, a brief song, a momentary gesture or dance move—into a single performance event. The focus of a Gegbadë performance is not entertainment, but the will of the spirits, who, moment to moment, inspire the *ge* to act in the most appropriate and effective manner. One minute, a song may be needed, the next, a spoken proverb, then a communicative gesture or dance move. The result is a masterfully improvised performance, in which Gegbadë integrates multiple arts into a single communicative flow in order to meet the goals for which the event is held. Even the music sound itself consists of small segments woven together as short sung phrases layered over the interlocking of short repeating drumming patterns.

Most of us still could not see the *ge*. During some of the pauses between the music, Gegbadë and elder *gedëmɛn* offered benedictions to various people present. The benedictions were punctuated at appropriate intervals by calls of "*Amina*" (Amen) from the crowd as they touched their foreheads with their hands to accept the blessings. When it was the *ge* who spoke, he emphasized certain points with occasional non-lexical growls.

As the music continued, Gegbadë's *gekianu* began bringing items out of the sacred house and placing them in the performing space. Dominique appeared with an hourglass-shaped power object (*geɓɔga*), roughly eighteen inches high, adorned with small mirrors, that Gegbadë uses to see into the mystical realm. In French, and even sometimes in Dan, Théodore refers to this power object as his *télévision*—an appropriate name given that he uses it to see images originating from afar, from another dimension.[10] Additionally, the *télévision* is used to test sorcerers; if Gegbadë accuses someone of sorcery and that person then denies his accusation, he or she could be asked to lift the *télévision* in front of the crowd. The *télévision* is in actuality very lightweight, but a guilty sorcerer allegedly cannot budge it from the ground. This was one of Gegbadë's methods for proving the guilt of an accused party. From this time on through the end of the performance, *gekia* Dominique also wore a mirror around his neck. From the time

Figure 1.2. *Télévision.* Photograph by Daniel B. Reed.

Gegbadë physically appeared until the end of the performance, Dominique positioned himself such that he had a clear line of sight between this mirror and the *ge.* This reflected Gegbadë's positive energy (*dusë*) back to him, helping prevent interference from negative sorcery (*duyaa*) attacks.

Patrice then brought out a large wooden chest, which was used to transport Gegbadë's effects when he traveled. On this day, however, it was merely used as a seat for the *ge.* Women began removing cloth wraps from their waists,[11] laying them on the ground to create a pathway from the entrance of the sacred house to the wooden chest.

After about forty minutes of music, two assistants, whom I had not yet seen, emerged from behind the raffia wall. First, Théodore's brother Jerome appeared, holding the *sraman*—a bell that spontaneously rings of its own accord when Gegbadë points it at a sorcerer or a sorcerer's power object (*fétiche* in French, *duga* in Dan). In his other hand, Jerome carried Gegbadë's *téléphone,* an object through which the *ge* receives messages from *yinannu.* This object consists of two parts: a bottle full of a secret liquid potion is connected by a cord to another *bisa* (sacred object), perhaps made of leather and stuffed with spiritually powerful materials, that is covered by the buildup from years of sacrifices of animal blood and kola-nut juice. This latter part is the "receiver" that Gegbadë holds to his ear to receive the messages.

Following Jerome, Théodore's close friend Lambert Celestin (who is also a powerful *zumi*) appeared, walking backward out from behind the wall, still facing the *ge,* who remained obscured behind the raffia wall. Finally, Gegbadë moved slowly to the edge of the raffia wall, tantalizing the crowd, as we could first see only his long beak, then finally, a portion of his full figure, dominated by his huge heavy raffia skirt. He lingered there for some time, alternately speaking to the musicians and initiating songs. I later learned that during the time that Gegbadë had remained behind the raffia wall, he was evoking not just his own *yinannu,*

Figure 1.3. Gegbadë
emerging from his sacred
house. Photograph by
Daniel B. Reed.

but also *yinannu* from many other sacred locations and *genu*. Every Ge performance is to some extent intertextual. Through music, gesture, and other means,
Gegbadë elicits many different sources of power to assist him in his spiritually
challenging work.[12]

Lambert then moved toward Jean-Claude and began dancing, his head low-
ered toward the drum, his rear end bouncing up and down, his long, cream-and-
dark-blue–colored *bubu* waving gracefully on his arms swinging through the air.
Finally, it became clear that the *yinannu* of joy had arrived: the *ge* himself began
to dance. Jean-Claude continued drumming in a dance style, with light and rapid
strokes producing cascades of high-pitched sounds, while Gegbadë extended his
arms from side to side in a rhythmic sweeping gesture, his body undulating to
the pulse of the drums. The *ge* danced out into clear view, and I caught my first
view of his complete physical form.

I was first struck by his size. Gegbadë's girth is substantial. His cream-and-
blue *bubu* spread wide as it draped down his abdomen toward the thick heavy
raffia skirt that hung to the ground, obscuring his feet. His colorful cone-shaped
leather hat rose high off his head, culminating in a tuft of white animal hair.
Cowrie shells rimmed the hat's brow. Long dyed cloth strips hung from the brow's
ends, framing the *ge*'s striking dark wooden face. Dominating Gegbadë's visage
was a long beak, extending downward from thin, feminine eyes, outlined in white.
Dark hair covered the end of the beak, looking almost like a long moustache. As

Figure 1.4. Gegbadë seated, attended by *gekia* Louan Dominique. Photograph by Daniel B. Reed.

he began to dance, his measured, graceful movements accentuated his physical form, bringing to life this masterpiece in shape and color.

Gegbadë danced bent at the waist, looking toward the ground, his raffia skirt bouncing to the pulse of the music, adding yet another timbral and percussive layer. Occasionally he rose up and looked or pointed to the sky in a gesture Jean-Claude later told me meant, "Give it to me," meaning the power of the *yinannu*. The *ge*'s attendants were attentive to his every move, following him around the performance space as he danced. After each brief period of dancing, one or two attendants rushed up to the *ge*, smoothing out his raffia skirt, straightening the long, colorful leather straps hanging from his waist, and generally making sure all elements of his physical appearance remained properly in place. To cool Gegbadë down after the exertion of dancing, attendant Dominique used each of the *ge*'s long baggy sleeves to fan his body.

After several segments of dance and speech, Gegbadë moved toward Djomande, the Mau man who had come for a consultation. For the next several minutes, Gegbadë alternated between speaking to Djomande and dancing immediately before him. Each time Gegbadë began speaking, Jean-Claude adjusted his drumming accordingly, playing more sporadically to allow space for the *ge*'s words. Then, when Gegbadë would resume dancing, Jean-Claude responded by playing more rapid virtuosic patterns. When he first stood before Djomande, Gegbadë delivered this proverb-drenched speech:

Ɓa fli da	Please excuse me
Ɓa we da	I ask for the floor
Zuluge we nin	It's the place [role] of the *ge* to seize sorcerers
Gba-ɓo Gba we nin	It's the place [role] of Gba

Figure 1.5. Gegbadë talking to Djomande, while *gekia* Louan Dominique holds a mirror reflecting positive spiritual energy back to the *ge*. Photograph by Daniel B. Reed.

Mεn yon puwon ɓa	People come to drink
Ke, waa yon gewon ɓa	But they do not come for the *ge*
Mεn yon puwon ɓa	People come to drink
Ke, waa yon gewon ɓa	But they do not come for the *ge*
Ɓö i tonto ɓa ge ɓa	You must listen to my *ge*
Ɓö i tonto ɓa ge ɓa	You must listen to my *ge*
Dεkpɔɗïö ɗo kpan ɓa kɔwɔ ɓa	The rising of the sun will find my words
ɗεkpɔɗïö ɗo kpan ɓa kɔwɔ ɓa	The rising of the sun will find my words
ɓa nin wo n Gegba kö	It is me whom they call Gegba.

The *ge* then initiated a song in Djomande's language, Mau, and went back to dancing. During this period of the event, the *ge* initiated several songs in the Mau language. Gegbadë was known far beyond the Dan region; often his clients were of other ethnic groups. Gegbadë sometimes sang songs in the language of the person who had come seeking help. For example, on this day he initiated the following song:

Masanɗe Allah ɗe Masanɗe Allah! Masanɗe	Masanɗe [a woman's proper name],
Allah i ko	Allah is with you

Jean-Claude later explained to me this song's meaning: it refers to the story of a woman (Masand'e) who was blamed for sorcery. A *ge* who was called to investigate this accusation found her innocent. To proclaim Masandʼe's innocence, the *ge* sang this song. In a different context, this song could be sung to announce that a suspect is innocent; here, the song was not serving that purpose. But through this song, Gegbadë situated himself on the side of Allah, the Muslim God. Dan religion holds that *genu* are intermediaries between Zlan, or God, and people. While my consultants sometimes had problems with *people* who identified as Muslim or Christian, they always asserted that there is only one God who simply goes by different names. This song shows that Gegbadë adjusts his performance to each context. He communicates with his clients in ways they will understand. In the process, he shows that, although he is an enactment of Dan religious belief and ethnic identity, boundaries between religious and ethnic categories are not absolute.

A little while later, in the middle of dancing, Gegbadë began walking in a distinctive way, back and forth across the performance space, with his hands on his hips. This, I later learned, was a walk of war. If this had been a context in which Gegbadë was pursuing sorcerers and he had walked thus, then Jean-Claude would have drummed in a way to attract the most aggressive *yinannu* of war. However, in this context—divination—Gegbadë danced in this way merely to show contentment; clearly, context affects the meaning of specific aspects of Ge performance. This context-specific dance step was here recontextualized by the *ge,* communicating something entirely different from what the same movement would communicate in its original context. Ge performance is full of such intertextual references. Master drummer Jean-Claude must remain alert to every little gesture and word of Gegbadë. Jean-Claude must be able to read every situation. He must know what is meant by the invocation of every song and dance step and be ready to respond appropriately with his drum.

After several more minutes passed, Gegbadë stood before Djomande and, by gesturing, asked his *gekia* for the *téléphone.* At the moment when the *ge* placed the receiver end to his ear, Jean-Claude drummed in a particular style that allows the message from the *yinannu* to arrive through the telephone. Soon thereafter, Gegbadë motioned for the music to stop. He took the *sraman* bell from his attendant. Holding the ringing bell in his hand, and looking to the sky, Gegbadë announced to Djomande that he had heard the message from the *yinannu*. He asked whether Djomande wanted to be informed of the necessary sacrifice now or whether he would prefer to return at a later time to hear the news in private, in the sacred house. When Djomande elected the latter, Gegbadë's work with him was finished for that day.

Several minutes later, the *ge* motioned for the musicians and assistants to follow him and he departed his compound, leading his group out onto the dirt road. Gegbadë toured Grand Gbapleu until late that night. At the compounds of several important families, he danced, gave benedictions, and delivered the news of his impending journey to Bofesso.

My first experience of a Gegbadë performance was relaxed and comfortable in a way that few others were. Most manifestations of *genu* from Théodore's sacred house directly involved the pursuit of sorcerers. Following this first event, I had no idea how important Gegbadë would become to my research, and, despite my initial reservations, I still had no idea what I was getting into. Could I be endangering participants in the performance by studying and later writing about these experiences? Were Jacques, Nicole, and I safe engaging in this kind of research?

At subsequent events, I found myself staring at a man who had just admitted to trying to kill his daughter, I found myself studying a situation in which nine members of the same family had died over the course of several months, I found myself worrying over Jacques when he came home bruised from an attack he had sustained while accompanying Gegbadë to a sorcery confrontation in a village near Man. And I found myself questioning what I believed and how I had become involved in this strife-filled phenomenon. *Zu ge* performance is serious business. It deals with peoples' misery. Gegbadë's role is frequently not just to put an end to this misery but also to assign blame. Performers make a living by throwing themselves into the center of grave conflicts. And at the center of Gegbadë performers' work is music.

By submitting to something I had originally tried to evade, I became exposed to a whole new set of ways that Ivorians use this old performance complex as a strategy to deal with postcolonial life. But I was surprised to learn how much there was in common between what I had embraced—entertainment *genu*—and the anti-sorcery *genu* I had avoided. Though many aspects of the performances, roles, and meanings of the two genres differ, both are clearly ways for performers to enact identities and accomplish goals in relationship to a complex world. Ge, this enactment of Dan social ideals, beliefs, and identity, is in practice a multi-ethnic and highly mobile affair. People of numerous ethnic groups travel great distances to seek out the services of both Gegbadë and Gedro, and the performing groups themselves are highly mobile, traveling throughout Côte d'Ivoire and even beyond the nation's borders to employ their skills. Like skilled popular-music performers, Gegbadë and Gedro draw influences from a wide variety of sources, adapting their performances to please their audiences and to best accomplish their goals. Unlike Gedro, Gegbadë does not incorporate popular-music references into his performance, but his performance is no less intertextual, no less intertwined with the world around him. In different ways, both Gedro and Gegbadë skillfully recontextualize and interweave disparate influences, reinscribing them with new meaning to accomplish particular tasks. And the music, *getan,* serves as the primary means through which performers accomplish their goals. Yet it is not only performers but also audience members and event organizers, among others, who meet differing and sometimes competing needs through Ge performance and discourse about Ge. Studying Ge performance helped me to better understand the world in which the Dan live, one in which people and their various domains of culture are "encountering, interrogating and contesting each other in new and unexpected ways" (Appadurai and Breckenridge 1988).

As the entertainment *ge* Kpaclöclö wandered the road to Man that hot morning in January 1997, he passed mosques, churches, regional headquarters of various government ministries, primary and secondary schools, and taxis with popular music blaring out of their windows. But a *ge* in this context is far from anachronistic. Ge performance is as much a part of modern life in Man as are the taxis and the government offices (cf. Piot 1999). Through "the tradition," my consultants express their own unique local views of modernity and enact views of themselves as complex beings in a complex world. Through Ge performance, my consultants place themselves in this world and position themselves in relationship to the difference surrounding them. Ge is not just their way of understanding and relating to the world, it is also their contribution to it; the road to Man is a two-way route.

TWO

Coexistence, Cooperation, and Conflict in the City of Eighteen Mountains

I first arrived in Man—"the city of eighteen mountains"—in July 1994. It was a rainy-season evening, and as our bus turned off the main highway onto the road leading into Man, mist was settling at the bases of the craggy green mountains that ring the city. My assistant Tiemoko Guillaume, Ivorian ethnomusicologist Adépo Yapo, and I clawed our way off the packed bus and went in search of a taxi. We carved out a spot on the side of a street, sandwiching ourselves between street merchants selling cigarettes and beef brochettes, a steady stream of pedestrians, and the sporadic flow of automobile traffic, mostly consisting of public-transport taxis and minibuses called *gbarkas*. Guillaume eventually flagged down one of the road-worn green taxis. We loaded in our gear and headed up the twisted narrow street through Quartier Air France to the Tiemoko family's compound. We were warmly welcomed by Guillaume's family, who generously included their surprise visitors in their dinner plans.

Shortly after a dinner of rice and sauce, I collapsed onto a foam mattress on a cement floor in one of the buildings in the family compound and listened to the sounds of my new environment. Recorded popular music from central Africa blasting from a nearby open-air bar. Jembe drumming. Human voices—talking, laughing, yelling. Children singing. Insects. Goats. Dogs. Eventually, this city symphony lulled me to sleep.

I awoke at 4:00 A.M. to the first phrase of the call to prayer coursing from the tower of a nearby mosque. The muezzin's voice, distorted by an overdriven loudspeaker, awakened people and animals alike. Dogs barked, roosters crowed, and I heard the shuffle of human feet on the dusty street. In the long sonic space between each phrase sung by the nearest muezzin, I heard several other amplified calls to prayer off in the distance, echoing off buildings, hillsides, and mountains.

Soon I heard the sounds of early morning women's work: the "swish, swish" of their brooms sweeping cement floors and compound grounds; the earth-shaking, rhythmic pounding of their huge wooden mortars and pestles grinding grain.

Around 6:00 A.M., we headed down the hill to find a baguette for breakfast. The streets were already filled with activity, as they were on any typical morning in Man. Balancing loads on their heads, streams of women made their way to the market. Street merchants laid out their wares—bananas, imported plastic-wrapped cookies, millet fritters. On charcoal burners, immigrants from the savanna boiled green tea, which they poured in long streams from pots held high above small clear glasses. Open-air bars served coffee and omelets. Kiosk windows opened, displaying rows of cassettes or cigarettes. Groups of uniformed children on their way to school stopped by a street merchant for a hot *gateau* (similar to a donut). Lebanese and Mauritanian shopkeepers opened their doors. Banks opened. The streets filled with taxis. *Gbarkas* bumped along, young men hanging out of their open doors soliciting passengers by yelling out intended destinations: "Bian-kouma Biankouma!" or "Fakobly Fakobly!" or "Danané Danané!" Women in high heels and waxed-print–fabric dresses joked with men in suitcoats as they headed to work in government ministry offices. Robed herders, immigrants from the savanna, guided cattle down paved streets in search of grass to graze. In the center of a roundabout at a prominent Man intersection, the herders, along with other pedestrians, taxis, and buses, regularly passed by a statue of a stilt *ge* (*gegblɛɛn*) standing high atop a monument. Indeed all of Man's citizens see everywhere images of the faces of *ge* (*gewëďënu,* or masks) as they move through their daily lives. On business signs and business cards, on walls in restaurants and tourist shops—masks are nearly ubiquitous symbols in the visual landscape. Despite the increasing diversity of the region, for many Ivorians nothing symbolizes the Man region more than the image of the mask. As elder Gueu Gbe Alphonse told me, "The mask is the emblem of the West [of Côte d'Ivoire] (Gueu Gbe 1997f).[1] The mask, and the institution of Ge behind it, is not separate from but is very much a part of the cosmopolitan flow of contemporary life in Man.

Set within a region that historically has been agricultural, Man boasts a diversified service economy. Banks and hotels, churches and mosques, residential *lycées* and *collèges* (near-equivalents to high schools and junior high schools, respectively), Koranic and *madrasa* schools,[2] government offices, nongovernment organizations, and shops of many kinds feature in the Man socioeconomic land-scape. At the center of the city is its vast market which, despite the fact that its central building burned down in 1997, still features a vast array of products, ranging from electronics to housewares to used books to clothing and fabric to tourist art. The continued prominence of agriculture in the region is also strongly evidenced at the market, where tropical fruits, vegetables, and grains abound. Sheep, chicken, beef, and fish merchants attest to the fact that animal husbandry and fishing also remain centrally important features of the local economy.

Dan villages in the Man region remain agriculture-centered. But even these villages are cosmopolitan, if, as Charles Piot argues, "by cosmopolitanism we mean that people partake in a social life characterized by flux, uncertainty, en-counters with difference, and the experience of the processes of transculturation" (1999, 23). Most villages around Man include, and for some time have included, residents who are not Dan.[3] Most have electricity, even if just in a few buildings. In the evening, farmers gather around wooden tables at village bars to relax, drink warm bottled beer or palm wine, and listen to popular music on the radio. Clothing alone reveals the pluralistic nature of village life. In a single-family compound one can see people wearing the blue, yellow, and cream of traditional handwoven Dan *bubus;* men sporting sheen city-style Muslim *bubus;* women wearing wraps of brightly patterned cloth made in factories in Holland and China; men in co-ordinated polyester slacks and shirts; and teenagers in T-shirts and jeans picked up on visits to Abidjan. Many youth come and go from the village to secondary school in Man or to work in Abidjan. Girls who spend time away are often conspicuous in the village, as their taste for jeans is not shared by the vast majority of village women, who prefer cloth wraps.

Gender roles are distinct and apparent. Village women work hard and nearly constantly—fetching water, pounding grain, planting and harvesting in the fields, feeding and washing children, cooking every meal. Men also work hard in the fields—growing crops such as rice, bananas, cassava, yams, and coffee—but tend to relax back in the village. Periodically, men busy themselves in meetings during which they govern village affairs. Daily interactions make plain the patriarchal nature of Dan life. Women are considered to be under the authority of their fathers during youth and their husbands during adulthood. Classes of gender and age are an integral part of the "taken-for-granted" world. Men expect to be able to command women, and older people—whether an older sibling, an uncle, a father, or even someone unrelated—have nearly absolute authority over anyone their junior. As Nicole observed, Dan patriarchy, like all patriarchies, is by necessity upheld by as many means as possible: land ownership, inheritance, and systems of social and spiritual power. The institution of Ge serves as one such means whereby gender and power relationships are reinforced. In these and other ways, Dan men dominate Dan women.[4] Yet the strict division of gender roles and the separation of gendered spheres of activity results in women having nearly absolute authority in their own realm. It is not only men who actively maintain the system of gender power relations; elder women also use their positions of power to uphold the system that accords them authority over their own affairs.

Boys and girls are circumcised in separate rituals that are part of the indigenous system of education, or initiation, into adulthood. This initiation—sometimes referred to as "the Mask school" in the case of the male version—is the point at which elders introduce the idea of Ge to the young. In initiation, girls become introduced to the women's version of Ge called Kong. A society consisting of (mostly) postmenopausal women, Kong is led by the powerful *zude*—an older woman whose roles include that of midwifery, excision (clitoridectomy), other traditionally female matters, and, often, spiritual consultation. Several *genu* are involved in boys' initiation, which is overseen by a type of *ge* called *dεn* and is the moment when inculcation into the multifaceted phenomenon of Ge takes place. In close proximity to every village is its sacred forest—a protected nature sanctuary where boys' initiation takes place, among other things. Most villages also have sacred mountains and sacred water sources. In addition to these communally recognized sacred locales, many individual families have their own sacred spots. A mountain, a spring, or other particular natural phenomena might serve as places for worship and sacrificial offerings of livestock and grain. And certain families have sacred houses—the village homes of *genu.*

I have chosen to use the term "sacred house," because these buildings take many forms. Dan-speaking French interchange the terms *"case sacrée"* (sacred hut) and *"maison sacrée"* (sacred house); in Dan, these buildings are called *gunkɔ* (sacred hut/house) or, more commonly, *gundïö* (sacred place). As is generally true, changes in Dan life are reflected in changes in things Ge. Just like the homes in which Dan people in the 1990s lived, some sacred houses are thatched-roof roundhouses, others are square cement structures with tin roofs, while still others are single rooms in elaborate European-style houses. Sacred houses, like sacred forests and indeed all sacred spaces, are marked by the presence of dried raffia at their entrances; noninitiates cross such a threshold at their peril.

While for the most part these aspects of Dan life are strongest in rural villages, they are also very much a part of life in urban settings. Conversely, "modern" life is very much a presence in many villages (cf. Piot 1999). People in both settings actively choose how to live their lives from a wide variety of options. Many villages have churches and mosques in addition to traditional sacred houses and sacred forests. While there is less mass media in most villages than in the cities, radio and cassettes are prevalent. Larger villages have their own primary schools and many children walk from smaller neighboring villages to join their compatriots at school. Local and national politics interpenetrate in village settings. Up until the coup of December 1999, one measure of the power and dominance of the national ruling party (Parti Démocratique de Côte d'Ivoire, or PDCI) was that most villages had a Président du comité PDCI. Always an important elder who was prominent in village affairs, this person served as a liaison between village politics and the subprefects and prefects at the regional branches of the PDCI-dominated federal government. Even the federal judiciary and indigenous systems of justice collaborate in handling sorcery matters through the performance of the *zu ge*.

Most important of all, people move back and forth from village to city so frequently that influences regularly flow each way, a pattern found throughout the continent of Africa. Previous studies of African arts have refuted the idea of an absolute rural/urban dichotomy. As Zoë Strother comments, "The constant movement between city and country of very large segments of the population calls into question any facile divisions between urban and rural populations" (1995, 31). It is common knowledge that throughout Africa, urban migrants remain intimately connected to village life. In many countries, one travels back and forth to one's "village" (both a physical and a conceptual "home") for weddings, funerals, during vacations, and at many other times during the year. Daniel Avorgbedor observes that through this interaction, rural Ewe significantly influence urban Ewe music (1986, 307). Sidney Kasfir discusses influence traveling the opposite direction: Samburu encounters with tourists in urban settings play back into " 'traditional,' non-commodified forms" when they return to the village (1994, 20). Strother notes that in the Democratic Republic of Congo, the notion of *sape*—a hip mode of being and dress usually associated with Kinshasa—is not limited to the urban setting. Aspiring chic young village men utilize this same aesthetic ideal in the creation of new forms of mask performance. Christophe Wondji describes the musical communication between villages and cities in Côte d'Ivoire as "intense and constant." Certain well-known performers and styles travel back and forth so regularly that they defy classification as either rural or urban; they are both and neither (1983, 182–183). As Karin Barber aptly asserts, "We are therefore looking not at a unilinear one-way process of change but at cycles of influence and counter-influence, borrowing and paying back, of great complexity and subtlety" (1987, 18).

Rural areas are far from static museums of traditional arts. In Côte d'Ivoire, styles of popular music distinct from popular music of the cities have developed in rural settings (Wondji 1983, 181). Avorgbedor writes that composition of new songs in new styles is normal practice in rural Ewe areas (1986, 295). These scholars recognize the agency of rural peoples. Rural Africans do not all uniformly adhere to traditions, nor are they blank slates upon which urban and other imported cultures are imprinted. Like most rural Africans, Ge performers select from a wide range of influences—some of local origin, some from other parts of Côte d'Ivoire, some transnational—and incorporate them into their own expressive acts. African village life is as much a part of the modern world as the African city; in both contexts, people see the mixture of the modern and the traditional "not only as unproblematic, but also as desirable" (Piot 1999, 172). This mixture is evident in artistic forms such as Ge performance.

Because of factors such as population mobility, trade, ethnic heterogeneity, and the media, my field "site"—itself a fluid and mobile "location" including both rural and urban Côte d'Ivoire—represents what Appadurai and Breckenridge call a "zone" of cultural debate, in which diverse peoples, their ideas and their expressive acts confront each other with increasing frequency and intensity (Appadurai and Breckenridge 1988). This is not to suggest that no interaction and mixing of different types of peoples and domains of culture occurred before the late twentieth century. Rather, as Ivorian society has become even more mobile, mass media has become common, and other changes have occurred, cultural give-and-take has become even more the norm. While cultural collision may be more readily apparent in urban settings, I maintain that the "zone" description applies equally to less populous regions of West Africa such as the rural areas around Man, where cultural intermingling has been the norm rather than the exception, both prior to and since colonialism. The range of influences surely differs according to situation, but "people are always adapting, whether in a city or in a village" (Avorgbedor 1986, 301).

This is the context in which Ge performances now occur. Just in the past century, western Côte d'Ivoire has seen the diversification of the local economy beyond agriculture, the introduction of mass media such as radio and TV and mass communications, the introduction of French-style systems of education and justice, centralized nation-state government, and Christianity. Islam also grew significantly during the previous century as great numbers of Muslim Jula[5] merchants from the savanna settled in the region, especially in the city of Man, where in the 1990s they probably outnumbered the indigenous Dan populace. Dan themselves have also converted to Islam in great numbers, and Muslims constitute a majority in Man and many Dan villages, a fact which has received little attention in scholarly literature (Gba Daouda 1982). Man features great ethnic diversity as well; the Dan and northern immigrants are joined by people from all over Côte d'Ivoire arriving for jobs in the governmental and service sectors. Because of this increased mobility and the introduction of many new institutions which serve functions historically served by the institution of Ge, *genu* have begun to manifest in new contexts, in different or extended roles. *Genu* often perform in contexts in which they are open to multiple interpretations and their religious dimension is not uniformly understood, accepted, or necessarily desired.[6] While some types of *genu* have receded from public view, remaining behind the walls of sacred huts where they are only privately consulted in times of need, others find themselves, as public entities, before an expanded and diversified audience.

MAN: A HISTORY OF MOBILITY AND ETHNIC AND RELIGIOUS PLURALIZATION

> We are all immigrants here.
>
> —Ge performer Gbongue Felix of Déoulé,
> August 29, 1997

The story of Man is one that reveals fundamental links between colonization, ethnic mobility, and the spread of religious ideas. This story begins with the migration of Dan peoples to the region. Oral histories of my consultants support other historians' claims that, beginning perhaps as early as 1300 C.E., Dan peoples began migrating south from the savanna region of present-day northern Côte d'Ivoire and Guinea (Person 1961, 47–49), eventually settling in the region around Touba. From the seventeenth to the nineteenth centuries, Dan peoples continued migrating south to their present locations (Loucou 1984, 63). In this location the Dan encountered Wè and Bassa peoples, whom they pushed south and west. Wè peoples, particularly the Wobé subgroup, remain a significant minority population in the Man region. Dan peoples have always traveled—to hunt, to trade, and to seek better fortune at times when political turmoil and population growth forced them to seek new land to farm (Johnson 1986, 1). Though I will concentrate in this book on the increasing movement of people and ideas in western Côte d'Ivoire in the late twentieth century and its implications for Ge performance, Gbongue Felix's statement serves as a reminder that mobility is not a new phenomenon in the Dan region.[7]

Stories about the founding of Man reveal its origin as a meeting point for traveling merchants exchanging goods. According to my consultants, Man was founded by people from two Dan villages—Gbapleu, known today as Grand Gbapleu (home of Oulai Théodore), and Gbépleu[8]—which in the 1990s rested about ten kilometers apart on the extreme southeastern and northwestern edges of the city, respectively.[9] Long ago, residents of Gbapleu and Gbépleu met periodically to exchange goods at a location roughly midway between the two villages. Over time, people began settling at this meeting point, which gradually developed and grew to become the town of Man. In recent times, Man has spread so far as to reach the edges of both villages from which its original inhabitants came.

Geographically, Man was well positioned to become a mercantile crossroads, and not just for nearby Dan. Man rests at a geographical borderland, near the northern limit of the coastal rain forest, just before the forest gives way to the arboreal savanna. Man furthermore rests at the confluence of two trade routes, one north to south connecting the forest to the savanna and another east to west linking settlements in the northern forest region (République de Côte d'Ivoire 1970(?), 5). The trade route heading north linked Dan peoples with the northern Mande world, connecting Man with Touba and Odienné and leading on into present-day Mali. This route would prove to be of particular importance during and after the colonial era, not just as a trade route but as an artery for peoples heading south.

During the era of French colonization and the ensuing postcolonial period, western Côte d'Ivoire witnessed dramatic social upheaval that fundamentally impacted Dan life and the practice of Ge. The French military campaign and ensuing occupation ushered in colonial and postcolonial waves of migration of Dan peoples out of and of other ethnicities into the Man region. Rather late in the colonial period, Man was subjected to one of the small but brutal "wars of conquest" that the French rationalized with the cruelly euphemistic term "pacification" (Manning 1988, 64–65). The French first established a military post in Man during the campaign of Captain Laurent in 1907–1908 (Cercle Militaire du Haut-Cavally 1911). For years, however, the military grip of the French on Man was tenuous. Finally, in 1914, it was reported that the conquest was "now complete," though resistance continued through skirmishes, defections, blockages of paths, and refusals to work and to pay taxes (Cercle de Haut-Cavally 1914; Benoit 1931, 605–691).

All across Côte d'Ivoire, once military superiority was established, the French set up *cercles*—administrative stations which oversaw large regions of anywhere from five to fifteen *cantons,* each of which were headed by a *canton* chief. Hierarchies of power were established; the colonial administrator governed *cercle* administrators, who ruled the *canton* chiefs (Manning 1988, 84). Soon after their triumph over the Dan, the French began setting up the Cercle of Man. This shift in the military and civil governance of the region altered certain key roles that Ge had historically played. No longer are war *genu* the ultimate protectors over the sovereignty of their land, and no longer are village affairs governed solely by chiefs and elders with the spiritual and political support of the *genu.* This is not to say that *genu* have ceased to play a behind-the-scenes role in decision making at the local level. Governance of local affairs still involves *genu* in many villages. But it also involves the power of the federal government, which shifts and complicates decision making and governance at the local level.

The Dan did not readily fall into step with the demands of the colonial power. Battles, blockades, and boycotts continued long after the French established military superiority. As late as 1922, even after the establishment of the Cercle of Man, colonial administrators complained that "they [the Dan] have not yet lost the hope of recovering their freedom" (Colonie de la Côte d'Ivoire, Cercle de Man 1922a). This hope was not realized, of course, and the changes wrought by the horrific colonial regime were far-reaching. The ethnic makeup of the Man region gradually began shifting, a process which continues up to the present day. At first, some Dan fled the oppressive regime by moving west into the mountains toward Guinea. To escape forced labor and taxes, young men began migrating east and south to search for work on plantations around Bouake, Dimbokro, and Abidjan (Colonie de la Côte d'Ivoire, Cercle de Man 1922). While many Dan had lived mobile lives prior to this time, the colonial occupation of Man initiated a period during which leaving their homeland would become an increasingly common choice for young Dan people. Gradually, small Dan settlements began appearing around the plantations in the southeast of the country. Today, Dan can be found living in many areas of the country. Individual Dan people and families have left Man for education and/or work of all kinds. Whole communities of

Figure 2.1. Gedro of Abidjan. Photograph by Robert Grossman.

migrant Dan exist as well, particularly in the south-central and southeastern areas of the country. The largest Dan settlement outside of the Man region is in Yopougon—a neighborhood of Abidjan.

Sizable immigrant communities such as that in Yopougon have brought with them many Dan customs, including Ge. Because Ge is a family affair, when a significant portion of a family relocates, their *genu* may well relocate along with them. Moreover, migrant Dan who were accustomed to meeting certain needs through *genu* back in the Man region continue to solicit them in their new setting. For example, migrant Dan hire entertainment *genu* to commemorate important rites of passage such as marriages, initiations, or other celebratory occasions. Such occasions are lucrative for the musicians, dancers, and ritual specialists who accompany a *ge*. When a community has become large enough, as in Yopougon, and there is enough of a market for a *ge* group to work consistently, one might migrate from the Dan homeland to fill the need. This is the case in Yopougon, where a number of *genu* reside to provide services for Dan people all over the Abidjan region.

Smaller migrant communities sometimes hire *genu* to come specially from the Man region. For example, Dan living in the southeastern town of Guitri, in the Dida ethnic region, hired the *zu ge* Gegbadë from Man to solve a sorcery problem. Having witnessed the effectiveness of this Dan *ge*, certain Dida themselves later hired Gegbadë for the same purpose. As Dan peoples migrate, their *genu* follow them and, as a result, Ge performances take place in new contexts. In this way, Ge—itself an expression of Dan ethnic identity—increasingly becomes a multiethnic affair, appealing to a transethnic clientele.

While the French occupation motivated some Dan to leave western Côte d'Ivoire, Dan emigration was far outweighed by the immigration of other ethnic groups into the Man region. The most significant population shift, which has continued into the postcolonial era, has been the sweeping immigration of Jula peoples into the forest region of Côte d'Ivoire. The French "pacification" led to the opening up of southern trade routes that had previously been monopolized or controlled by local ethnic groups such as the Dan. In the early twentieth century, the lucrative kola-nut trade was thus opened up, and Jula began migrating south into the forest in great numbers, settling in places such as Man which had heretofore been closed to them (Person 1982, 18). Merchants from the north began founding Jula neighborhoods around French military posts shortly after their creation. In areas where their presence previously had been relegated to that of itinerant traders, Jula peoples began to establish majority status. This immigration, made possible by the protection of the French military forces, amounted to no less than "a social and ethnic revolution" (Person 1982, 18).

As the twentieth century progressed, the increasing prosperity of southern Côte d'Ivoire attracted greater and greater numbers of immigrants from poorer regions in the north (Launay 1982, 80–97). As a result of this migration of northerners, by 1987 northern migrant workers constituted 25 percent of the population of Côte d'Ivoire, while over half of Abidjan's population was comprised of foreigners and recent settlers (Yacoob 1987, 120). No recent census figures are available for Man, but my consultants affirmed what I sensed to be true: at the end of the twentieth century, Jula almost certainly made up the majority of the population of Man. The Jula presence, while more strongly felt in some parts of town than others, is pervasive. In many parts of the city, Jula is the most commonly spoken language. French and Jula both serve as lingua francas for multiethnic Man. Even overwhelmingly Dan parts of town are home to large numbers of northerners. For example, in the neighborhood of Petit Gbapleu is the headquarters of the multiethnic *dozo*—the traditional hunter's society originally from the Mande heartland. A large population of *dozow* live in Man, where they hire out their services as a private security force for neighborhoods and private functions.[10]

But the greatest impact of the Jula migration on Ge performance has been religious, as the vast majority of these immigrants identify as Muslim. As peoples from the north have headed south (not only in Côte d'Ivoire but also in neighboring Ghana), they have often brought Islamic faith with them. Even non-Muslim northerners frequently adopt a Muslim identity upon arrival in the south, in part to aid in the transition to urban life by becoming part of the larger community of northern immigrants, the vast majority of whom are Muslim (Yacoob 1987; Grindal 1973).

While immigrants from the savanna and Dan peoples form the majority of the population in Man, the city is also home to a number of small minority groups. A substantial number of Wè peoples (Wobé and Guéré), whose homeland lies to the east and south of Man, live in the region, some in the city itself. Refugees from the Liberian civil war still constitute a small but significant presence, though the Ivorian government began repatriating them in 1997. Lebanese immigrants, who run video stores, groceries, and various other shops, have a small but vibrant community. Mauritanians work as butchers and own small shops as well. A handful of Europeans and Americans live in Man; some run businesses, others work in the mining industry,[11] some work for relief agencies, and still others are associated with the Catholic Church or work as missionaries. Volunteers from both the French and American versions of the Peace Corps occasionally stray into town, as do European and American tourists. While the tourist trade, and indeed the overall ethnic diversification, has opened up additional opportunities for entertainment *genu,* they have also led to a reduction of performances of many highly sacred *genu.* Some powerful *genu,* consultants told me, refuse to perform in a context in which so many of their neighbors are not initiated Dan and thus lack knowledge of the rules of Ge.

People from all over Côte d'Ivoire come to Man for jobs, often bringing their families with them. As capital of the region (a region is roughly equivalent to a state or province), Man is home to many civil servants, some of whom are Dan, but many who have come to Man from other parts of the country. The prefect's office, the police department, the judiciary, and a host of local offices of government ministries are staffed by appointees who represent many of the country's ethnic groups. People from other parts of the country also direct many local branches of nongovernment organizations such as the African Development Bank. Man has furthermore become an educational center. Students come to Man from all over the country to attend residential *collèges* and *lycées.* Many teachers in these schools and in the *écoles primaires* also come from other regions. Finally, the relatively thriving service economy of Man attracts job-seekers from all over who work as tailors, hairdressers, typists, secretaries, postal workers, and as providers of many other services.

The transition to a diversified monetary economy has had many implications for Ge performance. For an increasing number of people, Ge has become a business, a way of making a living. Making a living from the practice of this sacred tradition is no contradiction whatsoever for the performers with whom I studied. Master drummer Goueu Tia Jean-Claude considered that he was able to make a living drumming for Ge performances as evidence that he was on a good and righteous path. Jean-Claude's Muslim father at first questioned his son's decision to practice "the tradition," but when he noticed that his son no longer was coming to him for money, he gained respect for his son's decision and the spiritual path he had decided to follow. The two *genu* for whom Jean-Claude most frequently drums—Gedro and Gegbadë—are both extremely popular and thus work consistently for reasonably good pay. In an environment with a more diversified populace, tourism, and increasing opportunities for celebration, the entertainment *ge* Gedro meets many needs. Likewise, Gegbadë plays several important roles, primarily that of solving crimes of sorcery in an era in which the federal government has decided to begin relying on traditional agents to do so. In the diversified economy of contemporary Man, each of these *genu* provide important services for the increasingly diverse and mobile public.

RELIGION IN MAN

Linked to the flow of people in and out of Man has been the flow of ideas, customs, and beliefs, including religion. Ge performance, an enactment of religious belief and identity for many Dan peoples, today takes place in a context of many religious options. Practice of Dan religion itself involves many options and varies considerably from family to family and locality to locality in the Dan region. Two world religions, Islam spreading from the north and Christianity from the south, have impacted the Man area, as they have in other regions in West Africa. Both Islam and Christianity have been inextricably linked, at different points in local history, to invasive colonial and/or imperial powers. Since Islam has been a presence in the region for much longer than Christianity, I will begin there.

In the northern Dan region, where I conducted my research, Muslims constitute a majority in many villages, and in the city of Man, Muslims clearly are in the majority. Exactly when Dan began converting to Islam is difficult to pinpoint, however. First contact with Islam probably occurred, as it did in much of West Africa, through trade with itinerant Muslims from the Sahel and savanna. Drawn by the kola-nut trade, Jula began setting up the first permanent Muslim settlements in northern Côte d'Ivoire in the seventeenth century (Launay 1982, 14). Because the Dan are positioned at the gateway to the forest where kola trees grow, they have had a great deal of contact with Muslim traders for centuries. Still, Dan seem to have resisted conversion to Islam for the most part until the arrival of Samori Touré in the second half of the nineteenth century. Samori, the legendary empire-builder and leader of the resistance to the French military takeover of West Africa, forcibly converted those people whom he conquered and brought into his empire. That many northern Dan identify as Muslim could well be attributable to Samori, who was captured by the French in the Dan town of Guelemou in 1898 (Gba 1982; Person 1990).

One cannot deny the importance of Samori's campaign of forced conversion. Yet many Dan who have converted to Islam have done so by choice, as a result of the gradual spread of the religion through contact with the northern Mande world. Through trade and traveling clerics in precolonial times, and in more recent years through cohabitation as a result of the Jula migration, many Dan have interacted on a daily basis with Muslims and have over time begun to identify as Muslims themselves. The gradual Islamization of Man can be noted in colonial reports. In 1922, colonial administrators commented that no "confessional schools" existed in the entire Cercle of Man, though an influential Jula had asked for permission to establish a mosque and a Koranic school south of Man in Duékoué (Colonie de la Côte d'Ivoire, Cercle de Man 1922b). Much changed in just two years; a 1924 report stated that the *cercle* was home to nine marabouts who directed "embryos" of Koranic schools. "These schools are of no great importance," the anonymous writer continued, as each had just five to six students, all of whom were Jula (Colonie de la Côte d'Ivoire, Cercle de Man 1924). Twenty years later, an administrator commented on the celebration of Tabaski (the feast at the end of Ramadan) by the "numerous Muslims" of Man (Colonie de la Côte d'Ivoire, Cercle de Man 1944).

Islam would continue to grow dramatically over the next fifty years. When I lived in Man in the 1990s, I was struck by the prevalence and diversity of Muslims. No longer are all Muslims Jula—that is, depending on how one defines the term "Jula." Ethnic identity, as Peter Mark writes, is "far from being permanent" but is to some extent related to historical factors (1992, 113–114). Mark shows that as Mande peoples moved into the Casamance region of Senegal, other locals began speaking Mandinka and taking on their identity. Robert Launay describes a similar situation among the Senufo and Jula populations of north central Côte d'Ivoire (1982, 112; 1992, 49–103). Much like the Senufo, it is possible for Dan to "become" Jula by converting to Islam. However, in contrast to Launay's portrayal, I have not encountered Dan who identify themselves in this way (although some might well do so); rather, non-Muslim Dan would sometimes derisively call Muslim Dan "Jula" in a way that implied that they were not being true to themselves. Regardless, it is certainly the case that today many Dan identify as Muslim. In fact, some of my Dan consultants consider Islam a fundamental aspect of their identity as Dan peoples. Certain elders recounted genealogical histories that expressed the idea that Islam had been central to their families' identities for many generations (Tia, Gnassene, and Vahan 1997).

One can only speculate about why so many Dan identify as Muslim. Bravmann (1974) has noted that frequently non-Muslim West Africans associate Islam with economic and spiritual power. Viewing traveling merchants and clerics as successful, people become curious about what spiritual strategies enabled them to achieve this success. Launay writes that economics influenced many Senufo to convert in Korhogo. Becoming Jula through conversion to Islam gained converts access to lucrative business dealings (Launay 1992). Some of my Dan consultants (e.g., Kassia Noël 1994) affirmed Louis Brenner's observation that in postcolonial times, conversion to Islam has taken on a new meaning, that of an anticolonial, anti-Western statement (1993, 12–13). Many consultants explained to me that Islam is in many ways a natural fit for them, as it allows for the continuation of such traditional Dan practices as polygyny. Any and all of these factors, as well as others, might have played a part.[12]

Most Dan Muslims practice a relatively flexible Maliki form of Islam. They profess faith in Allah but regard the other four pillars of Islamic faith—prayer five times daily, fast during Ramadan, the giving of alms to the poor, and pilgrimage to Mecca—as ideals rather than requirements. As Bravmann notes in his study of Islam in northwest Ghana and northeast Côte d'Ivoire, deviations from the five pillars of faith occur widely. However,

> to stray from such observances does not exclude an individual from the community of believers, for in the end the crucial factor is that he recognizes the existence of Allah. Beyond the most basic commitment, a wide degree of latitude is allowed. Given the minimal requirements of Islam for the majority of the faithful, it is not surprising to find either individuals or whole communities retaining and incorporating into their new faith varying degrees of traditional life. (1974, 28–29)

For some of my consultants, the boundaries between Dan religion and Islam are very fluid in experience. Some profess faith in Allah and regularly pray at the mosque for general well-being for themselves and their families. Yet if a problem arises in their lives, they are as likely to go to an advisor/healer of the Dan religious system (a *zumi* or *zu ge*) for help as to an Islamic scholar/advisor (marabout). In fact, some people think of these simply as parallel options. Depending on the problem, one or the other might be more effective. Furthermore, many *zumi* and *zuďe* (male and female *zu,* respectively) are themselves Muslim. Traditional healer Mli Bakayoko Boulaman, a Mau person who is Muslim and lives in the Dan village of Biélé, explained to me that occasionally a marabout might defer a problem to a *zu* and vice-versa (Mli 1997b). Diagnoses from either a marabout or a *zu* might involve aspects of Dan religion. For example, a marabout or a *zu* might identify as the source of a client's problem that he has been neglecting his family's sacred mountain, stream, or *ge*. The recommendation would then be a particular sacrifice—perhaps a couple of chickens—to the appropriate source of the family's well-being.

Many Dan syncretically combine elements of Islam and Dan religion in their lives. Previous studies have found similar religious mixing in other parts of West Africa. What I find interesting in Man is that syncretic mixes of Islam and Dan religion occur to a greater extent within individuals than in events. Katherine Green noted that Sonongui people incorporate an indigenous dance through a sacred doorway into their celebration of Ramadan (Green 1984, 113). Bravmann found that among Jula peoples in Burkina Faso, the celebration of Ramadan included Burkinabé mask performances (1983, 65–67). In contrast, in the communities of Muslims in the Man region, people emphatically stated that no blending of these two religious domains occurs *in events,* and my experience confirmed this. *Genu* danced at none of the fêtes honoring the major Muslim holidays. Rather, blending of Islam and "the tradition" occurs in the lives of individuals who, as described above, practice aspects of Islam in certain settings and aspects of Dan religion in others; who fluidly range across different religious options. Many Ge performers are themselves Muslim. And sometimes leaders in the Muslim community double as leaders in the sacred house. Though they tend to keep the two domains separate in practice, people in many communities around Man have blended aspects of Ge with Maliki-style Islam for generations.

That is not to suggest that antagonism is absent between Muslims and followers of "the tradition." In more recent years, the stricter Wahhabi movement has spread to Man. The contemporary West African Wahhabi movement originated in Bamako between 1945 and 1958, where the Society of Young Muslims began a reform movement aimed at countering the "moral laxity of the old elites" (Kaba 1972, 14).[13] Soon after its appearance in Mali, Wahhabiya spread south to Côte d'Ivoire, arriving in Korhogo (Launay 1992, 84–91) and later in Man. Wahhabi followers oppose all mixing of local religions and Islam. Some Dan Muslims oppose Ge and seek to abolish it altogether.

Just as there are anti-Ge Muslims, there are also a small but growing group of anti-Muslim followers of "the tradition." When I first arrived in Man, I naïvely expected to encounter elderly adherents to Dan religion being challenged by youth abandoning the old ways in favor of Islam. While this stereotypical pattern does exist in Man, things are far from that simple. Islam has been around for a while, and today many Dan elders identify as Muslim. What I find surprising is that many youth are rejecting the religious ways of their parents and grandparents in favor of "the religion of [their] ancestors." This is particularly true in the Man neighborhood of Petit Gbapleu. A loosely organized group of people who are in their mid-30s and younger embrace Dan religion while opposing the kind of fluid mixture of Islam and Ge practiced by many of their elders.

Some of my consultants even argue that Islam is in general decline among the Dan. Biemi Gba Jacques insisted that it was mostly just older people who were Muslim. The young rejected Islam because "it stands in the way of the kind of cultural liberation many young people here seek." While he was hesitant to generalize about the Dan as a whole, Jacques asserted with confidence that this is the case in his home village of Biélé. In the 1970s and 1980s when Jacques was growing up, Muslim holidays were village-wide celebrations. His grandfather—the former village chief who died in 1999—and all his wives prayed fastidiously five times daily. Biélé began building a mosque in the early 1980s, but it was never completed, Jacques said, due to lack of interest. The young were not converting to Islam (Biemi from Biemi and Goueu 1997a).

Conflict, cohabitation, and mixing are all words that describe the interactions taking place between Muslims and practitioners of Dan religion in Man. Some Dan reject Islam outright. Others reject what they see as more orthodox forms of

Islam that are less tolerant of traditional ways. Others actively select, from their various religious options, techniques that are effective, regardless of their origin or what they are called. And finally, some embrace Islam while rejecting "the tradition." The picture that emerges is one in which people of differing religious approaches and identities coexist, some of whom are tolerant of each other and others who are not. What I do *not* see occurring is a unilinear, unidimensional movement from point A to point B—from the practice of a polytheistic traditional religion toward the practice of a "pure" version of monotheistic Islam (Fisher 1973). While this may be occurring in other parts of West Africa (Monts 1980, 1984, 1998), the situation in Man is complex; some are moving toward Islam while others are moving away from it. My research supports Peter Mark's hypothesis that movements away from Islam might be more common than has been represented in the ethnographic literature on West Africa (1992, 151). In Man, people select from numerous local options in determining their religious identities. Among those options are various forms of Christianity.

Christianity has a much shorter history in western Côte d'Ivoire than does Islam. Since the Man region was one of the last to be "pacified" by the French, missions were established very late there compared with other nearby regions of West Africa. It was not until 1933 that the first Catholic mission was founded in Man (Zinsou 1976, 73, 78). In the past half-century, various Protestant denominations have set up missions and churches in Man as well, but Catholicism remains the most prevalent form of Christianity. Catholics maintain an expansive complex near the center of town that includes a huge cathedral, a radio station, an audio and video production studio, mission schools, and various other administrative offices. On Sundays, a multiethnic congregation fills the cathedral. People from other parts of the country who have come to Man for work are joined by a large indigenous population of Dan and Wobé peoples. Dan and Wobé choirs alternate Sundays, singing songs of worship in their local languages and using indigenous instruments and musical styles. Mission schools have educated many local peoples for decades.

Despite its brief history in the region, Christianity has had a dramatic impact, attracting many converts in Man and surrounding villages alike. As in other parts of the West African forest belt (see, for example Eades 1980, 133), in individual families one can sometimes count several different religious persuasions. Goueu Tia Jean-Claude's family compound is a case in point: some are Muslim, some are Christian, others practice Dan religion, and some take no interest in religion at all. I encountered no Dan families whose members all identified as Christian, though surely some exist. On the other hand, many immigrant families, especially those from other parts of the forest region, are 100 percent Christian. In our neighborhood lived several Akan families in which everyone identified as Christian and attended church regularly.

The Dan Christians whom I met, unlike many (though not all) Dan Muslims, tend to distance themselves rather considerably from Dan religion and Ge. Chorale leader Loua Philippe told me that before he became Catholic he worshiped sacred water and *genu,* that he followed "the tradition of our ancestors. But before someone is baptized, they have to say they will renounce all that" (Loua 1997). A Catholic priest at an open-air baptism in the village of Biélé made this point throughout his service. Imploring the small group of *baptisées* to now go directly to God rather than through local Dan intermediaries, the priest said:

If before you accompanied your families to go worship the mountains, from now on, that's finished! Your mountain is here, at the hotel of Christ. It's here that you will come to offer God the true, real sacrifice. You will have no other sacrifices to make.

Among the Dan, many Muslims continue to practice aspects of Dan religion, but few Christians I met admitted to doing so. I met not a single Christian who was a part of a Ge performance group. My consultants unanimously told me that this would not be possible. Christianity seems to have been proselytized in Man as an either/or proposition. Christians and non-Christians alike told me that the kind of blending of Dan religion and Islam that many Muslims practice was not possible for converts to Christianity.

Some Christians will not go near even the least sacred types of *genu,* like those of the rejoicing or entertainment genre. However, others are a bit more flexible. For example, many Dan Christians I know attended the first annual Gueheva Festival of Masks and Traditional Dance that was held in the Man soccer stadium in March 1997. Still, I know no Dan Christians who openly approach more sacred *genu* such as Gegbadë for consultation about their troubles. But the same rule does not apply for Christians who are not Dan. Many non-Dan Christians have hired Gegbadë to solve sorcery-related problems. But many Dan themselves seem to publicly regard Christianity and Dan religion as something akin to oil and water—they don't mix.

There exists, in fact, a great deal of antipathy between many Christians and practitioners of Ge. Many Dan believe that Christians are bent on destroying "the tradition." Anthropologist Gba Daouda, himself a native of Petit Gbapleu, cites Christianity as "the premier instrument of destruction of Dan tradition" (1982, 44). Gba complains that Christians no longer visit the sacred forest or respect the *genu* and even engage in acts of vandalism aimed at demystifying the tradition (ibid.). Mameri Tia Thomas of Déoulé recounted a story to me that illustrates this conflict. A Déoulé man who converted to Christianity developed disregard for rules regarding the sacred forest and even began clearing a portion of it to plant crops. Two years later, Tia said, this man died mysteriously, and the portion of the sacred forest he had cleared grew back. Tia, a Muslim and ardent follower of Dan (Goh) religion, told me this story with pride and conviction as an example of what happens when foolish people defame manifestations of traditional sacred power (Mameri 1997). Conflict between Christians and traditionalists can be that hostile.

While I fortunately did not witness acts of vandalism, my field experiences otherwise confirmed Gba's portrayal of the relationship between Christianity and Dan religion. The situation in Man presents an interesting contrast to other studies of African religious contexts. Lamin Sanneh (1994) points out that Islam insists on one sacred language (Arabic) and one culture that cannot be translated and expressed in local vernacular terms, which has led to unity in worship and alienation from local culture. Christianity, on the other hand, has permitted the Bible to be translated, which has encouraged the vernacularization of religious services, nationalism, and the prominence of local culture. While a cursory examination of services in mosques and churches in Man bears out Sanneh's argument, overall, many Christians in Man pull away from local culture to a greater extent than many Muslims. One cannot overgeneralize though; as I have stated above, there are increasingly more Muslims in Man who refuse any contact with local religious practices and ideas. Overall, though, Christians I knew, though they might drum and sing in local languages in church, drew clearer boundaries between their Christian faith and local religion.

In this context of multiple religious orientations, people tend to distinguish themselves religiously from one another based less on dogma and more on *action*. On this point, my research supports what Launay observed in Korhogo. The Jula of the Koko neighborhood of Korhogo did not seem terribly concerned with issues of cosmology, nor for that matter with ideas generally, when discussing differentiations in religious identity. Religious controversy in Koko tended to center less on the realm of abstraction than on differences in ritual practices and other rules of behavior (Launay 1992, 27). Launay states, "The ideas of one's opponents are simply ignorant or silly; their behavior, on the other hand, is objectionable, if not frankly evil" (105). Likewise, it is behavior rather than the ideas of others that my consultants routinely cite as factors in differentiating Dan religious identities. The same can be said of ethnic distinctions—they are *performed*—recognizable in rhythmic patterns, the presence or absence of masks, types of masks if they are present, language, dress, and many other expressions that indicate ethnic identities. This is what makes public performances of Ge—en*act*ments of religious and ethnic identity—so important in terms of the negotiation of identity in the diverse social climate of contemporary Man. In the conflicts that invariably accompany the rapid diversification of a region, such performances take on heightened importance and expanded meanings. Nowhere is this more true than in the Man neighborhood of Petit Gbapleu, home of Gedro.

Many roads intersect in Man, bringing with them people and ideas that intermingle, by turns coexisting, cooperating, and conflicting with each other. The diverse peoples walking the streets regularly encounter images of the faces of *genu*. Meanwhile, *genu* themselves perform in these same streets, surrounded by difference arriving from all directions and by many means. And the *genu,* as mobile as the people and ideas surrounding them, also follow the streets through and out of town, negotiating boundaries between themselves and various competing forces as they perform throughout the increasingly pluralistic world of contemporary Côte d'Ivoire.

THREE

"When a rooster goes for a walk, he does not forget his house"

"The Tradition" and Identity in a Diversifying Context

Petit Gbapleu is an old Dan village that the growing city of Man has completely surrounded. In 1997, Petit Gbapleu maintained a kind of dual identity as a village and an urban neighborhood (Gba Gama 1997). While the majority of Petit Gbapleu's residents were Dan, many people of other ethnic identities lived there as well, including a great number of Jula immigrants from the savanna. Yet the Dan of Petit Gbapleu maintained much of the organizational structure and many of the customs of village life. Although many residents owned small businesses, agriculture remained the primary means of subsistence. Residents farmed the green hillsides and mountainsides that dominated the horizon to the north and east of Man, where they grew staples, including cassava, rice, yams, and bananas. An elected chief, Tia Sao, along with the president of the local committee of the Parti Démocratique de Côte d'Ivoire Gnassene Mamadou Cherif, led a group of powerful male elders in governing village affairs. Dan religious practices remained a part of the life experience of many of the Dan residents of the neighborhood. Boys and girls were circumcised and initiated at a young age. A powerful *zude* headed the women's Kong society. A sacred stream, the Kun, flowed through the neighborhood, though it remained sacred in name only; the Kun had become too polluted for ritual purposes, and residents traveled to a rural location to offer sacrifices they may have previously offered to the Kun. Individuals worshipped the sacred natural phenomena of their families. And many Petit Gbapleu residents worshipped *genu.*

In fact, in 1997, Petit Gbapleu had a reputation in the Man region for being

Figure 3.1. Gedro of Petit Gbapleu. Photograph by Daniel B. Reed.

particularly active in Ge affairs. Some people explained this reputation by refer-ring to a certain sacrifice elders made some time back, beseeching the ancestors to ensure that young people in Petit Gbapleu would always continue to practice Dan religion (Goueu 1997e). Many Man residents were aware not only of this sacrifice but also of what they considered to be its results—certain *genu* from the village earned local fame for their tremendously impressive performances. Even though these formerly well-known *genu* are now dormant, this reputation persists, as evidenced in a comment made by a master of ceremonies when Gedro arrived at the Gueheva Festival: "Petit Gbapleu. Everything is mask there. In each house, there are masks."

In addition, the majority of Petit Gbapleu's residents identified as Muslim. The chief and all the most powerful elder men; the *zude* and the majority of elder high-status women; indeed, most people in their 40s and older—all were Muslim. Petit Gbapleu was situated in a particularly Islamic area of the Muslim-dominated city of Man. Bordering Petit Gbapleu was the dense and sprawling neighborhood of Julabugu—the largest and most populous neighborhood of the city, which was home to the majority of Man's northern immigrants. Julabugu was filled with mosques, ranging from small, single-room mosques adjacent to family com-pounds to numerous storefront mosques to the massive white "grand mosquée de Man" which dominated the city's skyline. Five times daily, calls to prayer floated through Petit Gbapleu, some originating from Julabugu, others from the mosques in Petit Gbapleu itself. The Président du comité PDCI Gnassene Mamadou Cherif, a former healer/diviner in the Dan religious tradition and marabout who would no longer accept money to give spiritual consultations, had plans in 1997 to open up a Muslim mission bureau in the neighborhood, where he planned to continue working to lure people away from Dan religion and toward a more "pure" form of Islam—Wahhabiya (Gnassene 1997). Although Gnassene had a history of

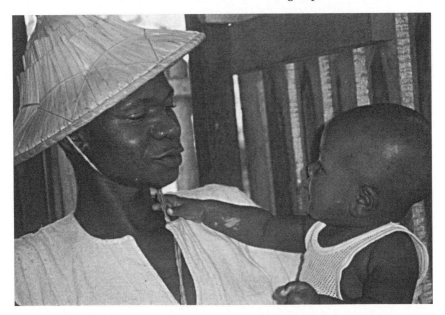

Figure 3.2. Gba Gama and his son. Photograph by Daniel B. Reed.

involvement in Ge and Dan religion, in 1997 he practiced what he called "true" Islam and was actively attempting to convert his neighbors.

One of the local Dan whom Gnassene wished to see converted was his neighbor Gba Gama. Gnassene joked with Gba about it, prodding him by reminding him that his father, his mother, even his older brothers all converted. But Gba barely cracked a smile when the elder Gnassene talked this way. Gba Gama considered himself the leader of the informal anti-Muslim movement in Petit Gbapleu. In his mid to late 30s, Gba had come from a powerful ancestral line going back to the founder of Petit Gbapleu, Gba Youda. Gba Gama's main livelihood, a bar called Bar le tombeau (The Tomb Bar) was literally constructed around Gba Youda's elaborate tomb, which remained publicly visible as a shrine to the neighborhood's founder. Though many in Gba Gama's family, including his deceased father who had been chief of the village, had been Muslim, they had also been centrally involved in Ge affairs. When Gba Gama's father and many of his contemporaries died in the early 1980s, a vacuum was left in the neighborhood concerning Ge and Dan religion. Since that time, many elders, led by Gnassene, who could have taken up the mantle of leadership in matters of Dan religion had instead begun leaning toward Wahhabiya, abandoning "the tradition."

Gba Gama resisted their overtures. Gba even refused to model himself after members of his family and other Petit Gbapleu elders who identified as Muslim but continued to worship *genu*. In reaction to the "purer" style of Islam gaining in popularity among the elders, Gba and others rejected any and all forms of Islam. Gba and Gnassene thus represented two sides of a battle for the religious future of Petit Gbapleu.

One of the reasons so many younger people such as Gba Gama rejected Islam was that they had observed conflicts that had arisen in their grandparents' and parents' lives as a result of their syncretic blends of Islam and Dan religion.

In previous times, many Petit Gbapleu residents had comfortably mixed Islam and Dan religious practices. By 1997, though, with the increased influence of a more orthodox Islam, many in the region began to view this *quartier* as a "Jula neighborhood" rather than one that was truly Dan (Oulai 1997b). Ge performers thus found themselves at the center of heated religious conflicts.

Before describing these conflicts, though, the lifestyle that Gnassene and others opposed—that which involved the mixing of Ge and Islam—must be described. Many Petit Gbapleu residents regularly prayed to Allah for general well-being for themselves and their loved ones. Many prayed five times daily and attended prayer services at mosques as frequently as possible. Yet if a problem arose or they had an imminent need, they often sought out Dan religious specialists.

In 1997, Petit Gbapleu elder Kpan Gbeu Antoine approached religion in this way, though many considered him to represent a dying breed. Dan religion is to some extent a family affair. Individual families have specific sacred entities that they worship. Kpan Gbeu told me he was "born within the affair of worshipping water" but "entered into the prayer" in 1967 as a result of working with Jula immigrants from the north (Kpan Gbeu 1997). "Worshipping water" is one of the most common ways Dan described their involvement in the tradition. This appellation reflects both the importance of sacred water—springs and streams—and the act of "pouring water," or libations of any liquid (usually alcoholic) that are common in Dan religious practice. In saying this, they were referring to the whole system of Dan religious practice. As Kpan Gbeu expressed, "Worship of *genu* and water go together" (ibid.). "Entering into the prayer" was likewise a common way of referring to the whole system of practicing Islam and identifying as Muslim. What is interesting is the emphasis on action in the religious thought of my consultants. Each of the metaphors Kpan Gbeu used for his involvement in religion describes an *act*—worshipping water and entering the prayer describe not belief but *action*. Like these two metaphors, the emphasis on action was prevalent in the religious experience of my Dan consultants.

All of my conversations with Kpan Gbeu about religion revolved around action. When Kpan Gbeu or members of his family were not in good health, he would take a kola to the water that he worships to ask for the restoration of health. He also prayed in an Islamic manner "at every moment" because "God is everywhere" (ibid.). He conceived of these two aspects of his religious practice to be distinct from one another. For example, on the day of our formal interview, he dressed in a Muslim *bubu,* because, he told me, he thought we were going to talk about Islam. "If I had known we were going to discuss the tradition," he said, "I would have worn my Yakuba [Dan] *bubu!*" Yet these two aspects of his life were not at all in conflict. To him, all of his religious practices united him with God; they were all pathways of communication with God. Both clusters of practices—those associated with "the tradition" and those associated with Islam—were routes to God, and both could bring good fortune.

The main difference between the two, Kpan Gbeu explained, was speed. For example, during a drought, one might seek a solution in Dan religious practice. Since I was having a hard time understanding Kpan Gbeu's Dan, Jacques translated:

> If he is desperately in need of rain for his fields and he goes to beseech the sacred water, it can happen immediately. He can be there, in the process of

worshipping the water, and rain arrives. But, usually, for the Muslim prayer, it's not the same thing. That's a matter of asking for protection every day, for every day. But when there is an urgent problem, something concrete to realize, when they go to the water, it is realized. . . . Water is like worshipping a fetish [*geɓɔga*]—the fetish acts immediately, in a spontaneous manner, concretely. (Biemi in Kpan Gbeu 1997)

Kpan Gbeu told me that he experienced no adverse reactions to his religious practices from Muslims or practitioners of Dan religion. When he went to the mosque, for example, no one asked him why he worshipped water. Yet I encountered resistance to Kpan Gbeu's syncretic style of religious practice from both sides—followers of "the tradition" such as Gba Gama and (self-described) "true" Muslims such as Gnassene Mamadou Cherif. In 1997, the chief and all the most influential and powerful elders of the neighborhood were of the latter category. This had not been the case in times past, when many influential Petit Gbapleu residents practiced both Islam and Dan religion. As Jean-Claude told me:

> The village chief, whom I knew, Gba Gama's father . . . I knew him during my childhood. He died in '83 or '82. . . . He was a Muslim! But he never held a celebration where he did not call a mask. . . . Otherwise, he was a Muslim! Very much a Muslim! He was never missing at the mosque! (Goueu 1997h)

In 1997, Petit Gbapleu chief Tia Sao told me that he does not support those who identify as Muslim but also worship *genu* because "you cannot have two Gods." The chief and Gnassene held the opinion that people who follow both traditions are not "true Muslims" (Tia, Gnassene, and Vahan 1997).

I learned a great deal about Gnassene's religious history during an interview with him one afternoon in Petit Gbapleu. Just as many interviews with practitioners of Ge began with a ritualistic offering of a kola and prayers to the ancestors, Gnassene intoned an Islamic prayer before he began speaking of his religious history. Gnassene was not unfamiliar with Ge, however. He had been a Muslim since childhood; yet, until fairly recently, Gnassene approached God not only through imams, marabouts, and prayers at the mosque but also through mountains, power objects, and *genu*. Gnassene came from a family that had been very active in Ge affairs. He shared with me his disdain for the religious practices of his family in times past:

> My grandfather is [buried] in . . . the sacred house. . . . They [his family] had masks. Every year, my father bought sheep, goats, chickens to worship those masks . . . after the harvest. . . . Before, it was evil—the sacred house! The elders said [of his grandfather], "He is not dead. We have placed him in the sacred house [to guard it]. Every year you must give him food. He who guards [the sacred house]—you take care of him." (Gnassene 1997)

Gnassene explained that when his grandfather died, they removed the skin from his hands and forehead and placed it in a cow horn that hung from the ceiling in the sacred house. Whenever there was a major decision to make, the elders sat under this cow horn in order to engage the presence of Gnassene's grandfather so he could make his will known to them. The elders would then inform village women of the requests of his grandfather. The spirit of Gnassene's grandfather would demand food and drink, and women would have to comply. "But this was really just a way to feed the elders of the village!" Gnassene exclaimed.[1] He claimed that:

> The sacred house—it was that which commanded Yakuba [Dan] country. All the bad people, it was there that they were. The most powerful fetishers, the sorcerers. . . . It was the elders who commanded everyone, but in the name of those ancestors buried in the sacred house. That's how life was in the old days. And now the change is complete. Everyone has begun to see clearly in their lives. . . . Before, we had masks. That's how life was before. The change came little by little by little, and it's changed now. (Gnassene 1997)

Like Gnassene, many young adherents of traditional religion in Petit Gbapleu found fault with the kind of mixing of religious options evidenced in Kpan Gbeu and other elders. "You cannot follow two vines at the same time," Jean-Claude once told me. Most of the time the different religious approaches in Petit Gbapleu seemed to coexist fairly well. In 1997, however, an event transpired which brought these tensions to the surface: the *zuɗe* died.

The *zuɗe* is the elder leader of the women's Kong society, the most powerful woman of any Dan village or neighborhood, and a leader in Dan religious affairs. Yet this *zuɗe*, like most members of the Kong society in Petit Gbapleu, had also been Muslim. Her syncretic religious approach did not seem to pose many problems until the day she died. Then a conflict erupted over whether her burial and funeral should be conducted according to Islamic or Dan tradition. To the dismay of many in the village, the powerful Muslim elders took the *zuɗe*'s body and buried her in an Islamic manner before followers of Dan religion could react. Some young women followers of the *zuɗe* were distraught by this. For example, Lien Sati Yvonne told me that the *zuɗe* had been a religious leader and should have been treated that way in death. People arrived from all over the region to stay up all night watching over her body but were unable to do so. Yvonne said that women who had been circumcised by the *zuɗe* should have had the opportunity to come to her body to offer blessings. "There was not even a dance. It was taken over completely by the Muslims!" (Lien et al. 1997).

All of the young women I came to know in Petit Gbapleu were ardent followers of the *zuɗe* and Kong, and not a single one identified as Muslim. When I gathered them together for an interview one day, they told me "No one prays here. We are women of the *zu*." Seeking clarification, I mentioned that the *zuɗe* herself had been Muslim (as was her replacement). They responded passionately, stating that they thought it was a bad idea for the *zuɗe* to be Muslim. As much as they revered the *zuɗe*, they thought it better to simply rest with the intermediary of Kong and not try to approach God through other intermediaries. Then there would be no problem when you die. Religious ambiguity is not good, they said. Tiemoko Christine summed up her thoughts on the matter by stating simply, "Kong is a religion, and praying at the mosque is a religion. Following a single religion is better" (Tiemoko in Lien et al. 1997). I asked if they were then rejecting the religion of their mothers and grandmothers for the religion of their ancestors. They responded by stating that it's the young women of Petit Gbapleu, more so than the elders, who are "conserving the customs" (Lien et al. 1997).

Funerals are an extremely important, if not the most important, life rite for many Africans. So it should not be surprising that religious conflicts about funerals surfaced in Petit Gbapleu. The case of the *zuɗe* was not an isolated one. One day Jean-Claude recounted to me several other examples, including the funeral of his close friend Gba Matthieu's father, who, like the *zucfe,* had been Muslim and had worshipped *genu:*

> Matthieu's father—he loved masks! Whenever there was a little fête at his place, he invited Gedro! But, when he died . . . Since he was an elder who loved us all, we wanted to go with the mask to his funeral. The Comité [Gnassene—the head of the PDCI committee] refused! He said, "But this is a Muslim matter! It's not a Ge matter, it's a Muslim matter! If you want to come with your mask, wait until after the funeral is over." So there were no masks there, and it was as if it was not *his* funeral. (Goueu 1997h)

Although Jean-Claude flirted with Islam for a brief period, by 1997, he was adamantly opposed to Gnassene and others who had converted to Islam and objected to the affairs of Ge. When Jean-Claude, Jacques, and I discussed this, they both recounted many examples of village Dan who were Muslim but also worshipped water and *genu.* Not so in town, they said, where more Jula lived and the pressure to become a "true" Muslim was growing from people such as Gnassene who had joined the Wahhabiya movement. Jean-Claude derisively asserted:

> It's our parents who have come into the city who *play* Muslim. It's our parents who do not understand. It's they who have become, how do you call it—Wahhabiya—who *play* Muslim. . . . Petit Gbapleu is a very dangerous case. A very dangerous case. Why do I say that? Because our parents in Petit Gbapleu have followed foreigners living in Petit Gbapleu, and they now want to abandon their customs. (Goueu 1997h) → Influence of Western foreigners

Jean-Claude's strong words—accusing his elders of merely *playing* Muslim— underscored the intensity of the generational religious disjuncture in Petit Gbapleu in 1997. Strother writes that Pende mask performances "build and cement communities" (1998, 16). Clearly, Petit Gbapleu residents created both community *and conflict* through their religious practices, including Ge performance. Identity is always formed in relationship to others; identity is *negotiated.* Jean-Claude expresses his own values and identity in direct opposition to the actions of others in his community, and Ge is at the center of this debate.

A GEDRO REVIVAL

It was in this context of religious conflict that young people in Petit Gbapleu began resurrecting Ge performance in the late 1980s. Gba Gama began recruiting young people to follow "the tradition" in the 1980s. Gba became a point man, a self-proclaimed "organizer," not just concerning the *genu* he had inherited from his grandfather and father but for many of the *genu* left in the neighborhood. He began inviting young people to his Tomb Bar every Saturday to practice drumming, paying for their drinks and encouraging them. Gba told me:

> We, the young who are left, we began to teach our younger brothers to drum and also to enter into the mask affairs so that they would not be totally forgotten. . . . Now the young try to ensure that the old attitudes continue. . . . I am an organizer. . . . There are some who play drums, others who dance, others who like to sing. So it's [a] shared [effort]. . . . I want, right up until I die, the customs to continue. So . . . I will not follow a religion, like the Muslim religion, where

they say that "If you are within, you cannot put your hand into the affairs of masks." (Gba Gama 1997)

Gba Gama, who in 1997 was Petit Gbapleu's Président des jeunes,[2] had become something of a booking agent for the *genu* of the neighborhood. Because of his family position, his passion for Dan religion, and the fact that he had a phone in his bar (a rare commodity in Man residences), he was well positioned to play this role. By far the most active *ge* from Petit Gbapleu during the time I spent in Man was Gedro.

In 1987, when Gba Gama was busy trying to resuscitate the practice of Dan religion, a *ge* who for years had been dormant reappeared. Fellow Petit Gbapleu resident Semlen Aimé's deceased grandmother came to him in a dream. This ancestral spirit instructed Aimé that a *ge* in their family should be brought back to life and that its name should be changed to Gedro, or "frog *ge*." Gedro is a common name for Dan *genu;* in fact, among the genre of *genu* called *tankë ge*—a kind of dance or entertainment *ge*—many share this name. Aimé's grandmother, though, suggested that their *ge* take Gedro as his proper name because the frog is their family totem.[3] If they resurrected and renamed this *ge,* this ancestral spirit said, then it would become very popular.[4]

Her prediction turned out to be true. From 1987 until 1999, Gedro, operating out of Semlen Aimé's sacred house, gradually became one of the most popular *genu* in the Man region. Unfortunately, Aimé, who was central to these revivalist Gedro performances, died young in 1999, bringing to an end an era during which the Petit Gbapleu Gedro group performed constantly, not just in the Man region but also around Côte d'Ivoire and beyond. During the 1990s, this group even toured several times, performing in India, China, and the United States. In Man, people attended Gedro performances who did not necessarily worship *genu.* Even Gnassene Mamadou Cherif attended Gedro performances. Gnassene would even give gifts to the *ge* (a practice usually associated with "offerings" or "sacrifice"), but "that is not worship," he explained. "[Worship] is what is evil" (Gnassene 1997). For Gnassene, giving gifts in this way was no different than what one would do during any secular performance of West African music, in which audience members offer monetary gifts to performers at peak moments as a matter of course. Many people considered *tankë ge* performances to be purely secular entertainment. Some Muslims and Christians felt they could attend Gedro performances without compromising their religious values. And many people who were not Dan enjoyed the artistry of Gedro performance as well.

AUTHORITY, VALIDATION, AND CHANGING CONTEXTS IN POSTCOLONIAL MAN

Gedro is one of the genre of *genu* called *tankë ge* who are called upon to dance at celebratory occasions. Historically these would include events such as harvest celebrations and rite-of-passage celebrations such as weddings and funerals. Today, however, one must add to that list an array of events including tourist-oriented festivals, speeches by visiting government ministers, and official political public-relations functions. During 1997, *tankë genu* danced at many political public-relations events: at a party thrown by the African Development Bank, at a ceremony honoring the opening of a new primary school in a nearby village, and to welcome the mayor back from a trip to France. In part as a result of these new opportunities in national political performance contexts, dance *genu* such as Gedro perform more regularly than in prior times and have grown in number compared with other types of *genu.*[5]

Expanding opportunities for dance *genu* can also be linked directly to other social changes, including the diversification of the economy and the religious and ethnic makeup of the region. Many Muslims and Christians who are unwilling to worship *genu* still permit themselves to attend events where a less sacred *ge* such as Gedro performs. Many Man residents are not Dan and lack the insider knowledge that would afford them understanding and appreciation of performances of more sacred *genu,* but they can easily appreciate a *ge* whose primary purpose is to dance and entertain. While the performance is sacred for the performers, it is not required to be so for the audience. The result is an expansion of opportunity for dance *genu* in today's Man. While all rejoicing *genu* had potentially greater opportunities to perform in 1990s Man, few were as popular as Gedro of Petit Gbapleu. In part because of the exceptional talents of the Gedro group, they were in extraordinarily high demand. Their clever incorporation of popular-music references also contributed to the Petit Gbapleu Gedro group's regional fame.

The federal government hires entertainment and dance *genu* to perform, which is another factor that has increased performing opportunities for the Gedro group. The presence of a *ge* is like a stamp of validation marking the importance of an event. Appropriation of both popular and traditional musical performance for political purposes is widespread in Africa. For instance, Waterman writes that Yoruba politicians hire juju musicians in order to "mobilize local support through the manipulation of traditional symbols of authority" (Waterman 1990a, 88), and there are numerous examples of former Ghanaian president Kwame Nkrumah using music and concert parties to spread political propaganda (Barber 1997b, 23). The inclusion of mask performance at political events, common in postcolonial Côte d'Ivoire, also occurred during the colonial era. While the most elaborate such productions were the mask festivals organized by the French to celebrate Bastille Day, colonial administrators also included mask performance at the ground-breaking ceremonies for the construction of government buildings, dedications of colonial monuments, and street-naming ceremonies (Steiner 1994, 94–95; see also Gorer 1962 [1935], 235–240).

While Christopher Steiner argues correctly that the association of mask performance with political events expanded during the colonial era (1994, 94–95), resulting in increased performance opportunities for dance *genu* such as Gedro, the appropriation of Ge performance by the Ivorian government is an extension of a historical Dan pattern. From all accounts, *genu* have always been present at important occasions in Dan life. This is in part because Ge manifests supreme authority in traditional Dan life. Chiefs come and go, but *genu* are eternal. Authority and governance in traditional Dan settings operate as a collaboration between humans and *genu.* Because they mediate between the spiritual world, where the ancestors (*ɓɛman*) reside next to God (Zlan), and the world of humans, *genu* are recognized by many Dan to be the ultimate manifestation of earthly power and authority. While there are certainly cases in contemporary Dan life in which conflict exists between chiefs and *genu,* my consultants generally recognize that the rule of chiefs is legitimized by their association with the most powerful *ge* of each village, especially the head *ge* of the village (*gunɗiöge*).

Contemporary politicians recognize that association with *genu* legitimizes and reinforces their political power. This is a mutually beneficial relationship. The members of the *ge* group are paid and are themselves honored to have been invited to perform at events associated with the most powerful chief of the land—the president—who in 1997 was Henri Konan Bedie. By recognizing local authority and respecting the tradition of honoring important occasions by inviting a *ge,* Bedie's government looked good in the eyes of the local populace. Just as they always had done, powerful agents were recognizing and working with other powerful agents in order to meet specific goals.

In fact, Gedro's presence at political functions served as a validation of importance not just for state politicians but for many people present at such events. Gueu Gbe Alphonse explained, "The Mask is the emblem of the West [of Côte d'Ivoire]. He has to be at all grand occasions" (Gueu Gbe 1997f). He went on to compare the late 1990s to the 1960s, when Hugo Zemp (1993 [1969], 1971, 1965, 1964) conducted research in the region:

> During Zemp's time, there weren't meeting places like the African Development Bank, like today. Masks were more involved in the agricultural cycle festivals. Now they do that too but also manifest at official events, parties, and so forth (Gueu Gbe 1997f)

The presence of a *ge* at an event not only validates the importance of the event but is also good for the performers. Discussing organizations that hired *genu,* Gueu Gbe continued:

> When they have a ceremony, they invite masks. They do well to do this. Behind the mask are at least twenty people. This is good for the community, because they get paid. When I used to be Regional Director of Tourism, I used to pay 25,000 CFA [about 50 U.S. dollars], often to Petit Gbapleu, for a mask to come to an event. (Gueu Gbe 1997f)

Thus, because of the diversification of the economy and the arrival of new businesses and institutions, Ge performance has increasingly become, for members of Gedro's group and others, a business, a way of making a living. It is therefore advantageous for the Gedro group to craft their performance in such a way as to appeal to a broad public, including people of various ethnic and religious identities. This is one factor that influences their aesthetic strategies.

INCORPORATION OF POPULAR MUSIC AS AN AESTHETIC STRATEGY

Gedro has become popular with a broad multiethnic and multireligious constituency in part by incorporating popular music and dance into his performance. It might strike readers as surprising that a sacred performance, which relies on specific music to attract spirits to the performance space, would incorporate references to popular music. My consultants informed me, however, that dance *genu* have always adapted their performances to please the crowd, no matter who they are. As Gueu Gbe told me:

> The mask dances for the population of the time. During the time of Zemp, there was no *zouglou* [a popular-music style]. The mask is always in the present, at the same time profoundly preserving his source. (Gueu Gbe 1997f)

On another occasion, Gueu Gbe told me that *ge* are "in fashion" (Gueu Gbe 1997a). He described certain *genu* who are called *ye ye*—a term which, as far as

I can gather, originated in France in the 1960s to describe a hip new music and lifestyle of that time. My consultants regularly used that term to describe *genu* who adopt "the new comportment" (Gueu Gbe 1997a), who make gestural references to Western movies and television programs, or who incorporate popular-music dance steps into their performances. In French, such *genu* are often called *masques ye ye*. *Genu* who dance popular-music dance steps often will be nick-named according to the names of the dances they incorporate. For example, I have heard *ge* called *masque zouglou, masque zaiiko,* and *masque gnakpa; zaiiko* and *gnakpa* are, like *zouglou,* Ivorian popular-music and dance styles of the 1990s.

That Gedro has become a *masque ye ye* is fundamentally in keeping with his traditional role. In performance, *genu* demonstrate their omniscience. Gedro has to demonstrate that he is in touch with the times. And many Dan consider Ge performance to be the performance of social ideals, or the performance of excellence. Each *ge* must be the best at what he does. In earlier times, when audiences would more likely have consisted primarily of Dan people, Gedro incorporated dances from other genres of Dan music to demonstrate his knowledge and mastery of his milieu. In the 1990s, Gedro was still the master of Dan dance styles, including dances associated with the elder women's society, dances of other *genu,* and dances of the Gedronu of the past. These Dan dances Gedro performers labeled as "traditional." Yet today, Gedro must also show that he is the master of a world of increasingly greater musical diversity. In today's media-dominated world, rhythms and dances from all over Côte d'Ivoire, Africa, Europe, and the Americas are present in Gedro's locale. In order to fulfill his traditional role, Gedro must demonstrate that he is aware of what performers called the "modern" dances in his environs and that he can master them all. As Petit Gbapleu Ge performer Gba Daniel told me:

> If [Gedro] has a person from Korhogo [in north-central Côte d'Ivoire] before him, he will incorporate Korhogolaise dance steps, to please the Korhogolaise person. If it's a European, he must know at least a funk dance step, or imitate a little Michael Jackson, something like that. (Gba in Biemi, Goueu, Gba, and Oulai 1997)

Gedro incorporates popular references in choreographed dance routines, which are usually between fifteen and forty seconds long, in which master drummer Goueu Tia Jean-Claude matches his rapidly moving feet beat for beat. Over the bed of the interlocking rhythms played on the accompanying instruments, Jean-Claude plays rehearsed solos that synchronize with the ankle bells on the dancing *ge's* feet. In this interaction, they quote rhythmic motifs from popular-music songs, which the crowd recognizes, having seen these rhythms and dances performed on television or heard them on the radio or cassettes. This is analogous to the "quoting" that occurs in jazz improvisation. In the context of a solo, for example, a saxophonist might quote a melodic motif associated, say, with Charlie Parker or John Coltrane. Educated listeners recognize and appreciate this kind of intertextual reference. This is what occurs rhythmically when Jean-Claude and Gedro quote popular-music rhythms. One summer evening in 1997, at a party thrown by the Ivorian government for the hairdressers of Man, the Gedro group made use of these strategies and other, more daring, methods of demonstrating their mastery over the many forms of music and dance present in their increasingly pluralistic world.

PDCI PARTY FOR THE HAIRDRESSERS OF MAN

By early summer 1997, my relationship with my drumming teacher Goueu Tia Jean-Claude had begun maturing beyond that of a professional researcher/musician student/teacher nature. It was becoming clear that he enjoyed having me around, not only because we liked each other's company but also because my presence at his performances reaffirmed his status as a superlative master drummer, one who had ascended to that role at a remarkably young age. Clearly, we were both meeting needs through our collaboration: he was earning extra money and renown and I was getting some of my most fascinating material. And we were becoming friends.

In the late afternoon of June 14th, I received a phone call from Jean-Claude. "We [the Gedro group] are going to perform at a hairdressers' party at the headquarters of the PDCI in an hour. We would like you to be there." And after a momentary silence during which I considered my response, Jean-Claude added, "*I* would like you to be there." For the first time, he had personalized an invitation; he did not merely inform me of the hairdresser's party but emphasized that he *wanted* me to attend. Sensing the genuine sentiment in his voice, I immediately agreed to go to the performance. I hung up the phone, touched, aware that our relationship had matured to another, more intimate level. Nicole and I packed our gear, headed down the hill, and flagged down a taxi to take us to the Man headquarters of the PDCI.

As Nicole and I entered through the gates surrounding the compound of the PDCI headquarters, Jean-Claude rushed forward and excitedly greeted us. Organizers in buttoned-down dress shirts made of cloth commemorating President Henri Konan Bedie were milling about and the guests were just arriving. The PDCI had organized this fête in honor of the hairdressers of Man as part of a broader public-relations campaign. During this period—just two-and-a-half years before the December 1999 coup that ended almost forty years of continuous PDCI rule—rival political parties were increasing in popularity. The PDCI periodically held such events as part of an effort to maintain their overwhelming majority grip on Ivorian political power. The regional capital of Man, with its population of roughly 100,000, was viewed by the PDCI as a vitally important source of support.

In addition to providing food and drink at the affair, the PDCI presented each participating hairdresser with a blue-and-white dress made of special commemorative cloth. Like many such public festivities in contemporary Côte d'Ivoire, the organizers created "ambiance" with a public-address system that blasted popular music out of huge loudspeakers. But this was not the only entertainment featured at this event. Also present was Gedro. Accompanied by his ensemble of drummers, percussionists, singers, and dancers, Gedro thrilled the crowd with his lightning-quick dancing, perfectly synchronized with virtuosic solos from master drummer Jean-Claude. Attendees included not just the women hairdressers, who were of various ethnic and religious identities, but also a small crowd of Dan people who had come to support the *ge* and participate in the festivities. With the pop-music beat pounding in the background, people gathered in a circle around the *ge* and his *gekia,* who accepted monetary gifts on his behalf.

Nicole and I joined this circle, videotaping and photographing as night began to fall on what would become an all-night party.

In the early parts of the evening, the circle enclosing Gedro and his *gekia* consisted for the most part not of the honored hairdressers but of Dan men, women, and children. Young boys wandered about wearing everything from Nike T-shirts to flowing cream-and-deep-blue handwoven Dan *bubus*. Middle-aged men danced in Muslim *bubus* or tattered sports coats over colorful T-shirts. The elder lead singer Gonëti sang and danced in his characteristic baby-blue plastic shoes and navy blue suitcoat and pants. Periodically, Gedro would take a break from dancing and a human individual would enter the center of the circle to dance for joy. Most memorable was an 8-year-old girl who, dressed in a worn patterned-cotton dress, wowed the crowd by dancing with a flair and skill beyond her years as her mother, in a handwoven Dan wrap topped with a Bedie T-shirt, smiled and proudly supervised. But proudest of all was Jean-Claude, who, though just in his early 20s, had risen through the ranks to become the most highly sought-after drummer in Petit Gbapleu. In his plaid cotton buttoned-down shirt, cut off at the sleeves, and knee-length khaki shorts, Jean-Claude directed the performing nucleus of youthful percussionists and singers while others in the circle sang responses, danced, and added layers of improvisatory clapping to the already richly textured polyrhythm.

Many of the Dan present were young, which is typical of contemporary dance *ge* performances, especially those featuring *genu* from Petit Gbapleu. Petit Gbapleu Ge performance has the air of youthful rebellion, as these young people defiantly enact religious identities in contradistinction to those of many of their parents and grandparents. Gedro himself embodies and manifests this youthful spirit. He carries himself with a cool but cocky demeanor, strutting more than walking. He exudes mastery in every respect and exploits both the fascination and fear that his presence elicits in spectators. He sports a tall brightly dyed leather hat, ornately decorated with cowrie shells and an animal-tail plume that rises above the crowd. Though his facial features are effeminate, his comportment is aggressively masculine. His dancing is athletic and insistent, his torso remaining stiff while his feet speed across the performance space. At the hairdressers' party, Gedro delighted in frightening the female honorees, who nervously laughed and scattered away when he danced directly toward them. The atmosphere that evening was one of jubilant expression. Gedro seemed to delight in using his forceful masculine sexuality to excite and intimidate his predominately female audience. In a setting where ultimate masculinity is respected and praised, Gedro was the hailed king of the roost.

The female hairdressers, though fascinated by Gedro, were wary and preferred to keep their distance outside the central circle made up of friends and supporters of the *ge*. Throughout the performance, when Gedro approached these women, his overtures were met with shrieks of mock terror and amusement. Although the performance was intended for everyone present at this gathering of diverse peoples, the "audience" was clearly divided into two camps. The performing nucleus and their Dan supporters indexed their own separate identity in a number of ways. By singing and speaking in Dan, by dancing in distinctively Dan styles, and simply by participating actively in any way in the performance, the Dan present demonstrated their cultural literacy in things Ge and presented a unified esoteric identity to the crowd of outsiders. And yet the performers also intentionally crafted the performance to please their crowd, using humor and suggestive dance moves and incorporating popular-music rhythms that are well known to the general public. In so doing, the Gedro group maximized the effectiveness of the performance and thus the reputation and popularity of the group while also projecting a hip, knowing, modern identity to the crowd. Balancing exclusion with inclusion, the performers put on an electrifying show that both attracted and frightened the honorees of the evening.

Yet another way in which the performers created the feeling of an "in crowd" was by calling attention to the fact that they had brought along a pair of researchers to document their performance. Gedro and his *gekia* on occasion danced directly toward my video camera, collecting monetary gifts and forcing me to join in by dancing with them. The ensuing eruptions of glee from the crowd further heightened the energy and intensity and served to mark the performers as important and unique. Just as he incorporates other outside elements such as popular-music references, Gedro incorporated Nicole and me into his performance, demonstrating his mastery over everything and anything in his domain. As I was observing and documenting the Gedro group with the intent of crafting my experience into something I could take home and share with my academic community, they were meeting their own goals through our encounter.

Yet despite the youthful zeal of the Gedro group, the musicians and the *ge* seemed somewhat rattled early in the evening by the loud prerecorded pop music. At one early point, the amplified music shot up in volume, causing Gedro and the drummers to pause mid-song and shoot angry glances over at the public-address system. But as the crowd gathered around the performers, the energy and excitement intensified, the drumming and singing grew louder, and Gedro's characteristic confidence returned. Gradually a feeling of competition between the prerecorded popular music and the Ge performance surfaced, a competition that Gedro, who is never content to be a sideshow, was determined to win. During one break between their songs, when the amplified popular music again stole peoples' attention, Gedro momentarily danced to the recorded pop music. Several minutes later he took this one step further. Lunging toward the human circle surrounding him, causing this circle to explode outward, Gedro strutted in long, flowing rhythmic strides toward one of the huge speakers. Followed by his assistant, Gedro paused in front of the speaker to dance to a hit song by Ivorian pop-music sensation Meiway.

This move was especially daring. Usually, popular influences are incorporated into Gedro dance and music only in the interaction between the *ge* and the master drummer over the bed of standard traditional drumming patterns. Dancing to completely non-Dan prerecorded music challenged the limits of acceptability for a *ge*. While this move may have been considered sacrilege by some elders, for the youthful Gedro group it was a momentary victory dance. To demonstrate his mastery and superiority over one of the country's most famous musicians, Gedro reinscribed Meiway's music with his own meaning, appropriating it for his own purposes. Dancing to the recorded pop music was an act of resistance for Gedro; he declared victory by inclusion, redefining the amplified pop music as just another aspect of his own performance.

No less meaningful for Gedro performers is the more typical manner in which they incorporate popular-music and dance references into their performance: in

Figure 3.3. Zaouli rhythm with main rhythmic pattern for *zi-k-ri*.
Transcribed by Timothy Reed with Daniel B. Reed.

the rhythmic interactions between Jean-Claude and the *ge*. Throughout their performances, Jean-Claude and Gedro interweave what they call "traditional" and "modern" dance routines. One of the "modern" dances they performed at the hairdressers' party was *zaouli*, a dance borrowed from a popular mask of the Gouro people of central Côte d'Ivoire. *Zaouli* became well known nationally in part because it was the favorite mask of former Ivorian president Félix Houphouet-Boigny. As a result, *zaouli* performances frequently were broadcast over state television and many Ivorians became familiar with this mask, which became a popular phenomenon. In fact, it was on television that members of Gedro's group first saw *zaouli*. Several *zaouli* rhythmic patterns and dances are so popular that they are etched in many Ivorians' minds. That night at the PDCI headquarters, Gedro performed a particularly sexual rendition of this dance, ending the routine by rhythmically thrusting his hips, his assistant mirroring his every move, as the crowd cheered them on. Figure 3.3 shows the complex relationship between the "traditional" time-keeping drum pattern (*zi-k-ri*) and the "modern" *zaouli* rhythm played by master drummer Jean-Claude.[6]

Yet another dance that is extremely popular for Gedro comes from a song of the popular-music genre *zigblithy*. *Zigblithy* is a style of music associated with one of Côte d'Ivoire's biggest stars since the advent of mass-mediated popular music—the late Ernesto Djedje. Djedje was Bété, an ethnic group from west-central Côte d'Ivoire. His style, *zigblithy*, drew upon Bété rhythms but placed them in a contemporary setting, with drum kit, bass, guitars, horns, and background singers. In many *zigblithy* songs, the bridge is a kind of breakdown, featuring a drummer playing Bété rhythms over the accompaniment of the bass, drum, and guitar groove. When Jean-Claude and Gedro play their *zigblithy* rhythm, the crowd recognizes it and responds with shouts, cheers, and loud applause.

Later that night, Nicole and I sat in a nearby open-air restaurant and bar, eating braised chicken. An interethnic mix of clients chatted and enthusiastically commented on a popular Ivorian-produced situation comedy broadcasting from a television set in the corner. Nicole and I were struck yet again by how interesting it was that "the tradition" of Gedro—this performance of Dan religious identity—had become a kind of regional pop star and was for many in Man just another form of popular entertainment. The hairdressers alternated between listening to the prerecorded popular music and watching the *ge*, while only a block away other Man residents watched television. Ge performance, commercially recorded pop music, and television shows all comfortably and naturally coexist in Man. The fact that Gedro is more than able to compete with such commercial forms of popular entertainment in this interethnic city speaks to the skill, adaptability, and ingenuity of these young committed performers and to the modernity of this tradition.

LOCAL INTERPRETATIONS OF TRADITION AND MODERNITY

While French-speaking Gedro performers regularly called the whole of Ge "the tradition," they also used the words "traditional," "modern" and "popular" when identifying the rhythms and dances they incorporate into their performance. Jean-Claude, Semlen Aimé, and other Gedro performers identified both *zigblithy* and *zaouli* as "modern" or "popular" dances. This is fascinating, since they told me that *zaouli*, performed by a *zaouli* mask in his home context in the Gouro region, would be "traditional." But when Gedro dances *zaouli*, they define it as "modern." Similarly, the rhythms they incorporate from *zigblithy* they consider to be traditional Bété rhythms. But they learned them through a popular medium—in a pop song, broadcast over radio and television. In the context of Gedro's performance, performers call this a popular, or modern, element.

By labeling these resources in this way, Gedro performers demonstrate that they understand that context affects meaning. This theoretical insight, central to the notion of intertextuality (see Kristeva 1986; Bauman and Briggs 1992; Duranti 1994), is here one aspect of the performers' own sophisticated local theory about what they do. Gedro performers' incorporation of modern elements works precisely because performers understand the contextual nature of meaning. Performers recontextualize *zigblithy* and *zaouli*, consciously altering their meanings, using them to demonstrate Gedro's knowledge and mastery of the dances in his midst. By incorporating popular or modern elements, performers show that the manifestation of Dan social ideals that they call "the tradition" is in touch with the times.

Gedro's incorporation of other Dan dances—those that performers call "traditional"—are, like his incorporation of popular music, intertextual references. In the new context, these dances carry different meaning. The dance associated with the initiation and excision of young Dan girls, for example, when danced by young girls who have just completed those rituals, carries quite different meanings than when this same dance is quoted by Gedro. For Gedro to perform such a dance manifests his awareness of and superior ability to perform the dances in his environs. And for Gedro performers who deliberately choose Ge as opposed to Islam, such a reference indicates the depth of their connection to Dan history and custom—in other words, their connection to their notion of the ways of the ancestors. Finally, Gedro's quoting of Dan dance genres reinforces the inherent social power of the institution of Ge. Alessandro Duranti states that access to and license to use certain genres "can be a crucial component of power relations in any given community" (Duranti 1994, 6), and I agree. Not just anyone can quote dances that otherwise are restricted to people of particular social groups in Dan society. But a *ge* certainly can, which underscores the ultimate authority accorded to Ge by many Dan people.

In every case, the original dances and music are adapted to Gedro's style of dancing and Jean-Claude's style of drumming. This last point has implications far beyond Ge performance. When Jean-Claude incorporates popular-music references into his drumming, he does not adapt them mechanically, imitating exactly what he hears. This cosmopolitan young Dan musician creates his own unique and appealing artistic style by combining his youthful fascination with popular culture with his knowledge of "the tradition." For example, in 1997, Jean-Claude was busy creating a new dance routine for Gedro based on the music and dance style of contemporary Ivorian pop star Ziké. Yet in the process Jean-Claude was adapting Ziké, mixing it with Dan rhythmic ideas. He does this with all "modern" rhythms that he plays. As he said, "For Ernesto Djedje, eh? When he dances *zigblithy,* they play only *zigblithy* steps. But, for me, I mix the *zigblithy* into the traditional steps" (Goueu 1997c). Of course, the *zigblithy* rhythms are played in the context of *getan*—the standard rhythms and songs of Ge performance. But Jean-Claude's comment goes beyond even that. Even when he plays his *zigblithy* solos, he creatively blends ideas from "the tradition"—Ge—with this contemporary style. He puts his own uniquely Dan imprint on *zigblithy, zaouli,* the Jula rhythm *simpa,* or anything, for that matter, that he plays:

> Me, for example, I can play a little of all sorts of drum rhythms. But if I want to play them, I am obligated to mix them with my rhythms. For example, if I want to play a reggae rhythm on my drum—I do it, and they are going to hear the sound of reggae, but I am going to mix it a little with the Yakuba [Dan] drum. For me, it's like that. . . . No matter what rhythm that I play, I always mix. . . . despite the fact that European music and American music is in abundance, we had before our *own* music. . . . If it was to be that because American and European musics were in greater abundance, that other musics were going to disappear, "the tradition" would have disappeared a long time ago. . . . Because modernism has come, and it has prospered. But despite all, "the tradition" still exists. So even though American and European music has become abundant, traditional music remains there. (Goueu 1997h)[7]

As Dan so often do, Jean-Claude underscored this point with a proverb: *"Tɔ ya niё, a zo yaa ɓɔ, a ɓa kɔr ka"*—"When a rooster goes for a walk, he does not forget his house."

As Jean-Claude asserts, he is not a blank slate upon which is inscribed the hegemonic imprint of mass-mediated popular culture. The economic and power imbalances that have resulted in the spread of North American and European popular culture to nearly every corner of the globe are undeniable. Yet, as Jean-Claude's example shows, this process does not necessarily "wipe out" local musics; "the world has not been reduced to sameness" (Comaroff and Comaroff 1993, xi). Rather, mediated musics are just new resources for creative local agents to draw upon as they create music and meaning in their lives. Results such as Gedro's inventive incorporations of popular musics demonstrate that people around the world are not passive recipients of global culture; they are, rather, active interpreters of mass-mediated cultural influences. The proverb Jean-Claude cites above does not describe a situation of passive response to invasion; rather, the rooster himself *goes* for a walk, trying out new things, and does not forget his house or his roots (here, Ge) as he creatively incorporates new material into his own personal expression of musical and cultural identity. And furthermore, of course, not all hegemonic cultural activity originates in Europe and North America. Ivorians are both consumers and *producers* of mass-mediated culture. Gedro incorporates dance steps of popular songs and of masks from other regions of Côte d'Ivoire as a result of members of his group having been exposed to them on Ivorian state television and radio.

Just as Gedro performers localize outside musical influence, they also localize the epistemological categories of "tradition" and "modernity." These concepts are, for Jean-Claude and his group, permeable, adaptable, and far from mutually exclusive. Eric Charry writes that the Mande musicians with whom he has studied similarly use the terms "traditional" and "modern" to make "meaningful local distinctions" as they interpret their own creative processes. He writes,

> Traditional and modern in the Mande context do not refer to opposing sides of battle with impenetrable lines, or to blind adherence to colonial lexical categories and mentalities, but rather reflect states of mind that can be fluidly combined and respected in innovative and often humorous ways. (2000, 24)

Regardless of their origins in European/North American social evolutionary discourse (Comaroff and Comaroff 1993, xii), these terms "traditional" and "modern" hold currency for my consultants, who imbue them with new nondichotomous meanings as they use them to interpret and understand their world. Within the context of performing "the tradition," Gedro performers articulate their own unique take on modernity (Gyekye 1997, vii). They embrace Ge not in a strictly conservative sense, but, like the Bamana performers of what Stephen Wooten calls the "traditionally modern" *ciwara* complex, as a means to express an "alternative modernity" (2000b). Gedro performers, like the BaAka as described by Michelle Kisliuk, "*perform* their particular view of the modern, constructing an aesthetic of modernity and placing themselves in the center" (1998, 16; italics in original).

"THE TRADITION" AS CREOLIZING PROCESS

The intertextual integrative processes involved in Gedro performance to some extent echo, but force us to extend, the process of creolization as formulated by Ulf Hannerz (1997 [1987])[8] and elaborated upon by Karin Barber and Christopher Waterman (1995). Barber and Waterman describe creolization as what happens when "locals selectively 'appropriate' elements from metropolitan cultures in order to 'construct' their own hybrid medium in which to articulate their own, historically and socially specific, experience" (1995, 240). Gedro performers clearly appropriate materials to articulate their own experience, yet metropolitan cultures are just one source for Gedro performers, who appropriate elements from sources as diverse as popular songs, masks of other ethnic groups, and numerous "traditional" Dan dances.[9] While the origin of the appropriated materials may differ, the process looks remarkably the same, leading me to wonder if the selective appropriation central to creolization might be found in many artistic forms, including those emically labeled "traditional." Gedro performance supports Strother's assertion that certain traditional arts exhibit a quality commonly associated with popular cultural forms in that they are fundamentally "open texts" (1998, 278) whose performers creatively absorb materials of various origins. Could it be that, as Hannerz suggests (1997, 17), "we are all being creolized"?

Barber and Waterman assert three advantages of the creolization model:

> First, it stresses the active, creative role of people as culture producers. . . . Second, it draws attention to the fact that in colonial and post-colonial African cultures we witness the creation of something qualitatively new, with its own dynamics, rather than just a dilution or corruption of something formerly authentic. And third, this new thing is represented as a language-like generative system; the function and significance of the heterogeneous elements are determined by their place in this system and not by the meaning they had formerly in their source culture. (1995, 240) → *Similar to Battle*

Two aspects of this model work very well to describe what happens in Gedro performance. The creolization model does indeed place the emphasis upon performers as agents and recognizes that the "heterogeneous elements" that agents draw upon in their creative process are given new meaning and significance in the new contexts. Gedro performers themselves recognize that as they recontextualize appropriated materials, they imbue them with new meaning. And yet, Barber and Waterman's second point can only partially account for Ge performance, which is neither a corruption of formerly authentic practices nor something "qualitatively new." Rather, Ge performance is an old form that performers today manipulate in new contexts to negotiate complex identities and get things done.

Quoting popular-music rhythms is a celebration for the young members of Gedro's group, as it shows that he, and by extension they, are in the know. My consultants describe Ge as a tradition that is timeless yet of the moment, eternal yet current. Performers assert that the tradition that is Gedro is one that has always inherently involved a responsibility to be in touch with and responsive to the various cultural influences in the local environment. This is a notion of tradition that is at its essence dynamic and fluid (cf. Chernoff 1979, 61). Though held as epistemologically distinct from popular-music performance by my consultants, Ge performance is no less responsive to the outside world—to mass media, to musics of other ethnic groups, to other religious persuasions, to the audience, and to the market. Just as one of Christopher Waterman's Yoruba consultants called the popular-music style juju "a very modern tradition," (1990b), one of my consultants called Ge *"une tradition modernisé"* (Biemi, Goueu, Gba, and Oulai 1997). Ge performance demonstrates that many of the same processes evident in the creation of African popular arts can also be operative in older indigenous forms that are emically defined as "traditional." My consultants asserted that Ge performance has always operated thus—in relationship to the world around it, performers selecting and incorporating "outside" materials toward particular ends. I view this point in political terms, in that it suggests that Africans have always been creative agents, not blind followers of some static or superorganic "tradition" that existed before colonialism and before life experience involved a cacophony of media (Barber 1997a; Diawara 1997). It is commonplace to assert that popular artists in the postcolonial postmodern eras creatively combine and juxtapose diverse influences; my consultants suggest that through the creative process they call "the tradition," they do the same. Keen and creative strategists and wonderful artists, my consultants use Ge performance to negotiate complex identities in the diverse setting of postcolonial Côte d'Ivoire and, in the process, try to make a living.

In the past century, many new roads have been built that lead into Man—some actual, bringing in northern peoples and ideas; others virtual, bringing mediated music and dance into radios and televisions around the city; still others paving new landscapes in which the authority and infrastructure of the nation-state interweave with indigenous authority and custom. As a result, today *genu* exist within a rapidly changing pluralistic social milieu where they are variously defined: as part of a moral and religious system, as a form of entertainment, as an economic industry, or even as a political tool. But through Ge performance, performers such as Jean-Claude define themselves as modern beings rooted in the ways of the ancestors. Gedro performers attach profound meanings to these performances, which are central to their religious and ethnic identities, even as they embrace the idea that for many this *ge* is a form of popular entertainment not unlike popular music and television. Through these performances, differing people meet differing goals: Petit Gbapleu youth earn much-needed cash and establish identities that distinguish them in terms of generation, religion, and their notions of what it means to be Dan; politicians align themselves with this popular *ge* as a strategy to increase their political power; and audience members appreciate the performance as entertainment, regardless of their religious and ethnic identities. Moreover, the mere presence of Gedro validates and lends a feeling of significance to the event, fulfilling the general expectation that important occasions in Man must feature a dancing *ge*.

Ge performance occurs in direct and deliberate relationship to forces outside "the tradition"; sometimes Ge performers reject outside forces, forming clear boundaries between what they define as tradition and what they see to be other possibilities (e.g., Gedro versus Islam); other times performers incorporate these other possibilities, mixing and blending tradition with them (e.g., Gedro and popular music); but never do they ignore these outside possibilities—never is Ge performance oblivious to the rest of the world. Ge performance, as a public enactment of religious belief, is a theater for the articulation and negotiation of identity and tradition in the ethnically and religiously diverse setting of contemporary Côte d'Ivoire.

[handwritten margin notes:]

there is collaboration here, b/w modern & traditional (NEGOTIATION)

What I think needs examination here is the idea of tradition. Yes, it is interesting how it is defined in religious/secular contexts but we should not abandon the idea that traditions can change

Correlation w/ Kislivk
· Outside forces
· re-negotiation of tradition

FOUR

What Is Ge?

Hours and hours of many days in 1997, I, often with Jacques and sometimes with Nicole, sat with Monsieur Gueu Gbe Gonga Alphonse, discussing Ge.

Monsieur Gueu Gbe's house, where we held all our interviews, was a 20-minute walk from the house that Jacques, Nicole, and I shared on the edge of Man. We followed dirt roads through the mostly residential Quartier Domoraud, passing women farming the spaces between cement homes, small street-food stands where women sold fried fish and *alloco* (deep-fried plantain), and children playing soccer in the streets using small stones to mark the goals. Approaching the center of town, we would pass a mosque and a rather large Islamic school just next to the bridge crossing the river Ko, which divided Domoraud from Julabugu—the neighborhood that was populated mostly by Muslim immigrants from the savanna. Gueu Gbe's house rested a stone's throw from the river in a small part of Domoraud sometimes called Quartier Résidential. Within his walled compound of multiple buildings, flowering bushes, and shade trees, the world seemed a tranquil place. Songs of tropical birds provided a constant background to our conversation, which was punctuated five times daily by the call to prayer emanating from the Islamic school around the corner.

Since Gueu Gbe had assisted ethnomusicologist Hugo Zemp with some of his research in the 1960s, I felt fortunate to have the opportunity to meet him and ask him how things had changed in the thirty years that had passed since that time. Because of his knowledge about and passion for Ge and his enthusiasm for discussing the topic, Gueu Gbe quickly became one of my primary consultants. There was from the beginning a kind of affection between Gueu Gbe and me. Because of his previous experiences with Zemp and as a politician concerned with cultural matters, Gueu Gbe understood my role as an ethnographer and enthusiastically invited us to his house immediately upon learning we were in town.

Gueu Gbe from the outset saw me and my research as a means to reach the outside world with the message that there was something wonderful, something powerful about Dan culture. He unabashedly said that he wanted me to go back and write about the Dan in such a way that would stir interest and inspire others

[margin notes: Profits used to reinforced social values — KEEP IN MIND]

to come to experience the riches of Dan culture. His was a very pragmatic idealism; he believed that the way to keep Dan culture alive was to publicize it, to write about it, to film it, in order to bring tourists and researchers to the region. A tireless promoter of Dan culture, and especially Ge, he argued that the way to keep "the tradition" alive was to make it relevant in the contemporary Ivorian and global economy, to make it profitable, which would keep people practicing it and keep the values that underpin Ge performance alive and functioning. It was from this point of view that Gueu Gbe sought us out. He was excited that there was a foreigner in Man to study Ge, and he viewed my presence as an opportunity to promote his culture to the outside world.

Although I had read previous literature about Dan *genu* and had conducted preliminary research in the Man region during the summer of 1994, it was only through my initial conversations with Gueu Gbe early in 1997 that my understanding of Ge began to deepen. Of course, Monsieur Gueu Gbe's thoughts about Ge represent just one person's take on the topic, and I argue that there are multiple interpretations of this phenomenon. Yet I begin with his thoughts here because they capture the essence of a notion of Ge shared by many of my primary consultants who practiced "the tradition."[1] Furthermore, I had a sustained, deep series of conversations on the subject with Gueu Gbe. As it was Gueu Gbe who initiated my understanding of the depth of Ge, I will begin my in-depth discussion of Ge here by focusing on his thoughts about this rich and fascinating concept.

During our many discussions on the topic, Monsieur Gueu Gbe artfully articulated the polyvalent nature of Ge. Gueu Gbe often spoke in poetic phrases, weaving together different aspects of Ge into a single multilayered metaphor[2] that demonstrated the subtle integration of religious belief, moral theory, and behavior—in everyday life and in special framed performance—that characterizes this word. Gueu Gbe emphasized to me time and again that "*masque*" is simply an insufficient French translation of the phenomenon I had come to study:

> Ge in Dan country, it's a history. It's a system. It's a philosophy. It has nothing to do with the act of taking an object to cover the face. . . . It's a school. A system of commandments. A philosophy of comportment. We must no longer accept the name "mask." There are words that you cannot translate in another language. "Ge" is "Ge." So it is my wish that you write in such a way that the name "Ge" be from now on the name retained for this phenomenon, of this system, upon which our society rests. (Gueu Gbe 1997g)

Monsieur Gueu Gbe stressed repeatedly the importance of distinguishing between the idea of a masked person and Ge. In other words, the image that immediately comes to mind when we hear the word "mask"—a piece of art that conceals the face—is but one small part of just one aspect of Ge—its physical manifestation among humans. This physical manifestation itself is just one aspect of the whole philosophy or system called Ge. Understandably, Monsieur Gueu Gbe and others argue that the translation of "Ge" as "mask" reduces a complex sacred phenomenon to something a person might wear to a masquerade ball.[3]

So, that said, what is Ge? Like any mystical phenomenon, Ge has no simple definition. Mystics around the world have often turned to poetic language to describe their spiritual thoughts and experiences. Gueu Gbe is no exception:

Ge is the beginning. Ge is the middle. Ge is the end.

Ge is a living entity!

It is polyvalent. It is omnipotent. It is a polytechnician. (Gueu Gbe 1997a)

Ge, it is unknowable. It is nonmaterial. (Gueu Gbe 1997d)

For Gueu Gbe, words can only approach Ge; the notion cannot be fixed in language, in definitive terms.[4] During one discussion we compared several divergent definitions and descriptions of Ge, some of which came from my consultants and others that I had read in previous literature. My goal was to clarify whether or not Ge is a manifestation of an ancestral spirit or a forest spirit that has direct access to spirits of ancestors. At one point, a somewhat exasperated Gueu Gbe said:

All these terms turn around the power of Ge—ghost, ancestor, *bɛman* ["ancestor" in Dan], *yinan* ["spirit" in Dan], all that. These are words we designate, that we choose, to approach the definition of Ge. But one can never succeed in finding a total single definition. (Gueu Gbe 1997g)

The absence of a clear, precise definition did not prevent Monsieur Gueu Gbe from describing Ge, which he did at length during many of our conversations. Drawing upon these conversations and many others I had with other primary and secondary consultants, I was able to slowly piece together common points that helped me to understand Ge and its role in Dan religious thought and practice. I approached this issue differently with different people in different situations. Never did I simply begin a conversation with the question, "What is Ge?" Occasionally, with secondary consultants with whom I had less time, I would ask that question toward the end of an interview to clarify the ways they had been using the term and thinking about the concept during the course of the interview. The material that comes from my primary consultants on this matter is much richer because we had many occasions to sit and talk around the topic, which is where my understanding of it really began to flourish. Occasionally, I would use previous literature or another consultant's opinions as a springboard to compare/contrast different peoples' opinions. I went back to primary consultants[5] time and again with my interpretations of their thoughts about Ge to be sure I was understanding them properly (Lawless 1993; Stone and Stone 1981). It was through this process that I developed the following general understanding. Fieldwork

GE AS FOREST SPIRIT

Ge is simultaneously spirit and matter. Ge can materialize in peoples' daily actions and in corporeal form in Ge performance. But *genu* are always extant and present in *geɓɔ*—the mystical plane—in spirit form. This aspect of Ge can be better understood by placing it in the context of the Dan religious system.[6]

Describing how Ge fits into the Dan religious system is not a task I take lightly. The notion of a religious "system" seems on the surface to suggest something monolithic, devoid of human agency, that people simply plug into. "Traditional religious system" is a phrase that has too often been used in just such a way, stripping individuals of active thought and choice. Many African ethnographies feature representations of ethnic groups as homogeneous blocks of people, at the center of which is their "traditional religious system" which is assumed to be uniformly shared, believed, and practiced. Postmodernism and its close cousin deconstructionism have exploded just this kind of essentializing, a necessary process in the growth of academic discourse. Yet, taken to an extreme, deconstructionism could render scholars unable to utter anything resembling a generalization for fear of being accused of essentializing and representing humans as will-less, homogeneous beings. Taken to an extreme, deconstruction could banish ethnographers to representations of individuals who share nothing, who are alone in the world. Such a representation would bear no resemblance to the life experience of my Dan consultants.[7]

The Dan religious system does in fact exist in certain of my consultants' experience. Many of my consultants identify as practitioners of this system. There is enough shared between and among their views, in fact, to permit me to make some generalizations. This is precisely because these people have community, which means they communicate, that they share ideas. Theirs is not a world where they are all faceless followers of some predetermined religious law, but neither do they think about and practice religion in radically individualized manners so different from one another that there is nothing shared, nothing to generalize about. Some of my consultants understand themselves to be, and experience themselves to be, actively engaged in a system of religious thought and practice. They want to create community through their religion, and they do so, by enacting their beliefs together. As van Beck and Blakely write, "The religious action that is the core of African religion is *group oriented*" (1994, 18; italics mine). The words "religious system" suggest a certain degree of commonality and generalization, but this phrase does not inherently remove agency. When my consultants refer to their religious system, they do so in individually unique ways, yet they are also intentionally referring to something shared. This is the nature of the intersubjective process of the creation of community. Like many religious traditions around the world, Ge serves as a resource for community-building. Through Ge, certain of my consultants accomplish the goal of creating community and solidarity.

Though they envision themselves to be participants in a religious system, my consultants do not share opinions about every aspect of this system. There are several possible reasons for this. The first is the nature of Dan religion. Dan religion, like many indigenous religions in Africa, is nondogmatic, is an oral tradition, and varies somewhat from family to family. Religious pluralism, then, did not arrive with the introduction of Islam and Christianity. At its core, Dan religion itself is pluralistic, in part because it is problem-oriented and action-oriented (van Beek and Blakely 1994, 16). The Dan system involves a somewhat cohesive set of separate systems of problem solving. One could view this system, in fact, not as one system, but as "an agglomerate of systems," a set of strategic means to ends. Still, as van Beek and Blakely assert, "the relevant sacrifices, words, dances, and associated beliefs" often end up being conceived of as *a* system (17). My consultants talk about "the tradition" in this way, even though the ideas they express demonstrate that this system is, like many in Africa, characterized by variability and flexibility.

Other interpretations may account for the discrepancies I encountered in my consultants' accounts of their religious beliefs and practices. Variation might well have emerged because of the sacred and, to some extent, secretive nature of the topic. It is possible, of course, that people were not always telling me the "truth" or what they really think. Yet postmodern anthropology has rightly questioned the very idea of searching for and constructing some kind of "truth" in ethnographic situations (Clifford and Marcus 1986). Rather, ethnographers interpret ethnographic encounters, encumbered as they are with all manners of politics, historical legacies, and interpersonal communications. And the translations of these encounters into something to be read by people in different social-historical situations further problematizes any notion of the representation of a "truth." I agree with van Beek and Blakely that "cultural expressions can be understood, but never fully, and can be communicated transculturally, but not without the loss of meaning and the creation of new meaning" (1994, 3).

To some extent, I am playing the role of "the native theologian" (van Beek and Blakely 1994, 16), assembling a coherent whole cloth from the various pieces collected from different consultants. Yet not all Dan theorize about their religious system. My ground base is constructed of ideas expressed by Gueu Gbe Al- phonse—someone who thinks a great deal about these things—and is supple- mented by ideas of others who are active experts in Ge affairs and performance and still others who frankly do not think about these things as much but share nonetheless in the intersubjective construction of ideas about Dan religion. It is possible these less informed people might not have known the "correct" answers but felt compelled to give me answers anyway, so they guessed or made something up. My methods thus had an effect as well; as I mentioned above, the material I learned from primary consultants is much richer because my relationships with them were far deeper. Yet, as Gueu Gbe stated of his interactions with me, all of my consultants taught me what they wanted me to know: I am now shaping those encounters into something for you to read. Mediation occurs at every step along the way, and the role of this intervention is intensified by the language transla- tion(s) necessary in this process.

Finally, certain differences of opinion might have emerged simply because all of my consultants are individual thinkers with differing experiences and unique ways of looking at the world.[8] The fact that they consider themselves to be fellow practitioners of a religious system does not make them a homogeneous mass. I will describe the Dan religious system partially as a means to avoid essentializing comments such as, "The Dan believe x" and "The Dan do y"; these statements suggest homogeneity. Rather, I will discuss the system of thought and practice to show that this system exists as one set of options for people as they select among their many possibilities in today's polyreligious climate. By describing the sys- tem, I am not intending to portray something everyone does; rather I want to describe certain options everyone has—options that exist as possible religious choices in Dan peoples' experience today, options that many of my consultants conceptualize as a coherent whole that they call "the tradition" or "the religion of our ancestors."

Religion for many in the Man region involves a creative process of selection and rejection, of problem solving and identification. Paramount to this process is religious action and interaction. Van Beek and Blakely write, "As much as African religions are systems, they are systems in action, their systematic properties being the net result of social interaction" (1994, 13). They continue, "In Africa, religion means performing or otherwise doing something." This is what makes Ge per- formance such an important consideration in the process of religious identification in Man. Yet the enactment in performance of Ge cannot be understood separately from the theory and ideas that undergird it. Dan religion is action-oriented, but it is not *solely* action. It also involves theory and a cosmological system of thought.

For my Dan consultants, there exist two parallel dimensions, one which is physical—the everyday realm of earthly existence—and the other a metaphysical
"mystical realm" called *ge6ɔ*.[9] The boundary between these two realms is fluid.
This fluid boundary is evident in many aspects of Dan religious thought and
experience. First, the corporeal world—including humans, other animals, and
various natural phenomena—is "animated" with a spiritual presence and power
called *zii* or *nii*.[10] My consultants translated both of these terms either as *âme*
(soul) or *ésprit* (spirit). Particular trees, forests, mountains, natural springs, and
streams are recognized as sacred and are periodically visited for ritual purposes,
including the offering of food sacrifices.

This system has as its ultimate power source and creator the supreme deity
Zlan. All of my consultants considered Zlan to be equivalent to the Muslim Allah
and the Christian God; that is, they understand Zlan, Allah, and Dieu to be Dan,
Jula, and French words, respectively, for the same supreme being. Like supreme
beings in many West African religious systems, Zlan is primarily transcendent of
earthly experience. Yet the Dan system entails multiple channels, or intermediaries, through which people communicate with the supreme being. Though humans can, and do, pray directly to Zlan (Himmelheber 1965, 84), they are more
likely to access him through an intermediary.[11] While it would be impossible to
identify all such intermediaries, as they are specific to families and/or individuals
(and their identities are often, for that matter, secret information), it is possible
and permissible to identify the different types of intermediaries—one of which
is Ge. Because of the emphasis on action in Dan religion, focusing on acts of
communication between people and intermediaries is an effective means to explain the roles of these intermediaries, including *genu,* in the Dan religious system.

COMMUNICATING WITH INTERMEDIARIES IN THE DAN RELIGIOUS SYSTEM

Communication between living Dan people and the spirit world is complex and
takes many forms. Dan people can send and/or receive spiritual messages through
several types of intermediaries, including power objects (*ge6ɔga,* often translated
into French as *fétiche*),[12] certain spiritually powerful people, and certain spiritual
entities. Of these, I will focus here on the spiritual entities, as they are the intermediaries most important to an understanding of Ge and Ge performance. Listed
below are spiritual intermediaries in the Dan language, as my consultants translated them into French, and my English translations:

DAN	FRENCH	ENGLISH
yinan	*génie*	spirit
dian	*génie; pygmée*	spirit (in times past); pygmy
bɛman or *diömɛn*	*ancêtre*	ancestor
Ge		no appropriate translation in French or English[13]

Yinannu, the most elusive yet most powerful of all intermediaries, are the
beings closest in access to Zlan in the "astral world." The word "*yinan*" almost
certainly has linguistic connections to the Arabic word "*jinn.*" The Mau, a southern Maninka group, and even some Dan for that matter, pronounce "*yinan*" closer
to "*jinan.*" Moving farther north to the Bamana, whose language (Bamanankan)
is more significantly influenced by Arabic, the word becomes "*jinɛ.*" Just as the

term varies geographically, so does the concept itself take on a different character in each region. For my Dan consultants, *yinannu* are beings that are in the form of spirit (*nii* or *zii*). In contrast to sacred places, animals, and people—who have *nii* but are manifest in a physical form—*yinannu* are purely spirit.

This was not always the case, though. Long ago, "during the time of our ancestors," *yinannu* would sometimes appear in a frightening form, looking somewhat like old, short,[14] and bizarrely misshapen humans called *"dian."* Though they frightened people, *diannu* were actually spiritual guides or messengers. They would pursue people when they were alone in the forest (which Jacques says partially explains why Dan people do not care to spend time alone). *Diannu* would most frequently appear at places of worship such as sacred mountains, water, or trees to deliver messages to people, often revealing to them powerful medicinal plant formulas. This was how the original powerful *zuminu* received their medicinal wisdom. My consultants argued that the manifestation of *yinan* as *dian* is rare today, if not impossible (Biemi and Goueu 1997b).[15]

Yinannu themselves are not manifest in the terrestrial realm but are *accessible* in the terrestrial realm in various ways. Humans call *yinannu* in many different settings and for many different purposes. *Yinannu* serve as messengers and empowerers. Much, though not all, communication between humans and Zlan moves through the channels of *yinan*. When people worship sacred places (*gbεgu*)—such as mountains, trees, or springs—or power objects, their prayers pass through *yinannu* on their way to Zlan. By observing family totems—for example, not eating or harming a certain animal—or by generally behaving in a proper manner, people attract the beneficence of *yinan*. Some Dan Muslims appeal to *yinannu* by praying at the mosque. A Muslim marabout or a traditional *zumi* can call *yinannu* directly to their service, to send messages to and receive them from Zlan.

Certain unexplainable occurrences are sometimes considered to be evidence of acts by *yinannu* themselves. Goueu Tia Jean-Claude taught me much about *yinan* and human behavior. If a person wakes up in a good mood, seemingly for no reason, that is because a *yinan* of joy has arrived. In musical performance, if a person suddenly is moved to get up, move to the center of a circle, and dance; if a drummer suddenly becomes inspired and drums in an especially passionate way—these acts are attributed to the arrival of a *yinan* of joy or inspiration. While some *yinannu* are general and are shared by more than one person, each person also has his or her own personal *yinan*. One of the explanations for musical virtuosity is the presence of a powerful personal *yinan* (Goueu 1997i). Indeed, many Dan attribute all acts that demonstrate extreme talent, and any extraordinary physical or intellectual achievement, to *yinan*. Once when attempting to explain *yinan* to me, Gueu Gbe found an example he thought I, as a researcher, would understand:

> You are engaged in scientific research, with your equipment, you have used all your formulas . . . and then suddenly, a luminous idea comes to you, to tell you—do it like this, do it like this! You do it, and then—whoa! The results that you had sought for ten years, they appear. That's *yinan,* that. You have had a brilliant inspiration. And you, you have done that, in the process you become a genius. This is how you must perceive *yinan* and its relationship to people. (Gueu Gbe 1997g)

To properly explain this fascinating example, I have to untranslate two words. The word Gueu Gbe used for "brilliant" (*génial*) shares a root with the French word for *yinan* (*génie*). Moreover, in articulating this example, Gueu Gbe deliberately exploited the homonymous nature of the French word "*génie*," which not only means "spirit" (specifically "*yinan*" for Dan people) but also means "genius." Thus, in an artful wordplay, Gueu Gbe demonstrated to me that an example of the presence of *yinan* is the kind of ultimately brilliant intellectual insight that English speakers call genius.[16] "*Yinan*" and "genius" are, in fact, etymologically linked through their shared roots in the Arabic "*jinn*" (Johnson 1992 [1986], 107).

Yinannu also come to people in dreams and revelations. Dan carvers say that *yinannu* come to them in dreams to tell them that they want to manifest among humans and to show them what form they have chosen for their manifestation. The form they choose could be that of a power object (*geɓɔga*) or a *ge* (Himmelheber 1965, 82; Johnson 1987, 3). Several of my consultants told me *ge* origin stories that involved *yinannu* visiting their ancestors in dreams. For example, Bleu Tiemoko told me that in the time of his grandfather, many people in his family dreamt each time they slept of a dancing *ge* they had never before seen. This was the *yinannu* coming to tell them that Dutipia, a comedic *ge* (*trukë ge*), wanted to manifest among humans (Bleu 1997).

Yinannu also come to the human realm during Ge performances. The relationship between music sound and *yinan* is vital to the process of the manifestation of Ge. This I will discuss below in the section on Ge performance. First I must introduce another category of spirit intermediary which is also critical to Ge performance—ancestor spirits, or *bɛman*.

The Dan social world is not limited to living humans but also includes ancestors. Generally, as Dan people age, they are understood to be wiser because they have had more life experience. A democratic aspect of traditional Dan religion is that all elders can become like priests. A person who is aged, who is closer to the ancestors, will usually lead prayers and offer benedictions to the younger. At death, the *nii* of an elder who has been a good person moves on to *geɓɔ* to reside next to the *yinan* and Zlan. The deceased from this point on is called a *bɛman*,[17] or ancestor. Death does not sever relationships between people but rather transforms them (Janelli and Janelli 1982, Chapter 3). Ancestors retain an active presence on earth. Their terrestrial home is the sacred forest—the nature sanctuary, next to each Dan village, in which very important male elders are buried and boys' initiation takes place. Ancestors also can be reincarnated in human form. For example, during the summer of 1997, a boy was born to *zumi* Oulai Théodore's brother Jerome and his wife. Since he is a *zumi* and can "see" (meaning into the mystical domain), Théodore immediately recognized that his newborn nephew was his grandfather reborn. Théodore inherited the mantle of control of the family's sacred house from his grandfather; his nephew has now been recognized as the probable heir apparent of his powers and position.

Ancestors also maintain influence in the earthly realm through the inheritance of abilities. As I mentioned above, talent can come from Zlan through the channels of the *yinan*. Another source of talent is the ancestors, who pass power and ability to living humans in the form of "gifts" (*ɓɔdɛ*). Biemi Gba Jacques explained that for each activity that is vital to Dan life, an ancestor at some point made sacrifices to Zlan to attain what was needed. Thus one can trace hunting, singing, or drumming skills or any talent vital to the functioning of Dan society to those ancestors' sacrifices. Since that time, these talents have been inherited in the form of *ɓɔdɛ* (Biemi in Biemi and Goueu 1997a).

Both ancestors and *yinannu* are germane to a discussion of the final category of spirit intermediaries—*ge*. There has been some debate in previous literature about exactly what *genu* are, and I can understand the confusion. Consultants regularly talked about *genu* as if they are actually manifestations of the ancestors. Yet they also regularly described *genu* as manifestations of forest spirits. I remain less than 100 percent certain about the matter myself but have decided that this is an example that demonstrates how problematic ethnography can be. As I mentioned above, many of my consultants consider themselves to be participants in a religious system, yet they differ on certain fundamental aspects of that religion. If I stubbornly attempt to seek the capital "T" Truth about what *genu* are, I am missing an important point—people have different ideas about, and different understandings of, this complex phenomenon.[18] → Key to Discuss of Prob of Ethnography Theme

All of my consultants consider Ge performance a way of paying homage to the ancestors. The living honor the ancestors through perpetuating their practices—participating in Ge performance and honoring the ways of life taught in initiation by *genu*. The ancestors are a part of the social world, and they must be regularly propitiated and consulted. Ge performance is one instance in which these acts can take place. Thus, ancestors may be spiritually present during Ge performances. But, some of my consultants hold, a performing *ge* is not *literally* an ancestor manifest but rather another type of spiritual power, or intermediary, which originated in the wilderness. This view upholds what Vandenhoute learned in his ethnographic study of Dan masks in the late 1930s: → Embodied / Represented Direction?

> The mask among the Dan . . . does not represent the ancestor as such, but is conceived of as an independent supernatural being, most often created by the Supreme Being and placed in the service of people to act as a mediator between the deceased and the living. (Vandenhoute 1989 [1952], 28)

According to this view, *genu* originally came to the ancestors from mountains, rocks, and trees in the forest, but their ultimate origin is, as with everything, Zlan, who sent *genu* to people through the envoy of *yinan*. As Ge performer Zogueu Anatole from Déoulé told me, "*Genu*, during the time of ancestors, were the dispatches of *yinan*. Ancestors kept them and passed them down to today" (Zogueu in Zogueu and Ve 1997). People today would not have this connection to God were it not for the efforts of the ancestors to accept and maintain the power of Ge. As Gueu Gbe said, "[The Dan person] leans on the patriarch to pass by the intermediary of a *ge* to address prayers to God" (Gueu Gbe 1997d).

Alternatively, some of my consultants hold views that define Ge, *yinan*, and *bɛman* in slightly different ways. They describe *genu* as manifestations of a kind of *yinan*—the kind who have lived here on earth. When the early patriarchs died, they became ancestors (*bɛman*) and went on to the mystical realm *gebɔ*. Thus, those *yinannu* who have lived on the earth *are* the *bɛmannu*, and when they return to manifest on earth, they are called *genu*. According to this view, Ge is not a type of spirit that is distinct from *yinan* but is rather a distinct *kind* of *yinan*— one who is an ancestor (Goueu 1997d; Bleu 1997). There are still other variations. Kong member Lien Sati Yvonne (Lien et al. 1997) and other young women whom I interviewed in Petit Gbapleu, along with Gba Ernest (Gba Ernest 1997f), contended that *genu* are manifestations of *yinannu* who were passed down by the ancestors but are not themselves ancestors. It seems that a range of opinions existed among followers of "the tradition" concerning what exactly *genu* are.

Gueu Gbe apparently was correct when he asserted that a search for a single definition of this "indefinable" phenomenon is futile (Gueu Gbe 1997g).

Two divergent opinions explain the form in which *genu* originally manifested among humans. Most of my consultants confirm the majority of the previous literature (Fischer 1978; Fischer and Himmelheber 1984; Johnson 1986) when they told me that *genu* originally announced their desire to manifest among humans in their ancestors' dreams, revealing to them the form in which they wished to manifest in the human realm. A minority of consultants argued that the first masks, or the faces of *ge* (*gewëdë*), were actually death masks, molded on the faces of the original family patriarchs before their burial (Harley 1950, 43). All of my consultants who practice "the tradition" agree, though, that the ancestors deserve reverence for having passed Ge down to people today.

I encountered two regenerations, or resurrections, of *genu* in 1997, examples of the reconfiguration of spirits that had manifested in the past but had become dormant. Gedro of Petit Gbapleu came back to Semlen Aimé's grandmother in a dream. In this dream, the spirit suggested that her family's *ge* wanted to manifest again with a new name—Gedro. In Biélé, I heard two different origin stories for the children's *gbage* (war mask) which was "born" in 1995. In an informal setting, I was told that this *ge* was created as a result of boys playing around during initiation, donning a soapbox for a mask and writing new songs in imitation of an old *gbage* named Gboko. When I asked about the origin of the mask in a formal interview setting, however, I was told simply that the new *ge* was not really "new" but was rather an extension of the spirit of the older *ge* Gboko. Elders during the interview told me that since Gboko was no longer needed, as this is not a time of war, its spirit effectively transformed into a new entertainment *ge* manifestation (Gbage group 1997). These two explanations are not incompatible. In the latter explanation, agency is attributed to the *ge,* while in the former, agency is attributed to the boys. But Gboko could well have been making known his desire to manifest in a new form by inspiring the boys' behavior in the sacred forest. Jacques and I concluded that the two explanations are just different aspects of the same story.

I can confirm that old *genu* are reemerging in new forms but not necessarily that new *genu* are continuing to be created. I did hear anecdotes about other new *genu* being created, but since I was not able to follow up on these leads, I cannot ascertain whether these were actually new *genu* or just reemergences of old *genu* in new forms. People in the Man region might well be creating new *genu,* as is suggested by previous research, but I have not learned of such practices during the time I have spent there. Rather, my consultants assert that all *genu* who are or ever have been manifest first arrived during the time of their ancestors. New manifestations are extensions of the spiritual power that first took form long ago.

TYPES OF *GENU*

In the ethnographic literature on Dan masks, one encounters various ways of categorizing *genu* and various names for the different types of *genu*. Names and classifications of Ge that I learned differ to greater or lesser extents from this previous research for a number of reasons. First, there are geographical variations within the rather large and diverse Dan region. Just as there are substantial dialectical differences in Dan language, there are other cultural differences. Much of the previous research was conducted in Liberia among southern Dan, which

to outsiders;
or ~~inside~~ among? insiders as well".

may well account for some of the differences I have encountered. Second, Ge, like all traditions, changes over time. Much previous research was conducted during the first half of this century. The Dan people with whom I studied are as distinct from their predecessors in the 1930s as I am from Americans who lived through the Great Depression and World War II and listened to big-band music on the radio. Previous literature and my own field research confirm that new *genu* can appear and others can become dormant, while functions of individual *genu* can change over time (Fischer 1978, 19; Harley 1950, 43). Third, the issue of Ge involves much secrecy. I regularly told consultants that I was primarily interested in learning what everyone could know about Ge rather than in publicizing their secrets. I was nonetheless told many secrets. Still, it is quite possible that some previous researchers were granted access to information that was not shared with me and vice-versa. And finally, because my goal was to study specific *genu* in more depth, other *genu* may well have been around that I did not experience. A comprehensive classification, given the diversity one finds in the region, would be extremely problematic anyway. As Gba Daouda writes, "The problem [of classification] is deeper than one can imagine" (1982, 57).[19]

Nonetheless, certain general statements can be made, based on previous literature and my own research. Dan generally classify *genu* in two different ways: according to the form in which they manifest and according to their functions. Previous studies have presented rigorous systems of categorization of both types; such is not my goal. However, I will briefly discuss the topic in order to provide a context for the two *genu* central to this book: Gedro and Gegbadë.

Regarding form, there are two types of *genu*: *ge ɓasi* (dressed *ge*) and *ge kpesi* (undressed *ge*) (Zemp 1993 [1969], 2). Dressed *genu* are those who are visible to everyone—initiates and noninitiates alike—and both Gedro and Gegbadë fall into this category. Undressed *genu* are those whom women and noninitiates are not permitted to see. However, everyone may hear these *genu,* which include some *genu* who have no visual form at all but manifest among people only in sound.[20] Each of these two categories can be further subdivided. For example, among dressed *genu* are the categories of *gegblɛɛn,* or "long *ge,*" which has a nonrepresentational black cloth face and dances on stilts; *gekpenë* ("short *ge*"), with a relatively flat oval-shaped mask and mid-length raffia skirt (e.g., Gedro); and *gegɔn,* or male *ge,* whose mask has a beak and who wears a heavier longer raffia skirt (e.g., Gegbadë).

Categorizing *ge* according to their functions is complex because *genu* fulfill many functions in Dan society. As Gueu Gbe once told me, "For every function that exists in society, there is a mask . . . that ensures this function" (Gueu Gbe 1997f). Moreover, functions that people can meet through *genu* can also be met in other ways. French-speaking Dan distinguish three broad groups: sacred *ge,* warrior *ge,* and entertainment *ge.* While consultants regularly used these terms, they are somewhat misleading. First, all *genu* are sacred by definition. Second, as Fischer and Himmelheber write, there is not a strict hierarchical order of *genu* but rather just some who are more important and powerful than others (1984, 103). The category "sacred *ge*" thus refers to those who are *more* sacred than most others. Third, as I have already noted above, *genu* can change functions over time. The most common example of such change today is that of sacred *genu* becoming entertainment *genu.* Finally, a single *ge* may fall in more than one category. For example, Gba Daouda lists the *gundïöge*[21]—the head *ge* of the

① SACRED / SECULAR
② DETERMINATION of RELIGIONS MEANING for DAN
③ CULTURAL INFLUENCE . .

Figure 4.1. Sakpe. Photograph by Daniel B. Reed.

village or of a neighborhood—in both the warrior and sacred categories (1982, 69–73).

Included in the category of sacred *ge* are highly powerful *genu* such as those who oversee initiation, those whom chiefs consult regarding important political decisions, and *zu genu* such as Gegbadë, who deal with matters of sorcery and healing. Some sacred *genu* perform on rare occasions, and an increasing number no longer perform at all. However, *genu* can be powerful even if they never perform (Fischer 1978, 18; Himmelheber 1965, 76; Vandenhoute 1989 [1952], 29). Many sacred *ge kpesi* are never seen but nonetheless are active with spiritual power which enables people to fulfill certain needs in their lives. Associated with many sacred *genu* are legendary stories of superhuman feats, such as walking through walls (Oulai 1997b; Adams 1986, 50). What ultimately makes sacred *genu* so much more powerful than other genres are the *yinannu* associated with them. Each sacred *ge* has three groups of *yinan*: the *yinannu* of manifestation of joy, who inspire the *ge* to dance; the *yinannu* who enable a *ge* to read someone's destiny; and the *yinannu* of war, who enable a *ge* to defend themselves and attack others in a mystical sense (Goueu 1997i).

Most of my consultants include in the category of sacred *ge* the *ge* of the women's society called Kong. This is the only *ge* operated exclusively by women. Men are not permitted to see the Kong. Even many females cannot see the Kong. Only women who are initiated to the highest attainable level, women who are usually postmenopausal, are permitted to experience the visual aspect of a Kong manifestation, though everyone is permitted to hear the Kong music (*dɔɔtan*). The Kong handles girls' initiation and excision, along with birth and other matters traditionally associated with women. The Kong is led by the most powerful woman of any Dan village or neighborhood—the *zud'e*.

The genre known as warrior *ge* are all mute keepers of social order. Certain warrior *genu* played leadership roles in times of war. Today their primary function is to survey villages to ensure that things are properly done. Some warrior *genu*

Figure 4.2. Warrior *ge* Zaclo of Déoulé being videotaped by Biemi Gba Jacques. Photograph by Daniel B. Reed.

watch over the sacred forest. Others ensure that women refrain from burning cooking fires at windy times of the day during the dry season. Some oversee public work projects and Ge performances, making sure that people do things in the appropriate way. The warrior *ge* I encountered most frequently was Sakpe, who was often present to keep public order during events when other *genu* were performing. In short, most warrior *genu* are like traditional versions of police and army officers (Gba Daouda 1982, 73). During the Yahabö (Yam Festival) in Déoulé, a whole corps of warrior *genu* emerge from the sacred mountain (Gohlan) as part of this harvest festival, engaging in violent acts to show their strength and fearlessness.

Gba Daouda (1982, 82–86) lists three main categories of *masques de réjouissance* (rejoicing or festivity *ge*): *tanɓo ge,* or singing *ge; tankë ge,* or dance *ge;* and *trukë ge,* or comedian *ge.* These categories blur. Many *genu* both sing and dance and could be listed in each of the first two groups. However, there are *tanɓo ge* who are *ge kpesi,* whose manifestation is exclusively aural. Some *genu* who might sing a little but are known more for their dancing than for singing—such as Gedro of Petit Gbapleu—would be considered *tankë ge* within this system of classification. *Tankë ge* and *tanɓo ge* perform at many types of community occasions, including weddings, funerals, harvest festivals, festivals organized by the Ivorian government, and political public-relations events (see Chapters 3 and 7). *Trukë ge* frequently come out when sacred *genu* are also manifest, such as during Déoulé's Yam Festival, to lighten the mood. *Trukë ge* specialize in parody and satire, imitating other *genu* and people as well. Specialists in current affairs, they commonly engage in pantomime skits in order to poke fun at local and national noteworthies. At the Yam Festival, among the subjects of *trukë ge* satire were other *genu,* Ivorian president Henri Konan Bedie, and bodybuilders of American movies and television. They even poked fun at Jacques and me, using sticks to imitate microphones and video cameras that they used in a mock silent interview of the visiting ethnographers. Comedian masks who behave thus are common in many West African societies who practice mask performance (Reed et. al 2001). They often appear during performances of more serious and/or sacred masks and frequently engage in miming and parody much like *trukë ge* do among the Dan.

GEDRO - Female

Much easier than describing the various functional categories of *genu* is describing which functions particular kinds of *genu* can provide in Dan society. Gedro is a rejoicing *ge* who can perform in many contexts and for many reasons. Compared to a highly sacred *ge* such as Gegbadë, Gedro is a Jesus Christ Superstar–like figure.[22] Gegbadë performs for serious reasons for smaller crowds to solve problems that affect just one or only a few people at a time. Gedro, on the other hand, is a *ge* of the masses. Anyone can hire him, and he can perform at virtually any type of celebratory occasion. Gedro can be categorized in several ways. Considering form, Gedro is a *gekpenë*—a short (meaning not on stilts) *ge* with an oval-shaped, beautifully carved wooden face. He wears a light raffia skirt (*dua*) that is roughly knee length. Like most *ge 6asi,* or *genu* who manifest visually, Gedro wears traditional handwoven Dan clothing beneath his raffia skirt and a tall, elaborately decorated leather hat.

Functionally, Gedro is a *tankë ge,* in that his primary purpose is to dance and entertain, although, like many *genu,* he can also "pour water," or give blessings to people. Dan often call the giving of blessings, or benedictions, "pouring water" because this act is generally accompanied by the pouring of libation onto the ground for the ancestors. "Water" in this context can refer to any liquid, though it is most frequently some form of alcohol such as palm wine. Blessings can be silent; even mute *genu* can bless children simply by picking them up and holding them.

French-speaking Dan often call *tankë genu* such as Gedro "women's masks," for several reasons. First, while some *ge*'s faces look fierce and frightening, *tankë genu* faces are effeminately beautiful, with finely shaped features. They are frequently adorned with earrings or other jewelry associated with women. More important, women involve themselves in *tankë ge* performances to a greater extent than with more sacred *genu.* Not only do women enjoy watching rejoicing *genu* perform, they also more frequently sing and dance along with the *ge,* taking important roles in the manifestation of the spirit in performance. For all these reasons, many women cite rejoicing *genu* as their favorite type of *ge* (Lien et. al. 1997). One must not confuse this term, however—women's masks—with the *ge* of the women's society called Kong, which is an entirely female affair that is never seen by men.[23]

Although Gedro's primary stated responsibility is to entertain people and dance, one should not forget that there is far more to it than that. He valorizes political events and reinforces the importance of any event to which he is invited. He also serves as an important expression of Dan religious and ethnic identity for many of my consultants, as do all performing *genu.* But given the few "totems," or restrictions, placed on a Gedro performance, he is able to perform more frequently in today's pluralistic climate than are many other *genu.* For that reason, his role as an expression of identity is increasing.

GEGBADË

In terms of form, Gegbadë is a *gegɔn,* or male *ge.* According to Fischer and Himmelheber (1984, 81), *gegɔnnu* are found exclusively in the north of the Dan region; while I cannot confirm their absence in the southern Dan region, *gegɔnnu* were certainly prevalent in the northern region stretching from Man to Touba during the period of my research. *Gegɔnnu* are easily distinguished by their *gewëdënu,* or masks, which feature protruding beaks that have led some researchers to call a *gegɔn* a "bird masquerade" (Fischer and Himmelheber 1984, 81), though my consultants did not associate the beak or this type of *ge* with birds. Oulai Théodore, head of the sacred house in which Gegbadë resides, explained to me that the beak and the round face each represent different *genu.* The beak, according to Théodore, is a visual representation of the male circumcision *ge* called *dɛn.* While not permitted to see the *dɛn,* who manifests only during male circumcision, women are allowed to hear the *dɛn*'s voice, which is the part of the *dɛn* manifestation that is present when a *gegɔn* is outside. The round face represents the *gegɔn.* A *gegɔn* does not speak, though; it is the voice of the *dɛn* who speaks when a *gegɔn* performs.

Théodore explained to me the history of the relationship between the *dɛn* and *gegɔnnu:*

> When boys go for circumcision, it's the *dɛn* who watches over them so that sorcerers don't come kill them, so that at the moment when they are in the process of circumcising ... they don't have any surgical problems. So this mask, *dɛn,* it's he—since he has provided so much service to people, and people [meaning women and noninitiates] don't get to see him, men decided to invite him into the village—in another form. Since women are not permitted to see him, they dressed him, and they gave him the name *gegɔn.* That's his origin. ... That's why his voice is different from the voices of other masks. Because, he, when we see him, we say, "His name is *gegɔn.*" But when he speaks, he does so with the voice of the mask who is in the bush, whom women do not see, who watches over the *circumcisées.* ... So it's a cover that is there. That's why I tell you the *gegɔn* represents several powers. (Oulai 1997b)

A *gegɔn* is thus actually two *genu* combined into one especially powerful manifestation.

Given the value that my consultants placed on circumcision, it is not surprising that *gegɔnnu* are very highly revered. "The master of masks, the tutor of masks, the director of masks, the most powerful mask—all those qualifications are associated with *gegɔn*" said Théodore (Oulai 1997b). Many Dan also call *gegɔn* a *masque de sagesse,* or a mask of wisdom. As Jacques told me, "He is the sage of the sacred house. The historian of the sacred house" (Biemi in Biemi, Goueu, Gba, and Oulai 1997). Ge performer Gba Daniel explained that *gegɔnnu* are

> like griots, they sing praises about all those things your ancestors, from long ago, did, that you must now assume the responsibility to do. ... You must not forget the past. He is there to reveal all that to you. (Gba in Biemi, Goueu, Gba, and Oulai 1997)

Daniel described the way a *gegɔn* regulates and comments on young people's behavior. If someone is doing badly at school, for example, a *gegɔn* while performing might remind that person of the good examples set by his ancestors to get him or her back on the right path (Gba in Biemi, Goueu, Gba, and Oulai 1997). *Gegɔnnu* thus teach about the past, bringing the past into the present. *Gegɔnnu* offer a specific example of the perpetuation of ethnic, religious, and family identities through Ge performance.

The educational, historical, and value-enforcing aspects of *gegɔnnu*, though, seem to be on the decline, according to several consultants. Goueu Tia Jean-Claude said that many *gegɔn* performances today emphasize singing and dancing over recounting stories and history. Jean-Claude asserted, "*Gegɔn* now is obliged to dance more because the young of today are not so fond of things from the past" (Goueu in Biemi, Goueu, Gba, and Oulai 1997). Oulai Théodore agreed and argued that "Since the whites have come . . . people have need of a dance mask," so there has effectively been a new genre of *gegɔn* created—*gegɔn danseur* (dancing *gegɔn*) (Oulai 1997b). Théodore mentioned that a *gegɔn* from the Man neighborhood of Libreville—a *ge* who I had noticed was quite popular—was created just eight years ago for this purpose.[24]

No one would accuse Gegbadë—the *gegɔn* from Théodore's sacred hut—of being a mere dancer. Théodore is adamant about the fact that his *gegɔn* remains true to "the tradition." Gegbadë will not come out of the sacred house simply to dance for pleasure. Furthermore, Gegbadë is not just a *gegɔn* but also a *zu ge*—a type of *ge* who consults, divines, and exorcises. Théodore stresses that *zu ge* performance is serious work, a fact which is proven by the amount of money people are willing to pay. People sometimes will pay Gegbadë 350,000 CFA (around $700 U.S.—a very hefty sum by Ivorian standards) just to transport his group to the site of a problem, not to mention the extra fees that are expected during the course of the work. Théodore asserted, "People won't pay that kind of money for mere entertainment" (Oulai 1997b).

Théodore's sacred house has several *zu genu*. He sums up the work these *genu* do in the following manner:

> The masks that my ancestors gave me were the types that chase evil spirits, exorcise places that are ruined by sorcery, speak of the destiny of an individual or a people, and identify sacrifices which are appropriate to an individual. Gegbadë disinfects places, heals, gives sacrifices. (Oulai 1997b)

Other types of *genu*, called *dɛɓogenu*, also do consultation (*dɛɓo*)—that which Théodore describes above as "reading the destiny" of a person. *Dɛɓo* is essentially divining—a "means of knowing" (Peek 1991, 2) what a person should do in a given situation or predicament. Gegbadë is able to predict what will happen and give advice accordingly. As Théodore says of Gegbadë, "What he says is realized" (Oulai 1997b). Gegbadë also "identifies sacrifices." Giving sacrifices to an appropriate source is a common way of solving a problem for many Dan peoples. Dan will sometimes consult a *zu ge* to identify a source (a mountain, a tree, another *ge,* or a power object) to which a sacrifice should be offered, as well as what that sacrifice should consist of (usually some food—a chicken or chickens, for example, or in rare instances something as expensive as a cow). A *zu ge*, like his human counterparts of *zumi* and *zuɗe,* also acts as a kind of traditional physical and metaphysical healer in Dan society. Gba Daouda identifies the *zo gue*[25] as a *ge* who serves as a specialist in the pharmacopoeial use of plants and what Gba calls "therapeutic magic" (1982, 71). When Gegbadë consults people who are ill, he applies his encyclopedic knowledge of medicinal plants and his ability to "see" into the mystical domain to find the problem's cause and solution.

"Seeing" is also used by Gegbadë in his battles against the negative use of spiritual power called *du*.[26] According to my consultants, *du* is a neutral spiritual force which, through use, can become either positive (*dusë*) or negative (*duyaa*). "*Du*" is often translated as *sorcellerie* (sorcery), a word that in Ivorian French is generally used to refer solely to socially destructive spiritual action. In the Dan dialect that my consultants spoke, however, *du* is not inherently negative.[27] In fact, many Dan hold that the only way to effectively combat negative sorcery, or *duyaa*, is through the use of positive sorcery, or *dusë*. All forms of *zu*—*zumi*, *zuɗe*, and *zu ge*—make use of *dusë* to combat *duyaa*. In other words, *zu*, like negative sorcerers (*duyaami*), possess the capability to manipulate *du*, but they use this capability toward positive ends. This capability is called in French *dedoublement* (doubling)—the ability to send one's spirit into the mystical realm to interact with others who share the ability to double and to see what they are doing. Everyone is capable of doubling in dreams, but a *duyaami* or a *zu* can do so consciously. This ability is the subject of a proverb that is sung during Ge performances:

Example 4.1. Text of sung proverb *"Tungë ɗɛ man"*

Tungë ɗɛ man,	The bird who passes on high,
Ko ko kɔnyan-wo	We all see one another.

Ge performer Gbongue Felix interpreted this proverb to mean, "Those of us who are sorcerers (good and bad), we know each other, because we see one another there in the mystical plane."

Jacques preferred to think of *du* not as a force but as action. To explain, he used the metaphor of a knife. One can use a knife, which is itself neutral, for good or bad purposes. If the knife is used to prepare a meal, then that is *dusë*. But, if it is used to senselessly kill someone, that is *duyaa*. *Du* is thus not the knife itself, but the *use* of the knife. For Jacques, *du* is a form of behavior, a manner of comportment—an action, not an objectifiable force. For example, *duyaami* consciously double themselves to meet in the mystical realm to plan and engage in destructive acts. In order to build the power to act, *duyaami* must eat the *nii*, or soul, of another person. *Duyaami* tend to work in groups, trading off sacrificing family members whose souls they eat in order to build their power. A person whose soul has been eaten tends to wither away and die a slow, medically unexplainable death. Sorcery is illegal in Côte d'Ivoire, and Gegbadë plays a role in enforcing anti-sorcery legislation. ~~INSEPARABILITY OF LEGAL ACTION & RELIGIOUS BELIEF~~

Zu genu are like spiritual policemen who combat the illegal (by Ivorian law) practice of *duyaa*. *Zu genu* are hired to identify malevolent sorcerers and, if possible, locate and destroy their power objects (*duga*). *Genu*, and especially *zu genu*, as embodiments of good and just behavior, also actively promote positive spiritual behavior (*dusë*). But protecting the innocent from *duyaa* is messy and dangerous work; in so doing, *zu genu* place themselves in harm's way. Any *ge*, but especially a *zu ge*, must be prepared to ward off attacks of *duyaa*. He must have the knowledge and the ability—in other words, the power[28]—to combat such attacks. And he must be alert and vigilant. At any Ge performance, there could be people present who are opposed to the *ge* and who might attempt to mystically attack him.

While *zumi* are also called to solve sorcery problems, there are advantages to having a *ge* do this dangerous work. Writing about sacred *ge* in a general sense, Siegmann and Schmidt state:

> In the process of enforcing rules, the masked spirits must punish, or be able to make fully credible a threat to punish, all wrong-doers, regardless of family allegiances, ages, or social status, and thereby establish their credibility, impartiality and flexibility as a rule-making and-enforcing entity. Since the mask is conceived of as a spirit, there is no person to blame and no recrimination or retaliation within the community. (1977, 3)

One could say that a *zumi,* as a fellow human, is more vulnerable. He is a recognizable person who can be held personally accountable for his decisions and actions in enforcing traditional rules. A *ge,* on the other hand, has the authority of the ancestors behind him and is a spirit who should not be questioned and cannot be held accountable. A *zu ge*'s work is contingent on his reputation and the authority that he assumes. His reputation is built through years of experience successfully doing his job; this reputation thus builds respect for his authority. One can question the authority of a reputable *zu ge* such as Gegbadë, but at great cost.

The argument that a *zu ge* is more invulnerable than a *zumi,* however, needs some clarification. Depending on the will of the *yinan,* Théodore, himself a *zumi,* will investigate and solve a sorcery problem. But this, Théodore insisted, is still a manifestation of the *zu ge.* In other words, Théodore himself can physically direct an investigation by drawing on the spiritual power of the *ge.* On these occasions, Théodore himself manifests one or more *ge.* One should not confuse the physical evidence of a *ge*—the mask, the raffia skirt, and so forth-with the *ge* himself. *Genu* can manifest in many forms, including in the actions of a powerful *zumi.*

OULAI THÉODORE: AFFLICTED BY SPIRITS, ACCEPTING HIS FATE

Ge is generally the province solely of particular families that have sacred houses, and Ge performers usually inherit their roles, and the knowledge associated with these roles, from older family members. Yet not everyone of a particular generation can hold key roles, and knowledge of the process of determining who might inherit a particular role is critical to understanding how Ge manifests in the human realm. In the case of *zu genu,* one is sometimes pursued, in a spiritual sense, to become a performer. Oulai Théodore inherited the capability to work as a *zumi,* as well as a sacred house full of *zu genu,* from his grandfather. As Théodore tells the story, he had little choice in the matter of his career. The *yinannu* chose him to inherit his grandfather's ability, and though he resisted for years, he now makes his living by the grace of their powers. Théodore grew up in Zoba, a village west of Man, though his family traces its roots to the northern Dan town of Yorodougou west of Biankouma. As a child, Théodore was vaguely aware that his grandfather somehow supported their family, though he never farmed. As Théodore grew older and was initiated, he realized why: his grandfather was a *zumi* and had a sacred house in which he kept several powerful *genu.* When he was in his late teens,

Figure 4.3. Oulai Théodore with the author. Photograph by Biemi Gba Jacques.

Théodore was told that his family had known since his birth that he had inherited his grandfather's powers. Théodore learned that he was the one chosen to continue his grandfather's work. → How .

At this time, Théodore was still in school and was not at all attracted to his grandfather's line of work. He was a Catholic and a serious student. When I asked him how he had become involved in the affairs of Ge, he told me:

> I really liked my studies, eh? I want to tell you that. I was already quite old. But when they told me [that I had inherited the power], that did not immediately break my spirit [to continue in school]. Because at school, I had never had to repeat a class. . . . At each stage, when I slept, what they were going to teach us the next day, or even a week later, I could foresee as early as one week before in my dreams! Do you see? I asked myself, silently, if that was what they call sorcery, or what was it? Introspectively—I kept it to myself, secretly. . . . So it did not really surprise me when they told me, "Voila—this is how you arrived at birth, and this is what you must do." (Oulai 1997a)

Théodore continued in his studies, however, going on to Abidjan where he enrolled in school to become a hotelier. He continued:

> I then saw that running a hotel would be much better than what I would have done back here [in the Man region—meaning follow in his grandfather's foot-steps]. That's where I fell into error. It was at that time that I became insane.

. . . it was then that I had problems. I had a nervous breakdown. . . . And they sent me to Bingerville [to a mental health facility], and my grandfather back at the village said, "No, it's not Bingerville where he will be healed." That's how I came back to the village. I came back, and they worked on me [using traditional healing methods], and when things began to work again, I left again. And after two years, I had my diploma, and I went to work in San Pedro [a coastal city south of Man]. (Oulai 1997a)

Théodore worked in the hotel industry for several years, eventually landing a job at the Hôtel Beau Séjour in Man. It was there that his problems resurfaced:

One day, I woke up, I opened my eyes, and I could see nothing. I became blind. . . . I could not even discern colors. And my grandfather was aware of *everything* that was happening. That time, people said [Théodore] must return to the village, and [my grandfather] said, "No. If he comes back to the village, he will die. So take him to someone else who can heal him. And this person will give him advice." . . . And it was then that I was sent to Gbagblasso [a village north of Biankouma in the Dan/Mau borderland region]. It was at Gbagblasso, I can tell you, that I had a master. It was he who gave me advice. He said to me, "My young man, if you want to succeed in your life, [you must follow your grandfather]. If you continue in your ways and your grandfather dies, you will die as well. And you will die mired in problems." . . . This man who gave me this advice, he is there, he is still alive—he is an owner of masks as well. So I studied a bit with him, and he gave me advice. (Oulai 1997a)

Théodore spent two years studying with his master, a Mau *zumi*, in Gbagblasso, who taught him how to use his inherited gift. He learned that the madness and the blindness he had experienced were just "warnings." These were "revelations," or attempts by the *yinan* to sway him toward his true path.

When Théodore finished his studies, he did not return to live at Zoba. Since his grandfather was still alive and working there, Théodore left to set up shop in a location where his skills were needed. After several moves, he eventually ended up in Grand Gbapleu, on the edge of Man. He has led a remarkably successful career since that time. He has traveled great distances to work with his Ge performance group—in many locations around Côte d'Ivoire and neighboring countries. He has worked for prominent West African politicians and military leaders.

If Théodore has had to make sacrifices as a result of giving up his career in the hotel business, they have not been financial. In 1997, he was constantly in high demand. His compound filled up day after day with people in need of spiritual consultation. He had a sizeable staff of musicians and religious specialists and was in the process of building a large, brand-new family compound in Grand Gbapleu. And if he was once mentally unstable, he revealed none of this troubled past during the time I spent with him. In 1997, Théodore was well-spoken, kind, and charismatic. He was confident almost to the point of arrogance. ^{7}

And he has to be that way. This persona is required of a high-profile *zumi*. He has to command authority. To be able to accuse others of sorcery, he cannot question himself, or others will question him. He carries himself in a convincing manner, which demonstrates to people that he has a highly sacred *ge* behind him whose power cannot be matched and whose authority cannot be challenged. By acquiescing to the will of the *yinannu,* Théodore has found a life in which he can fight evil as a livelihood—the livelihood of Ge performance.

GE IN PERFORMANCE

A manifestation of Ge can take many forms, from simply a combination of certain sounds (Lifschitz 1988; Majima 1997; Zemp 1993 [1969]) to an elaborate production involving a masked dancer, a percussion ensemble, singers, power objects, specific dance moves, specific songs, proverbs, and other standardized performative tendencies. Whatever form a particular *ge* takes, all aspects of the manifestation become *ge*. Regarding the physical, visual aspects of a performance, Gueu Gbe said,

> The mask, the wearer . . . there is the raffia, there is what they put on the head, there are the pants, the *bubu* (shirt) . . . that whole ensemble, which is material, and worn by a human who, from the moment that he is dressed like that, and that he is in that disposition, becomes spirit. . . . From the instant that he places himself behind the mask, he becomes different. He is inhabited by a wisdom, he is transported, he transcends, and at the moment, he becomes at the same time the physical mask that you see, and he becomes at the same time, spirit. (Gueu Gbe 1997b)

But for many *genu*, the donning of the clothing and mask is not all that is required for the spirit to arrive. The "disposition" that Gueu Gbe mentions above arrives with the *yinannu*, who arrive with the sound of the music. The music in a Ge performance is not mere accompaniment. Rather, it is a necessary part of the manifestation of the *ge*.[29] Elder Zogueu Anatole from Déoulé used the following metaphor to express the idea that a *ge* performing without his music is not a *ge*: "A fish out of water is not a fish" (Zogueu in Zogueu and Ve 1997).

Ge can be embodied simply by a person. In early 1997, on my first night back in Déoulé where I had spent some time in 1994, a party was held for Nicole and me. Beginning in early afternoon, dozens of people began gathering in the compound of *zumi* Mameri Tia Thomas, with whom we stayed whenever in Déoulé. Young men drummed, played iron bells, and sang, while the swelling crowd of at least 100 children and adults swirled around me while I videotaped the occasion. In the late evening, after many speeches and much dancing and food, people began heading home and things seemed to be winding down. Nicole and I, exhausted from the day's activities and our first serious bouts of amoebic dysentery, went to bed.

But before we fell asleep, a magical sound began emanating from the courtyard at the center of the compound. Ecstatic drumming. Impassioned group singing. And above it all, a male voice resonating so intensely that it nearly buzzed, like the voices of certain *genu*. Certain that a *ge* had manifested, Nicole and I got up, opened the door of our room and walked down the steps into the center of the dark compound. But much to our surprise, we found there no visually manifest *ge*, just a group of human performers gathered in a circle, playing some of the finest music I have heard in the Man region. Master drummer Ge Bernard drummed with hurricane-like force, while he punctuated his solos with his characteristic growls, thickening the texture of the sound. The lead singer, a young man visiting from the neighboring village of Zagoué, improvised intricate, snake-like lines over the call and response of several men and women of Mameri Tia's family.

Although no *ge* was visually present at this event, at a certain point, Mameri Tia, who was singing, dancing and playing the gourd rattle, exclaimed, "It's the

Mask himself who is here." Later, I asked him what he meant by this. He told me:

> If I am outside, seated, that's one person who is seated there. But when I get up, and I enter into the dance, into the group, with movement, that creates a presence of the mask. . . . The face of the mask is resting in the sacred house over there, but . . . since it is the drum which makes the mask move, the drum which wakes up the mask . . . when the drum resounds in my presence . . . the mask which is over there [in the house] acts within me. When it acts on me, on the spot, I do the dance steps of the mask. . . . So [it's] the joy that animates you, the joy that animates you by the sound of the drum . . . That's why that night, it was the mask himself who was there. But who is the mask? That's why I tell you, it's spiritual. . . . It's the drum that builds the joy of the mask. . . . It's the sound of the drum that gives the power to the mask. (1997)

This example underscores two very important points about Ge. First, in performance, whether or not a *ge* is present is to some extent a matter of the heat of the moment. Excellence and intensity in performance, just like brilliance in intellectual pursuits as described by Gueu Gbe above, can be interpreted as evidence of the presence of *yinan* and *ge*. Second, this example highlights the importance of music in manifesting certain types of *genu*.

In Ge performance, the idea that all aspects—sonic, material, and otherwise—become spirit deserves further elucidation. A sense of physical/metaphysical ambiguity surrounds Ge performance. Everyone but very young children know that a person is "behind the mask" of a performing *ge*. Many people, not just initiates, know who the person dancing a particular *ge* is. Yet this information cannot be spoken in public. In public discourse, the *ge* is a spirit manifest. There is no human present. What people see is not a person possessed by a spirit but rather the spirit itself, present in the form in which it has chosen to manifest.[30]

It would be a mistake to interpret this as mere symbol. Ge performance certainly does symbolize certain things, including the west of Côte d'Ivoire, the importance of honoring the ancestors, of engaging in Dan tradition, of behaving according to accepted norms. But more fundamentally, Ge performance *enacts* those values. The *ge* and everyone else present enact values through their behavior. They embody Dan tradition, the will of the ancestors, and proper Dan behavior through behaving in such a way as to embody the spirit of Ge. My understanding of this began to unfold back in 1994 during my initial field experience. I was trying to understand exactly what a Ge performance was. Talking with Ge performers in Déoulé about the rejoicing *ge* called Gua ta Ge, I asked, "Does he resemble anything? Is he symbolic of anything? Why does Gua ta Ge have this physical appearance and not the same appearance as some other *ge*?" To all these types of questions, the response was simple: when Gua ta Ge decided to manifest for the first time, he chose his form. He chose everything about his manifestation—his outfit, his mask, as well as the songs, drum rhythms, and dance steps that would accompany him. As Fischer and Himmelheber write, Ge performance does not represent, but *is*, a spirit (1984, 8).

This is generally how *ge* performers talk about the specifics of any particular *ge*'s manifestation. They usually say that the *ge*'s physical form first arrived in dreams during ancestral times. Yet Ge is not an ahistorical static phenomenon. Even though each *ge* originally chose the form of his manifestation, aspects of each manifestation change over time. Jacques explained this to me with a visual

Relates to idea put forth earlier about the continuation of community through Ge

relates to fieldwork - process of asking indirect questions to get answer metaphor. He held up a book, saying "This represents Ge." Then he laid sheets of paper on the book, removed them, and replaced them with still other sheets of paper. The book, he said, does not change, even if the papers lying on top of it, "dressing" it, do.

Change occurs in various aspects of the manifestation of Ge, including its sonic and visual dimensions. Most obvious in the sonic dimension is the incorporation, by Gedro and other *masques ye ye*, of popular-music rhythms in recent times. Regarding the visual aspect of Ge performance, Himmelheber and Fischer, writing together (1984, 8) and individually (Himmelheber 1965, 83; Fischer 1978, 19) assert that *genu* cannot wear human-made clothes, only those constructed from forest materials such as raffia, feathers, and furs (though photographs in their publications do show *ge* in human-made Dan clothing that is made *of* forest materials but made *by* humans on traditional looms). My experience differs on this point. While some *genu* adorned themselves with forest materials such as leaves, they all wore human-made clothing. Some wore exclusively traditional Dan clothing made from local materials, but even this was not an absolute rule. I saw *tankë genu* in jeans, *biansëgenu* (racing *genu*) in sweatpants and T-shirts, and many types of *genu* wearing shoes, from rubber boots to sneakers. Oulai Théodore said a *ge* from his grandfather's sacred house was responsible for the introduction of shoes into *ge* fashion. In the early 1940s, his grandfather's *gegɔn* was invited to visit the French colonial installation at Grand Lahou on the central Ivorian coast. Théodore explained:

> So the first masks who went to greet the whites, [the whites] gave them boots, during the 1940s. They have kept that, like a souvenir of this first greeting of the whites. It's like if I went to visit you in America, and you give me a T-shirt. You must wear it, so that people know you have been to America! So it's since that time that other masks . . . have begun to wear shoes. (Oulai 1997b)

Change is thus a recognized aspect of the tradition of Ge. My consultants understand Ge to be an ancient, historic, and sacred tradition. It is not completely porous in relationship to things "modern." Gegbadë, for instance, would never dance a popular-music style. For each *ge,* the relationship between "the tradition" and outside influences is uniquely constituted. And for each *ge,* this relationship is *performed*. In looking at the form in which each *ge* performs, and the processes of such performances, I saw my consultants demonstrating and perpetuating their ethnic and religious identity in deliberate relationship to their world. In performing Ge, my consultants show the modernity of their tradition (Waterman 1990b).

THE PROCESS OF PERFORMANCE

Before any *ge* can emerge from a sacred house, a performance must be approved. Arrangements for a Ge performance generally follow a standardized pattern. The person or persons interested in hiring a *ge* must approach the proper authorities—the *gedëmɛn* of that *ge*'s sacred house. A request will be made regarding why, where, when, and for how long the *ge*'s presence is desired. The *gedëmɛn* then do a "consultation" in the sacred house. I cannot divulge exactly what this process entails, as this is the domain of secrecy. But, basically, the *gedëmɛn* consult the appropriate *yinan* by "throwing the kola." In this case, I am talking about real kola nuts, which Dan people use for divination. I am at liberty to explain how this works in public ritual settings, by way of comparison. In public, to determine if the ancestors or *yinannu* have accepted a blessing or a sacrifice offered by an elder, people split a kola nut in two, place the two halves in liquid in a calabash bowl, and then toss them onto the ground. Dan interpret the way that the two halves of the kola land as follows: if both halves land with the inside of the nut exposed, this is an unequivocal "Yes" from the spirits; if both halves are upside down, with the outer shell facing up, this is a definitive "No"; and one half up, one half down is read as a "Maybe" which will require further consultation. In the sacred house, the *gedëmɛn* engage in a more complex version of this same process to determine whether or not the *yinannu* accept the request for the *ge* to manifest.

If the answer is yes, then the *gedëmɛn* will announce what kind of "kola" (and here, they use the term metaphorically) will be required for the *ge* to manifest. The price for a performance can vary dramatically, depending on the seriousness of the occasion and how sacred the *ge* is. Usually, some money will be involved, to buy food and palm wine for the *ge* performers. Often a chicken or two, or a goat, must be sacrificed (their necks are slit in a ritual manner, the blood dripping onto the ground in offering to the ancestors). Women then prepare the food to accommodate the performers and other guests, which is just one of the ways in which women's participation is essential to Ge performances (cf. Adams 1986).

If all these demands are met, then the performance can take place. As in many West African performance contexts, monetary gifts are also expected during the course of the performance. Monetary gifts are one thing that most inspire the *yinan* to animate the *ge,* who will usually dance especially energetically in front of a donor immediately after receiving a gift. Speaking *genu* such as Gegbadë will also announce gifts to the crowd in a verbal display of thanks. How often gifts are given and how much is given are some of the main factors determining how long a performance will continue.

Another stipulation for all Ge performances are each *ge*'s totems (*tiyin*), or the proscriptive rules that must be followed in order for each *ge* to manifest. Some rules apply to performers in the time before a performance. For example, Gegbadë performers must abstain from sexual intercourse for one week prior to a performance. If this is not possible because a job has come up quickly, then performers who have had sex must be washed in a special "medicated" water (which probably contains medicinal plants—a specialty of *zumi*). Other totems apply to the performances themselves. During Gegbadë performances, smoking is prohibited because, as Théodore told me, "Cigarettes chase *yinannu* away, so you cannot smoke around serious *genu,* only dance *genu*" (Oulai 1997a). All such rules exist to ensure that the necessary *yinannu* will arrive. Usually, the more sacred a *ge* is, the more totems he will have.

Many rules concern women. Perhaps the most common is that women are not permitted to see certain *genu.* I heard many explanations for this. One of the most prevalent was that although women are mystically more powerful than men, they are also more sensitive and vulnerable to mystical danger. The powerful *yinannu* of war who come out when certain *genu* are manifest are thought to be dangerous for women's reproductive faculties. If a woman sees such a *ge,* she can become sterile; if she is pregnant, the child could be born crazy. Another explanation is that women, because of their nature—"a spirit and heart of possession" (Gueu Gbe 1997c)—cannot be trusted to refrain from trying to wrest power and control from men. As Gueu Gbe explained,

> Women want to keep everything. They have the power of adoption. And it's women who have men. Even, a man can be full-grown, but as long as his mother is alive, he's a baby! . . . If you give her that which enables you, in life, to command? You put it away or you give it to her? It's finished. Man will no longer be anything. . . . Society will change direction, because the Dan have come to this point with a patriarch at the fore. (Gueu Gbe 1997c)

[handwritten margin note: SPEAKS TO POWER & GENDER INEQUALITY IN RELIGION new plane]

Some researchers have encountered in Dan myths the idea that *genu* originally belonged to women and were taken away by men (Zemp 1965). Seen in this light, if the power behind Ge originated with women, then men's hold on this power might be tenuous, which could help explain why men so jealously guard the secret information associated with Ge that helps them to perpetuate their power and dominance over women. Myths aside, in Gueu Gbe's eyes, women are potentially threatening to men's hold on power, a position that Ge enables men to maintain. Ge thus could be seen as a legitimator of the gender power imbalance in Dan society.[31]

If women are accused of intentionally gaining sight of a prohibited *ge,* they can be severely reprimanded. I heard several anecdotes about incidents when punishments were administered. For example, although I did not witness it myself, two young girls told me that a woman had deliberately stayed outside on the final night of the 1997 Yam Festival, when the head *ge* of the festival tours the village and only initiates are permitted outdoors. I was told that this woman's penance was to shave off all of her hair and sit in the sun, all the while accepting ridicule and insults from *gedëmεn* while she prepared them meals until the time that they dismissed her. This kind of humiliation acts as a very effective deterrent to breaking the rules of sacred Ge performance. Rocking the boat of established power relations in Dan society is not taken lightly.

Though nonvisual, *yinannu* and ancestors are critical participants in the manifestation of Ge. Ge cannot manifest among humans without the help of *yinannu.* Each *ge* has a certain number of *yinannu* associated with him. The *yinannu* who make manifest the *ge* must be drawn to the human realm in order for a performance to take place. Music sound is vital to this process.

For some less sacred *genu* such as Gedro, this process is less complicated than for other more sacred *genu.* As soon as a rejoicing *ge* comes out of his sacred house, the *yinan* of joy arrive. Still, music "wakes up" the *yinannu,* which gives the *ge* "*fan*" or strength/power (Bleu 1997). If Gedro wants to bless someone, then he has need of the *yinan* of benedictions. Certain music is required to attract these *yinannu* to Gedro to enable this to happen. For Gegbadë, music is required to call the *yinannu* even to manifest the *ge.* Before exiting the sacred house and taking form among people, Gegbadë must call the *yinan* of his master drummer. When the drummer's *yinan* arrives, he drums in particular ways that attract other more powerful *yinannu* who enable the *ge* to manifest and accomplish his goals.

The *yinannu* of *genu* are much more powerful than those of people. As Goueu Tia Jean-Claude said, "Just look at the behavior of masks and you know— they do things people cannot do" (Goueu 1997g). Speaking of sacred *genu,* Gueu Gbe said, "Often those [people] who accompany powerful masks are phlegmatic old men. But by the time they are dressed, they have the power of a chimpanzee. *Yinannu* give them that energy" (Gueu Gbe 1997g). The power of a *ge* lies in his ability to enter into contact with his *yinannu,* and it is music that facilitates this process. Music is thus literally a part of the manifestation of the *ge.*

The *yinannu* for each *ge* enter the world of humans at particular locations in the natural environment. Gba Ernest, discussing night *genu* called *gbɛnge,* explained:

> Each *gbɛnge* has his good fortune. . . . It's *yinannu* who give good fortune! He [the *gbɛnge*] has his sacred river over there, at Krikouma, or a sacred spring there at Krikouma, or a sacred mountain. If he cites their names [the names of the *yinannu* who come from those places], the *yinannu* will come to give him courage! To give him good fortune! . . . When a mask wants to sing, he calls all those *yinannu.* (Gba Ernest 1997g)

A *ge* is not limited to his "own" *yinannu,* however, when seeking power to accomplish his goals. If a *ge* wants to accomplish something difficult or extraordinary, he might elicit the aid of other powerful *genu* or *yinannu.* In the following passage, Gueu Gbe describes this process, using the words "spirit" and "god" to refer to *yinan*:

> When a mask sings and dances, he turns his head toward a huge mountain and says, "Spirit of that mountain, help me. God of that spring, come to my aid. You who live in that tall tree, which has resisted all winds . . . If you are still alive, it means you are inhabited by something that is very powerful—come to my aid." He solicits all that help. "Sacred mask of such and such village—you whom I have never seen but whom I have heard of, you who surround me, whom I see and whom I don't see, come!" (Gueu Gbe 1997e)

Boundaries between entities and dimensions are fluid in the Dan religious system. Boundaries are fluid between *genu* and *yinannu,* and between the realms of the living and the dead. Ge performers invoke their ancestors and the *yinannu* each time they enact their religiosity.

Overall, then, in the process of Ge performance, communication takes place between and among the living and the dead, *genu* and *yinannu, geɓɔ* and earth, the past and the present. Ruth Stone, writing about performance of the Woi epic among the southern Mande Kpelle, notes that "the past, in epic, is dynamically manipulated in the present." For example, "performers incorporate departed ancestors and deceased great musicians in the music event" (1988, x). Stone shows that Kpelle past and present time frames are not mutually exclusive, and identifies this conflation of time as a critical element of Kpelle musical experience. Likewise, the social world for Ge performers is not just the world of humans presently walking the earth but also includes the world of ancestors and the forest environment as well. As Jackson writes of the Kuranko, for the Dan, "being is not necessarily limited to human being" (1982, 17).

Though the original patriarchs are said to live in the mystical realm, they are also said to inhabit the sacred forest. And these domains—*geɓɔ* and sacred spaces on earth—are the sources of power and possibility for practitioners of "the tradition." Ge performance does not just symbolize the fact that Dan must recognize their dependence upon their environment and their ancestors. Rather, a manifest *ge* is a participant in Dan experiential existence in the *act* of connecting forest and village, a participant who exemplifies the fact that forest spirits and ancestors are an interactive part of peoples' lives (cf. Jackson 1982). A dancing *ge* is an embodiment of the literal, experientially grounded connection that exists between forest and village and between the mystical and corporeal domains.

GE AS INITIATION, BEHAVIOR, THE PERFORMANCE OF EXCELLENCE, AND IDENTITY

Ultimately, Ge performance is far more than the performance of a spirit. For some, Ge performance is also the performance of their ethnic and religious identity. This is linked to the fact that Ge is the spiritual base of boys' initiation, where young Dan boys learn what it means to be Dan. Ge in this sense is the performance of ideals—the ideal of proper behavior, the ideal of power and ability, the ideal of beauty. Art historians and collectors have long admired the beauty of finely carved Dan masks. Vandenhoute describes the style of the more representational Dan masks as "idealized realism" (1948, 8). This phrase gets at the heart not just of this style of carving but of the very idea of Ge and Ge performance. Ge represents the ideal of what humans can aspire to. These ideals are taught in initiation, and they are expressed in every aspect of Ge performance. The ideal of beauty, the ideal of dance, the ideal of music, the ideal of behavior—Ge performance is the performance of ideals, the performance of excellence.

Gueu Gbe Alphonse expressed this idea in his typical sublimely poetic way:

> Ge does not permit mediocrity. Ge, he is excellence. He is excellence. All that which he does is beautiful. All that which he does is powerful. All that which he does is good. Because Ge is the beginning, is the middle, is the end of the Dan. It's his environment, it's his system. (Gueu Gbe 1997a)

Gueu Gbe continued, "The greatest dancer other than a mask in Dan country, there is not one. . . . They always have to be the best, at the top level" (Gueu Gbe 1997a). Ge must be the best at whatever he does.[32] If he is a *ge* who dances, he must be the best dancer of the community. If he is a *ge* who sings, he sings better than any human around. If his job is to seize sorcerers, no ordinary human can do it better. Ge thus bears some resemblance to the ways many people around the world idealize life through art. The European male body is idealized in Michelangelo sculptures; romantic love is idealized in countless popular songs and movies. For the Dan, this idealization is expressed and generated through the sacred enactment of Ge. Ge manifests the ultimate expression of things Dan, of how to do things Dan properly. For practitioners of "the tradition," Ge represents "Dan-ness." Gba Daouda writes, "Ge is above all and especially the foundation of Dan being" (1984, 19).

The time and place that Ge begins playing this role, for males anyway, is in the initiation school. Gueu Gbe told me:

> If you would want to put a marker at the entrance of the schools of education and initiation, a mask would suffice, as behind that design is everything that the Dan must learn to enter into life, to enter into an active life, to enter into the life of people. The Mask is a school. The Mask is a system. (Gueu Gbe 1997a)

Dan, unlike many ethnic groups in the Guinea Coast region of West Africa, do not adhere to the multiethnic Poro (male) and Sande (female) initiation societies. Dan have their own school of initiation, called in the Man (Ka) dialect *gbannë* (which also means "circumcision"; lit., *gban*—sacred things + *në*—children) or *gbɛguwon* (*gbɛgu*—sacred forest + *won*—affair; thus, "affair of the sacred forest"). Dan initiation is much shorter than the Poro initiation school, which can take years. Even back in the 1930s, Vandenhoute was taught that Dan boys' initiation took anywhere from three weeks to three months (1989 [1952], 21). *Genu* literally direct boys' initiation and circumcision. Biemi Gba Jacques taught me about his own initiation; Jacques' story of his initiation experience sheds light on the links between Ge, initiation, and behavior.

Since so many young people are now enrolled in the French-styled national educational system, traditional education now takes place during official school vacations—at Easter and during the summer.[33] Even those who live in cities often go back to their "home villages"—usually the village of their paternal ancestry—for initiation. Jacques, however, who was living in Abidjan when his time came,[34] did his initiation partly in Petit Gbapleu (where he has a great deal of extended family) and partly in his mother's home village, Biélé, because of his father's estrangement from his home village.[35]

Boys' initiation has two steps. Jacques underwent the first step during sixty days of the summer vacation of 1985. It all began with the circumcision operation. Following this operation, the boys were sequestered with the initiation *ge* called *dɛn* for forty-five days in the sacred hut in the middle of the sacred forest. These forty-five days were spent learning many virtues of Dan behavior. First of all, the boys were taught the importance of courage and stamina. Jacques recalled, "The first step is the operation and with that operation they torture you to teach you that life, life is very hard, that you must be courageous in life" (Biemi 1997c). The boys were forced to work, even when already enduring pain from their healing wounds. They were given rotating responsibilities, such as cleaning the hut, and were beaten if they made even the slightest errors. They were denied food for long periods, denied the chance to bathe, and forced to sleep crowded together in spaces too small to accommodate them. This was all to teach them courage and how to withstand suffering.

Additionally, the boys were taught practical life skills. Elders and recent initiates visited the boys and recounted to them their life experiences. The boys were taught how to hunt and how to survive in the wild. More important, the boys were taught the virtues necessary to participate as adults in Dan society, virtues that are required before one is permitted to marry and found a family. They were taught how to farm, including how to cultivate one's own field and they were taught how and at what stages in the agricultural cycle the Dan come together to farm communally in each others' fields. They were taught how to manage a family, as Jacques explained,

> How do you behave with your wife. How do you treat women. For example, they tell us that women must not know all the things that are in the sacred house. Otherwise, at that moment, she is your equal, because she knows what you know. For example, women have the responsibility for the education of the children, to take care of the children. And so it's not good to involve yourself in the taking care of the children, to try to mix up what women do naturally.

... [We are taught] why a woman is important to a man. ... She contributes to the stability of a man in the village. .... It's the woman who is tougher than the man. It's the woman who gives important advice. It's the woman who directs the life of men. It's the women who organize all this. In the village, a man without a woman ... it's a man who doesn't have organization in his life ... But with a woman, all that you have to do, you are going to do it in relation to someone, so you reflect more upon it, you aren't going to do just anything. (Biemi 1997c)

So during this stage of initiation, gender roles are clearly defined. Jacques' words demonstrate a fascinating mixture of control over and yet respect for women that Dan boys are taught is essential to the proper functioning of society. As he says above, imperative to the maintenance of norms, of the ways of the ancestors, is to deny women access to the knowledge of what goes on in the sacred hut, to deny them knowledge of Ge. In this case, that knowledge clearly equals power, because Ge is the source of power in Dan life. Though women have their own *ge,* the Kong, men conceive of their *genu* as a part of their secret knowledge that provides, maintains, and justifies their dominance over women. Participating in Ge thus upholds the patriarchal structure of Dan society by perpetuating the ways of the original patriarchs. And yet, as Jacques' comments about childrearing exemplify, women are accorded authority over their own domain. In initiation, men are taught to respect the knowledge and abilities that women have and not to interfere in their affairs.

During initiation, the boys learn how Ge works. They are taught the secret preparations for Ge performances, how to drum, how to sing; they are taught the songs and dances that are part of the manifestation of Ge. While they are not taught the details of how Ge works within the Dan system, they are taught specific aspects of this system and how to *do* things, through which a thinking person can piece together an overview of the system (Biemi 1997c). I found in my initiation-related discussions with Jacques an emphasis on action, on behavior. Initiation is in part experiential education. They are taught "that when we do a libation, you call your ancestors, you offer [it] to God—'when you pour water, you see what we do.' . . . How do you learn for example to pour the water? You watch someone pour the water!" (ibid.). Yet they are also taught *why* they do certain spiritual acts:

The goal is to understand why we do all this. . . . So when someone is in the process of doing it, you are up-to-date now as to *why* it is being done. . . . For example, we worship the Nyon [Biélé's sacred mountain]. . . . We worship the Nyon because the Nyon is filled with water. It's the only mountain in that sector, perhaps within fifty kilometers . . . that is filled with water. At every place on the Nyon there is a spring—everywhere, everywhere! So that's why, during the dry season, the Nyon becomes important. So you have to take care of the *yinannu* of that mountain so they don't stop the water, for example, during the dry season. (Biemi 1997c)

Jacques went on to say that they also worship the Nyon because during ethnic wars, their ancestors used to hide out on the top of the mountain for protection. After they were told these reasons why Biélé residents worship the Nyon, they took the initiates to the locations on the mountain where they make sacrifices to demonstrate how this is done:

We sacrifice animals—sheep, chickens, and so forth. Before killing the animals, we speak, we speak, we speak, the name of the mountain, and so forth, and so forth, then we slit their throats, and then it's finished and we cook. Everyone eats, everyone has a fête there, and then we return. . . . [What we speak are] prayers to *yinannu,* it's benedictions, it's requests, all that. For protection. . . . That, for example, is a specific case, that's something that we worship and why we worship it. (Biemi 1997c)

Initiation, like Ge generally—indeed, like any tradition—is part theory, part behavior.

The final stage of the first step of initiation was a survival test. The boys were split up into small groups of two to five each and forced to fend for themselves in the sacred forest—preparing traps, finding edible foods, making fires, and cooking for themselves. During this stage, the mute *ge* Sakpe roamed through the forest, watching over the boys' progress and gesturing suggestions to them if they needed help. During this stage, the Sakpe and the elders watched carefully over Jacques and his brothers, since "we were the Abidjan kids, so they paid a lot of attention to us!"

The second step of Jacques' initiation took place the following summer. It consisted of an extended version of the same test that concluded the first step. This time they spent one whole month alone in the forest, applying what they had learned, proving their courage and their knowledge of how to survive in the wild. Following this stage, the boys came out of the forest and into the village to celebrate their transition to adulthood (though many were, of course, still children in years). Jacques described this as a ceremonial celebration in which the village came together to drum, sing, and dance with them to honor their successful completion of initiation.

Yet the official two steps of initiation are in many ways only the beginning. Initiation does not end when the initiates reenter the village; initiation is rather "a continuous university" (Gueu Gbe 1997a). Character flaws exhibited during the formal initiation process persist for the rest of their lives. "Everything you leave the sacred enclosure with, you have for the rest of your life. I was stubborn there, so today I remain stubborn," confided Gueu Gbe (1997h). The *genu* and the elders are hard on such behaviors during initiation, but if these behaviors persist despite the teachers' best efforts to correct them, then they will last a lifetime (Biemi 1997c).

Likewise, the respect for the authority of the elders and the *genu* must continue after the boys return into the village. Much has been written about *genu* and social control among the Dan. In 1950, George Harley wrote, "The *gɛs* exercised all the functions necessary for control of society on the religious, the executive, and the judicial levels" (1950, 42). While this authority has encountered numerous challenges during the second half of this century, Harley's observations nonetheless remain relevant in many Dan villages today.

On a hot afternoon in 1994 in the village of Déoulé, Mameri Tia Thomas, Tiemoko Guillaume, and I gathered under a shelter made of woven palm leaves and a wooden frame to discuss *ge* and authority with elder Yoro Victor. This issue had interested me because Déoulé, like many other communities in the region, featured a mix of competing authorities. The vast majority of Déoulé's residents identified as Muslim and regularly attended the village mosque, where they prayed to Allah. Many children attended the primary school where their authority figure was their teacher and where they were taught to respect the authority of the state. Meanwhile, Yoro himself was at that time the village's *comité* (president) of the village committee of the PDCI, the ultimate political authority of the nation and the power behind everything from local police to the judiciary. "Despite all the changes in the Man region," I asked Yoro, "do the young in Déoulé continue to respect and submit to the authority of the *genu*?" Leaning his tall wiry frame forward on the wooden bench where he sat, Yoro gazed at the ground briefly, deliberating over his response. Finally, he looked up and replied, "I don't know about other villages, but in Déoulé, everyone—man, woman, and child—has very much respect for the *genu*. If a *ge* says that the children will not go to school on a particular day, then the children stay home." "And Muslims and Christians," I countered, "Do they submit to the *ge*'s authority?" Yoro, himself a Muslim, emphatically replied, "If a *ge* is manifest and says that there will be no prayer, then the mosque is closed" (Yoro in Mameri and Yoro 1994). → *So what could be the reason for the Christian / Muslim affiliation?*

At this point in our conversation, Mameri Tia Thomas took the opportunity to remind me that the authority of Ge had been corporeally demonstrated to me several times during the Ge performances that I had attended a few weeks earlier in Déoulé. I had been mildly forced to submit my body to the demands of *genu* on several occasions, including once when I was forcibly instructed, along with other young men, to lie down, after which a *ge* crashed somewhat violently onto my knees. "As you remember," Mameri said, "when the mask says to lie down, you lie down. Automatically" (Mameri in Mameri and Yoro 1994). His recollection of this scene inspired laughter from all those present, and I remembered the feeling that that moment had instilled upon me: that in fact, when I was in Déoulé and a *ge* was manifest, *I* had to physically submit to its authority. The point that everyone must submit to the *ge*'s authority was not explained to me verbally that day, it was taught to me experientially, bodily, as part of my experiential education into the way things work in their village. → *RELIGION AS EXPERIENTIAL KNOWLEDGE*

This is just how things are taught to young men and boys in initiation. And, Jacques explained to me, this kind of experiential education continues for Dan after the formal initiation period. Jacques stressed the point that initiation is continual by arguing that, for him, our fieldwork had been an intensive continuation of his initiation. He explained that after the initial two steps, individuals can experience specific initiations into specialized aspects of Dan life. For Jacques, initiation is life experience. Initiation is "continual. It never ends. It's a manner of living. It's the experiences. . . . true knowledge comes from experience" (Biemi 1997c). If a person shows a predilection to a particular skill, such as hunting or drumming, and he pursues deepening his knowledge of this skill, this, Jacques argues, is a continuation of initiation. Moreover, simply by living with other Dan, people advance their initiation. This is why elders are accorded such respect and are often called "great initiates." Jacques argued that a person is not a called a great initiate

> because we have given him some kind of powerful medication or . . . because he is more mystically powerful than everyone else. No. The word initiate itself, in its true form, that goes with wisdom, knowledge, all the virtues in our society. That's what an initiate is—someone who knows. . . . The initiate is someone who knows how the society in which he lives functions. (Biemi 1997d)

This is why Jacques argued that, for him, our fieldwork was initiation: "So it's like I spent one whole year, I dedicated my time, to initiation. And so, during the time that you did your research, I initiated myself [laughs]" (Biemi 1997d). For Jacques, who lived his first four years in Biélé but then was taken away to city life in Abidjan, our year of fieldwork was a way of making up for lost time, a way of deepening his understanding of his own culture; in other words, of continuing his initiation. That he felt this way was satisfying for us both. As he said, "You understand that if I am initiated, that is very enriching for me!" (ibid.).

Life experience is thus viewed as a continuation of initiation, and behaving according to the rules learned in initiation is considered to be manifesting Ge. Jacques and I had one experience in Biélé that made this idea particularly clear. One thing that is learned in initiation is how meetings take place among the Dan. There are formalized rules about how meetings work—who sits where, who speaks when, how the word is passed from one person to another. These rules apply to any kind of formal ritual gathering, whether a *ge* is visibly present or not. I learned aspects of these rules by accidentally breaking them. I began an interview with the elders in charge of the children's *gbage* by introducing myself and why I had come, an inappropriate behavior. Since we had come to discuss Ge, we could not proceed without first offering the elders a monetary gift, or "kola." Jacques and I quickly recovered and offered a kola, and, though somewhat embarrassed, continued the interview. At the interview's end, we discussed the meaning of Ge. The elders emphasized that Ge means the spirits, the education, and all aspects of the manifestation of the spirits and the education. The elders reminded us of the interview's beginning, clarifying why the gift of a kola had been required. A kola is required for any manifestation of Ge, and "even when we speak of Ge, Ge is present." They went on to explain to us that for this reason, even our interview had been a manifestation of Ge.

So Ge is a spirit—maybe an ancestor, maybe from the forest, maybe both. Ge is the spiritual base of initiation and the behavior that is learned there. Ge is all aspects of its manifestation among humans—the masks, the outfits, the dances, the benedictions, the songs, the rhythms, the styles of singing and drumming— all of which are learned from *genu* in the sacred forest. Ge would not be defined thus by just any Dan or by just any resident of western Côte d'Ivoire of another ethnic identity. But Ge means this for those practitioners of "the tradition" with whom I studied. The older brother of some of my primary consultants—ethnographer Gba Daouda—asserts that Ge fulfills a role that "is beyond that of an informant of knowledge and techniques, but also it is . . . the image of the whole society" (Gba Daouda 1984, 14). That is why Gueu Gbe argues that initiation, which he calls "the Mask school," is *the* thing most important to the continuity of tradition, of Dan identity (Gueu Gbe 1997a).

One day, Gueu Gbe Alphonse and I were discussing the competition between various religions that characterizes contemporary Man. Gueu Gbe, who is old enough to remember the early days of Christianity in the region, recalled that early missionaries demanded that converts renounce everything associated with Dan religion. He explained that after some time, church organizers recognized the need to permit some aspects of local culture—language, dress, music—in church services. This trend was common in Africa. In many parts of the continent, Africans themselves began "Africanizing" Christianity by creating their own churches, incorporating music and even in many cases certain beliefs from local culture into their Sunday services. Many European- and American-led churches, suffering from declining numbers in their congregations, then began permitting elements of local culture in their services in order to compete for followers.

In Man, this trend led to the creation of "chorales," or choirs, in the Catholic church. In the Man vicinity, both Dan and Wè choirs sing traditional music, using traditional instruments, with Christian-oriented lyrics. Gueu Gbe explained that permitting this was a wise move by the Catholics, as it enabled Dan people to be Christian yet retain a sense of their own cultural identity. He reasoned, "If we don't have the drums in the church, people will leave the church and return to the villages, to the masks" (Gueu Gbe 1997a). I found this all interesting, if not unusual. But my ears really perked up as Gueu Gbe continued: "The have sent our Mask songs to the church, and they call that 'Choir.' . . . They add 'Jesus,' 'Father,' [or] 'Savior,' but the refrain, the melody, the drums—it's the same thing!" (ibid.). He went on to say that this showed the power of Ge. Christianity could not survive in Dan country without transferring power from Ge. Since the rhythms, the manner of singing and drumming—indeed, in some cases, even the *very songs themselves* that are taught by *genu* in initiation and are themselves considered to be a part of the manifestation of Ge—are being sung in the church, that means that *Ge is in the church.* → HYBRIDIZATION of RELIGIONS

I continued to explore this compelling idea for the remainder of my 1997 stay in Côte d'Ivoire. I encountered many people who agreed with Gueu Gbe and numerous examples supporting his claims. Dan choir leader Loua Philippe, who composes songs for his choir, explained his creative process to me. He takes traditional Dan songs, changes the words to make reference to his Christian faith, and then teaches them to his choir, who sing the songs to the accompaniment of a Dan drum ensemble. Particularly effective are songs that already have religious associations—*getan*—the songs which are the sonic aspect of the manifestation of Ge. Following is an example of a song I heard his choir perform at a baptism, and that I later heard sung in its original form:

Example 4.2. Text of a choir song and its original form as a *getan*

Zlan ye dö	God exists
Mɛngban waa wondo Zlan ye dö	Not everyone knows that God exists
Gewon ye dö	The affair [matter] of Ge exists
Mɛngban waa wondo gewon ye dö	Not everyone knows that the affair [matter] of Ge exists

In this typical example, Loua simply substituted, "Zlan" or "God" for "Gewon," a word that literally translates as "affair of the Ge" but refers to the whole system and school of Ge. It is important to note that for Loua Philippe, his use of Getan as original source material does not indicate that he has invited Ge into the church. Changing the words, he says, changes the meaning. The songs no longer attract the *yinannu.* Rather, in the church, when his choir sings, they are animated by the Holy Spirit. For Loua, the style of singing and drumming and the melodies are not a part of Ge. For him, they have taken on a new meaning.

Biemi Gba Jacques is one person who disagrees with Loua Philippe. For Jacques, Ge is a spirit, all aspects of that spirit's manifestation on earth, an education, and a manner of behavior—to the extent that when *getan* is played in the church, Ge is in the church. Ge is something that is deeper than affiliation with another religion; it is the theory and action that some call "the tradition," a concept at the base of a notion of religious and ethnic identity. I have chosen to close this chapter not with my own words, but with those of Jacques, who articulates below, as well as anyone could, the connection that some Dan feel between their music, their culture, their identity, and, the source of it all, Ge, which Jacques here calls "Mask." Discussing the use of *getan* in the church, Jacques said:

> If the rhythms which were taught by the mask [*ge*], under those circumstances, if the songs which were taught—because it's the *same* refrain—if it's those songs, if the drum that was created to manifest the victory of a mask, to manifest the glory of a mask, to glorify a mask in song, if all that is found in the church, I say that it's the Mask [Ge] that's in the church. . . . If the accoutrements, that's to say the clothes that we wear to accompany a mask, are found in the church, I say that the Mask is in the church. What they didn't want! And that's what they don't know. . . . We [Jacques and I] will go to the church, and we will listen. . . . You will see that it's the same thing! The difference is that it's "Mask" that is sung, and the other it's "God" that is sung. . . . That will be palpable proof that the Mask is in the church!

> . . . All that comes from the Mask school. Even if a mask doesn't go to dance in the church. But what they [the *genu*] have taught, we find in the church. And that also is the Mask! They [the Church] think that the Mask is he who accompanies a mask with a face covering. But no! That's what they don't understand! That's what they don't know! They don't know that the Mask—it's an education. The Mask, it's a comportment. The Mask is the clothing. The Mask is the manner of speaking. The manner of singing. In short, the Mask is life. The manner of living that [the elders and the *genu*] inculcate in a person. That they teach someone. That's what the missionaries didn't know at first. . . . The Mask has its metaphysical manifestation that has entered into the mentality of people, in the people's manner of thinking, in peoples' manner of living! In short, in the sociocultural comportment of the people. (Biemi 1997b)

FIVE

Manifesting Ge in Song

One hot May morning, Nicole and I sat on our porch, looking at the mountains, waiting. The day before, Gba Gama had invited us to a Gedro performance at a funeral in the village of Douélé Doumba, some twenty kilometers west of Man. Gba had told us that he, along with many of our friends from Petit Gbapleu, would arrive to pick us up around 6:30 the following morning. About 7:30, the phone rang. It was Gba Gama. "Our transportation has not yet arrived," he told me. "We'll be there soon." Finally, around 10:00, Gba Gama showed up at our front door, and the three of us rushed off to a nearby intersection to meet the minibus (*gbarka*) in which the group was traveling to the event.

We stood along the side of the road in the sun for what seemed like hours. Just as Nicole and I were beginning to feel fatigued and lose hope that the *gbarka* would ever arrive, Gba Gama shouted, "That's it!" Lunging out into the road, Gba flagged down a typically overloaded *gbarka* careening down the road in our direction. As the *gbarka* pulled alongside us on the edge of the road, we saw that stuffed inside were many of our friends and acquaintances: my teachers Jean-Claude and Gba Ernest, the young singer and Kong prodigy Lien Sati Yvonne, and many others who had become familiar to us during our time in Petit Gbapleu. And there, seated among the people and drums, was Gedro. This was the first time I had seen a *ge* using public transport. The sight of this sacred phenomenon riding a minibus caused me to chuckle and ponder the reality in which these people live, one in which "the tradition" exists so naturally in—indeed is so much a part of—modern life.

But I was abruptly jarred out of my theoretical reverie by shouts of anger. Not surprisingly, Petit Gbapleu residents, many of whom were interested in participating in the day's festivities, had packed the *gbarka* before it had even left their neighborhood. Not a single seat remained. Gba Gama, the neighborhood youth leader who had booked the event, *had* to go along. Waving his right arm in the air as he spoke, Gba argued vehemently that some room should be made not just for him but for us all. Nicole and I stood to the side sheepishly, holding our recording gear, aware that we were the source of the conflict, feeling awkward, in the way, and very expendable.

Suddenly Gedro rose to his feet, and the shouting ceased. Followed by several assistants, the *ge* made his way off the bus, athletically climbed onto its roof, and took up position with his assistants for the ride of twenty or so kilometers to Douélé Doumba. We were touched and relieved by this gracious move, which made room for us all. Though I was at first delightfully shocked by the site of a *ge* atop a mini-bus, I later understood this move as pure Ge. Gedro, by giving up his seat on the *gbarka,* had manifested ideal behavior, both leading the way to a resolution of the conflict and demonstrating compassion for Nicole and me. Yet this gesture also provided him an opportunity to show off his physical prowess and mastery of the human realm. Riding atop a *gbarka* on the paved road for a dozen or so kilometers at high speed was challenging enough. But how the *ge* and his assistants hung on to the roof rack for the final 7- to 10-kilometer ride on the dirt road to the village is beyond me. Bumping along, tree branches whacking its top and sides, the overstuffed *gbarka* reeled and tipped its way up and down steep inclines, through deep ditches, and around sharp curves. When at last we arrived at the village, the *ge* and his roof-riding entourage aggressively and triumphantly hurled themselves down onto the ground. Having demonstrated his masculine bravado and invulnerability, Gedro was primed and ready to continue embodying excellence for the funeral crowd.

By the time we arrived, a considerable crowd had already gathered in the center of the village. Douélé Doumba was quite small, consisting of just a dozen or so mud brick buildings, some with thatched roofs, others topped with sheets of tin. In the center of the village was a temporary shelter consisting of a frame of tree branches with a woven palm-leaf roof and no walls, which villagers had constructed for the day's event. Most of the crowd had gathered under the shade of the shelter, where an elder women's group, probably representing the village Kong society, danced and sang. This stage of Dan funeral ritual, the seventh day after a person's death, is an event when religious offerings, or sacrifices, are made and the person's life is celebrated. The deceased was the widow of a canton chief whose three sons were prominent Man citizens—a doctor, a teacher, and a civil servant who worked at the office of the mayor. Given the status and relative wealth of the family, they sent this woman off in style. In addition to the elder women's group singing for their departed sister, a *trutan* ensemble—consisting of musicians playing side-blown wooden trumpets and drums—performed to protect the soul of the deceased from negative spiritual energy. To counterbalance these heavier, more serious performances, Gedro was hired to do what he does best: bring joy to the crowd with his superlative dancing.

Shortly after our group had all piled out of the *gbarka,* an older man who had come with the Gedro group sang the first "*weɓoo wenze.*" "*Ee-a-ee-a, weɓoo wenze*" came the response from the rest of the group. This short musical interlude, called a *tankwi,* served as a cue for the group to come together and pay attention, as someone was about to initiate a song. From the perspective of the crowd at the funeral, the singing of "*weɓoo wenze*" marked the beginning of Gedro's performance. For Gedro and his group, however, the *tankwi* merely marked the beginning of this stage of the performance; Gedro is in performance mode from the moment he emerges from his sacred house, and his *gbarka* adventure was clearly performative. Responding to the call of the *tankwi,* the performing nucleus—the percussionists and several key singers—drew together under a tree, remaining on the periphery of the funeral site some distance from the shelter, so as not to compete too directly with the singing women.

Perhaps emboldened by Gedro's nearly heroic ride on top of the *gbarka*, the group immediately began performing with a riveting intensity and fervor. The group featured some of Petit Gbapleu's best. Lien Sati Yvonne was among the principal singers, often initiating songs and singing the call to which the others responded. She was supported by the stirring combination of Goueu Tia Jean-Claude on the lead mother drum (*ɓaaɗe*) and Gba Ernest on the accompanying *ɓaanëyakwade,* while two young men played the *lökö'së* and *sekpe,*[1] completing the ensemble. Gba Ernest has gained local renown for his skill in playing, and the whole group was clearly feeding off his passion and brilliance. And Gedro began to dance. Ever the showman, Gedro performed not just for the crowd but also for the camera, dancing directly toward me, doing some of his best moves at close range.

The Gedro group is unaccustomed to being a sideshow, and the energy of the performance, fueled by the spectacular rhythmic communication between Gedro and Jean-Claude, the impassioned improvisatory singing (*gbakwi*) of the group, and Gba Ernest's creative variations on the standard *ɓaanëyakwade* patterns, began drawing people away from the funeral's main activities. A human circle quickly formed adjacent to the shelter, marking a secondary performance space. In the spaces between songs, the women's group could still be heard above the murmur of the crowd encircling Gedro; during songs, the women were completely drowned out. About twenty minutes after Gedro had begun performing, one of the sons of the deceased, who had organized the event, approached Gba Gama and invited the group into the shelter. The movement of the group into the shelter did not mark a break in the performance; rather, the music continued to intensify. In response to the invitation, an older man intoned a song:

Example 5.1. Text of *getan "Mii nu we ɓo"*

Mii nu we ɓo	I have come for a reason (lit., I have not come for nothing)
response: *Wɔ nɗɛ nɔɔ*	It's because they have called me.
(*zagoa/zaginɛ*)	(vocables)

In typical Dan fashion, a young man sang parallel fourths beneath the elder man's improvised vocal melody. Two duos—the two men and Yvonne and her good friend Tiemoko Christine—alternately made the call. The rest of the group sang the response.

Led by Gedro, the group slowly and deliberately marched into the shelter, layering this song over the rich polyrhythm of the drums and *sekpe*. In this context, singing "*mii nu we ɓo*" communicated that the group was happy to have been invited. But this song expresses a deeper meaning as well—the idea that as long as people have need of *genu, genu* will come to them. In the context of contemporary Man, in which Dan have so many options—which religion to practice, which profession to choose, which lifestyle to adopt, which problem-solving method to choose, and many others—practitioners of Ge take pride in the persistence of their tradition. By singing this text at the moment when they were invited into the center of the performance space, Gedro performers asserted this pride, their belief in the supreme authority of Ge, and, by extension, the importance of Ge to their identities as Dan people. Like Gedro's behavior during the *gbarka* ride to the funeral, this song manifested a self-assurance and superiority

Figure 5.1. Gedro of Petit Gbapleu in performance at Douélé Doumba.
Photograph by Daniel B. Reed.

that is central to the very idea of Ge. On a more basic level, that the Gedro performers sang and danced their ways into the center of the performance space at Douélé Doumba underscores the point that singing and dancing are themselves at the center of the idea and process of Ge.

Song texts are a vital component of the communicative process of Ge performance and serve as a window into the meanings associated with Ge. But these texts are far more than that; conceptually, song texts are one component of the sonic aspect of the manifestation of Ge. Taken as a whole, this sonic aspect is called *getan.* Though it is fundamental to Ge performance to the extent that most performances could not occur without it, *getan* has received little attention in previous literature on the subject.

GETAN GENRES AND REPERTOIRE

Getan translates literally as "*ge* song/dance." As has been noted by Hugo Zemp, the dialect of the Dan language (Ka) spoken around Man includes no general term for music in an abstract sense (1971, 69–70). The closest equivalent is the word "*tan,*" which translates as "dance," "song," or "instrumental music," depending on context. A crucial distinction is that *tan* refers only to songs and/or instrumental music to which people dance. Lexically, then, song and instrumental music are integrally linked to dance. Furthermore, dance, song, and music do not exist as abstract concepts, separate from some activity, institution, idea, or action. In verb form, "*tan*" is used in conjunction with two different verbs, distinguishing between dancing and singing: "*tanɓo*"—to sing, and "*tankë*—to dance."[2] In compound noun constructions, "*tan*" appears as a suffix connected to an activity, institution, or idea, as in "*dɔɔtan*"—the dance of the women's society—or "*gian-*

tan"—war dance.[3] Each word refers to the genre of songs associated with these activities: women's-society songs and war songs, respectively. In the same manner, the word *"getan"* refers to the dance of the *ge* as well as the songs that are sung when the *ge* dances.

Far from being mere musical accompaniment to a dancing masked figure, the sound that Western music theorists would call "music" is an essential part of the manifestation of *genu* among humans in performance. Not surprisingly, then, it cannot be just any music that fulfills this function. I had returned from my initial field experience in 1994 with the erroneous impression that each *ge* has songs specific to him and that only those songs specific to each *ge* could be sung when that *ge* was manifest.[4] Although specific songs are associated with each *ge,* the pool of possible songs for each *ge*'s manifestation extends far beyond each *ge*'s specific songs. In fact, a vast pool of *getan* exists for performers to draw upon during Ge performances. Some *getannu* can be sung in many contexts and for many different *genu.* Certain *getannu* can even be sung at events at which no *ge* is present. Others are appropriate only for a specific *ge* or a specific genre of *ge.* Knowing when, in which context, and for which *ge* it is appropriate to sing a particular song is a skill that comes from experience.

While it is not true that only certain songs can be sung for each *ge,* only songs of the appropriate *genre* can be sung for each *ge.* Over time, specific songs begin to become associated with certain *genu,* simply because they are popular and are frequently repeated during certain *ge*'s performances. This process leads to the development of *ge*-specific repertoires, as Jacques explained:

> When a *ge* is outside, there is a specificity of activity. And it's in the activity of this *ge* that the songs that we sing are inspired. And it's like that—that forms a specific repertoire for each mask. If it's a *ge* who seizes sorcerers, all the words that will be in the songs will be words of insult, words of denunciation, words of sorcery—that's what will be in the songs. If it's Gedro, it will be words of enjoyment, words of comedy, words of mockery. (Biemi in Biemi and Goueu 1997a)

I once asked Goueu Tia Jean-Claude how many songs exist in the overall *getan* repertoire. "It's impossible to say," he said. "Can you give me an estimate?" I asked, to which he replied, "One cannot say. It's too many to count. . . . We can give you two days of dance without singing the same song twice. There are hundreds, thousands of songs" (Goueu in Biemi and Goueu 1997a). The pool is enormous, even potentially infinite because it is continually growing. Good singers count as one of their talents the ability to spontaneously compose new *getannu* that comment upon the context in which they find themselves. "A good singer is a good liar," Gba Ernest once told me, meaning that a good singer must be adept at improvising on the spot, especially texts appropriate to the situation at hand. For example, a *ge* performing at a soccer match at Biélé might look up to the sacred mountain Nyon and improvise a *getan* calling the spirits of the mountain to support Biélé's team (Biemi in Biemi and Goueu 1997a). Not every song sung at a Ge performance is necessarily linked to things Ge. Especially in the case of entertainment *genu* such as Gedro, performers may improvise songs that are simply an expression of personal joy or that refer to a personal story.

As I began to learn more about the songs in the *getan* repertoire, I began to notice qualitative differences between them. Finally, one day Jacques and I developed a diagram to represent what we were beginning to understand to be

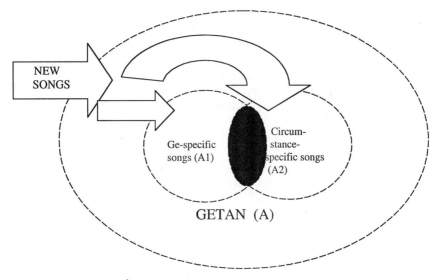

Figure 5.2. Diagram of *getan* genres.

different genres of *getan*. I need to stress that these are analytical categories that Jacques and I developed; I know of no Dan terms for these genres. While I support folklorist Dan Ben-Amos's (1976) call for ethnographers to seek out "ethnic genres," I cannot claim that these *getan* categories fit that rubric.[5] Like anthropologist Peter Mark's categories of Jola masks (1992, 14–15), these *getan* categories represent a convergence of my concerns with those of my consultants. When I shared these genres with consultants, they agreed that our diagram accurately represented how they think about and use *getannu*. Since this diagram helped me to better understand *getan* repertoire, I reproduce it in this text (Figure 5.2).

The large oval in Figure 5.2 represents the great body of general *getan* repertoire (A), including songs that are appropriate to sing in many contexts and for many different *genu*. Some songs in this general category can even be sung at events at which no *ge* is present. This vast pool contains two more specific categories—songs associated with particular *genu* (A1) and songs specific to certain circumstances (A2). *Getannu* of these two categories are less generally applicable; that is, they can be sung in fewer contexts. These more specific *getannu* tend to be older songs with the weight of history, tradition, and connection to the ancestors behind them. Many of my consultants, especially elders such as Gba Ernest, attributed to these songs a greater spiritual efficacy and reacted to them with a special kind of devotion and enthusiasm. These songs, above all others, most inspire a *ge*. Categories A1 and A2 overlap for the simple reason that each type of *ge* has certain functions and responsibilities in society and tends to find himself in certain circumstances on a regular basis. Gegbadë, for example, frequently engages in pursuing sorcerers, so people associate with him certain songs that are used to pursue sorcerers. I use dashed lines to demarcate all three categories (general, circumstance-specific, and *ge*-specific) to indicate that these are open repertoires; new songs are introduced on a regular basis. The distinctions between these categories also are fluid, as new songs can become over time songs that are associated with a circumstance, a *ge,* or both. Like the tradition of Ge generally, the *getan* repertoire is not fixed but dynamic, constantly evolving and transforming according to individual innovation and the ever-changing circumstances in which Ge is performed.

The fluidity of these categories can also be seen in the fact that one *ge* can, in the right context, dance to a song associated with another *ge*. For example, a *tankëge* such as Gedro can dance to a song associated with a *gegɔn* such as Gegbadë, but if he does so, he will not dance in his usual rapid manner but more slowly and gracefully as would a *gegɔn*. Likewise, at a moment when a *gegɔn* wants to fire up the crowd, he or someone in his group may initiate a song associated with Gedro. During this song, the *gegɔn* himself would probably not even dance, as his style is not suited to the rapid tempos of Gedro's *getan;* rather, a person or people would ask for the *ge*'s flywhisk, which gives humans temporary permission to enter the center of the circle to dance. Similarly, on one occasion I saw Gedro dance to a rhythm of the women's *ge* called Kong, but the song was adapted to suit Gedro's style. In lieu of the iron pellets and kitchen utensils that would normally accompany a Kong song, Gedro's group accompanied the song with their standard ensemble of drums and a gourd rattle. In every case I witnessed or was told about, a *ge* performing a borrowed song always adapted that song to his own style. Just as popular musicians regularly incorporate and shape outside influence into new forms and Jean-Claude puts his own unique interpretation on popular-music influences he incorporates into his drumming, so does each individual *ge* interpret and shape outside influence according to their individual identities and performance tendencies. "When a rooster goes for a walk, he does not forget his house."

Context-specific songs also are potentially interchangeable, as a *ge* can sometimes dance a song connected to a context with which he is not generally associated. For example, at a moment when he wants to "heat up" the crowd, Gedro might dance to a song of the *giantan* genre—war songs—which tend to inspire an intense visceral euphoria in many Dan people. Gegbadë might initiate the same song but for a different reason—to call upon his *yinan* of war, perhaps in order to mystically attack a sorcerer. The context in which a song is performed can significantly affect that song's meaning. While genres of songs are associated with both *genu* and contexts, the relationships between these genres are fluid in experience, in performance.

In using the term "genre," I indicate, following my consultants' leads, not a concept with fixed meaning but rather something that changes and is negotiated over time. My research affirms folklorist Amy Shuman's assertion that "generic boundaries, the systems for classifying different sorts of texts, are never fixed, and our investigations usually tell us more about the edges and crossovers than they do about the centers" (1993, 71). Both the boundaries of the genres I discuss and the songs that together make up the repertoire of each genre are in flux. As Bauman and Briggs (1992) and Duranti (1994) have argued, intertextual genre-crossing referencing demonstrates interlinkages not only of text (or, in the case of Ge performance, text, sound, and movement) but also context. Gegbadë's incorporation of war music makes a point (that he is about to make an aggressive move) because his audience members implicitly carry these generic categories in their minds. They understand the reference, and communication occurs. Furthermore, only certain *genu* are permitted to incorporate other genres into their performances, which supports Duranti's argument that the license to perform certain genres is an indicator of power relations in a community (Duranti 1994, 6). Ge and *getan* genres are used to benefit certain people, enabling them to meet certain

1st soloist / duo (A):	(zɔngo wa dɛ) ge nin nu-- ba.	(vocables) It's the ge who has arrived.
Chorus (B):	go-wa-dɛ	vocables
2nd soloist / duo (A):	(zɔngo wa dɛ) ge nin nu-- ba.	(vocables) It's the ge who has arrived.
Chorus (B):	go-wa-dɛ	vocables
etc.		

Figure 5.3. Standard form of *getan*. Transcribed by Daniel B. Reed.

goals. Powerful old men and (in the case of Kong) old women attempt to determine *getan* boundaries based on the precedents of previous elders having done the same. Yet things change, and others challenge these boundaries. Encounters with challenges to the boundaries were precisely what inspired Jacques and I to attempt to graphically represent the repertoire in the first place. Only in exploring the edges of these boundaries was it possible for us to discover that something resembling a genre concept could be construed.

GETAN FORM

Getannu have the same structure as much Dan vocal music. As in the performance of "*mii nu we ɓo,*"[6] the basic pattern is that of call and response in cyclical ABAB form, although the A "call" is sung alternately by different people as follows: one soloist sings a melodic call (A), sometimes with an accompanying singer following in parallel fourths below, after which the chorus sings a response, or refrain (B). Then, rather than the first soloist or duo repeating the call, a second soloist or duo (singing in parallel fourths) sings the call (A), to which the chorus again responds with the refrain (B). Figure 5.3 demonstrates this form with a very popular *getan* that is frequently sung at the beginning of a *ge* manifestation, when the *ge* has just arrived.

People distinguish one *getan* from another by their texts and melodic refrains. The soloist's initial call usually features lexical text, although it may include vocables as well (as in the "*zɔngo-wa-dɛ*" in Figure 5.3) to add "taste" to the song (Goueu 1997d). The refrain sung by the chorus often consists exclusively of vocables. In performance, *getan* texts are never as static as Figure 5.3 suggests. Soloists, called *geatanɓomɛn,*[7] improvise words as a song progresses. The responding chorus might also alter the refrain, adding and dropping words, sometimes breaking the refrain apart into sections hocket-style (individuals or small groups coordinating to create the refrain's melody). The words I reproduce in Figure 5.3 and in the following examples represent what is generally sung when a *getan* begins. But good *ge* performers are master improvisers, both of text and of sound. My consultants place high value on improvisation, which is one of the most important aspects of an effective performance of *getan*.

GETAN TEXTS

It is no accident that texts are an important factor distinguishing *getannu*. *Getan* texts play an important role in enacting Ge. The proper text, sung at the appropriate moment, can activate spiritual power. Other texts verbalize aspects of the values that undergird the concept of Ge. Not all *getan* texts directly concern things

Ge. Still, sampling and analyzing the texts is an effective way of approaching the meanings Ge performances hold for the people with whom I studied.

Figure 5.2 describes a particular stage in a *ge* manifestation—when the *ge* has just appeared. A number of *getan* texts I collected refer to stages of Ge performances. Example 5.2 uses a concrete bodily metaphor to comment on the arrival of a *yinan* who accompanies *genu* from the spiritual realm to the world of humans:

Example 5.2. Text of *getan "Zo-ma-ɛ"*

(*zo-ma-ɛ-ɓoo*) *Ba kɔ da ɓɔɗɛ kwin*	(vocables) My hand has entered into the hand of a gift (in this context, "gift" [*ɓɔɗɛ*] is a metaphor for *yinan*)
refrain: (*zo-ma-ɛ*)	(vocables)

Some *getan* texts offer advice and/or promote the values that many of my consultants consider to be the base of proper behavior in Dan society, often making use of proverbs:

Example 5.3. Text of *getan "Pö mɛn diankë gbɛng"*

(*gi-la-mo-zoo*)	(vocables)
refrain: (*i-yo-yo*) *Pö mɛn diankë gbɛng*	(vocables) Things trick people during the night.

As is often the case with proverbs, they require interpretation. The *getan* whose text is in Example 5.3 was composed by young boys from Biélé who are the principal singers for a children's *gbage*. In an interview with Jacques and me, they explained this proverb's meaning: the night serves as a metaphor for any situation in which one cannot see things clearly (Gbage group 1997). They explained that one must be very vigilant in such situations. When Jacques and I later discussed this interview, he extended the metaphor, interpreting it to mean, "During the day, verify things you experience at night." Dan proverbs, however, are inherently ambiguous, which allows for multiple interpretations. Like *getan* generally, this proverb could surely have different meanings for different people in different situations.

Another *getan* underscores the emphasis placed on community values and working together in Dan life:

[handwritten margin note: relates to hermeneutics]

Example 5.4. Text of *getan "Ba gbaa to"*

Ba gbaa to	If my field is left unfinished.
refrain: *K'o to ko ko nyan*	We have all left my field unfinished together.

As Ge performer Gue Tin from Biélé explained to me, the idea behind this text is that should an individual's field go unfinished, it will be everyone's fault. The implication is that everyone will have seen that the individual was having difficulty finishing the field and will have failed to act to help the individual in need. If a family fails to complete the planting of a field, they risk going hungry.

Using a metaphor from the most central activity (historically and for many still today) of Dan life—agriculture—this text promotes the idea that the whole community is responsible for the well-being of each individual (Gue Tin 1997).

While some *getan* texts concern the values associated with Ge, others have little or nothing to do with Ge. In dances of entertainment or rejoicing *genu,* singers may spontaneously compose songs that express personal joy, recount personal stories, or comment on a situation at hand. These spontaneous songs are frequently humorous. Jean-Claude once improvised a song using veiled metaphors to surreptitiously mock a beautiful but conceited young woman present at an event. Singers frequently use *getan* to communicate messages that only "insiders" will understand. Jacques recounted a time when a *ge* improvised a song to tease another performer in his group about something funny he had done the prior day in the fields. In so doing, the *ge* demonstrated to the crowd that even though he was not physically present when the incident occurred in the fields, he, like all *genu,* sees and knows all. By singing this song, the *ge* affirmed a fact of the concept of Ge—that *genu* are omniscient—while adding to the levity of the joyous event.

Certain genres of *genu* who sing (especially *gegɔn,* but also others) regularly praise people of high status. Some *getan* texts praise national political leaders. Jean-Claude, Gba Ernest, and others from Petit and Grand Gbapleu sometimes sing a *getan* during the manifestation of Gedro praising colonial-era politician Ouezzin Coulibaly. And at the 1997 Yam Festival in Déoulé, singers performing with a dance *ge* called Gbinge sang a *getan* about President Henri Konan Bedie, lauding him as the chief of all Ivorians.

This association, through text, of *genu* with humans of high status and power is not surprising. As an intermediary between the world of humans and the world of Zlan and the ancestors (*bɛman*), a *ge* manifests authority and power of the highest magnitude. In times past, *genu* effectively ruled all aspects of Dan life. Today, living within a contemporary nation-state with its rules, laws, police, judges, and politicians, the traditional power structure of Dan villages has had to be renegotiated. Still, the power of Ge continues to be recognized and reinforced when, for example, chiefs and other powerful elders consult *genu* when making important decisions or when politicians invite *genu* to important political events or laud them in political speeches. I regularly witnessed evidence of these power relationships in performance; *genu* always ritually greet chiefs and elders of high status during their manifestations. Associating *genu* with powerful political figures in song has the same effect. When figures of authority work together or even simply reference one another (call it "musical name-dropping"), they reinforce each other's powerful positions.

Some *getan* texts discuss behavior during Ge performances. Certain songs implore people to support the manifest *ge,* to do their part in the performance:

Example 5.5. Text of *getan "Ka nu kwɛwo ɓaa"*

Ka nu kwɛwo ɓaa	Come to the sound of clapping,
refrain: *n ɗoo ɓaɗe*	wife of my older brother.

Of the musical roles women often play during Ge performances, none is more important than clapping, which enhances the rhythmic richness of the song and thus its overall effectiveness. This is crucial, since the *yinannu* who accompany a *ge* from the spiritual realm must be drawn by the quality and intensity of the music. This song reminds people of the important part they play in ensuring the success of the event.

Still other *getannu* remind people that codes of behavior must be adhered to when a *ge* is manifest. One strict rule is that fighting is absolutely prohibited. For example, during the Déoulé Yam Festival, if a person strikes another while a *ge* is present, it is tantamount to striking the *ge* himself (Zaclo group 1997). Though on numerous occasions I did witness verbal conflict between people at Ge performances, the ideal is that even arguing and insulting people is considered inappropriate in the presence of a *ge*. This ideal is expressed in the following *getan* of the women's *ge* called Kong:

Example 5.6. Text of *getan "Waa dɔ ge gu"*

Waa dɔ ge gu	One does not stand before a manifest *ge*.
Waa ɗian yaa zë	One does not say negative things.
refrain: (*za-ko-pe, ko-pe-ɗɛ*)	(vocables)

Some *getan* texts discuss aspects of the institution of Ge, a system of education and values that is said to preserve and perpetuate fundamental notions of Dan life that originated during the time of the ancestors:

Example 5.7. Text of *getan "Ɓa mun ge ka"*

Pö ko dënu wo to,	Of the things our fathers (ancestors) have left us,
Ɓa mun ge ka	For me, I choose Ge.

This text speaks of the strong connection between Ge and the ancestors. Some of my consultants went so far as to state that *genu* are literally manifestations of ancestors. Most of my consultants, however, hold that there is simply a strong association of Ge with ancestors, since *genu* first manifested among humans during the time of the ancestors and ancestors have passed this gift down to people alive today. This is the sentiment being expressed in Example 5.7: of everything passed down to us from the ancestors, it is Ge that I choose to practice, that I decide to keep.

The flip side of this sentiment, expressed from the perspective of a *ge*, is found in the text of the *getan* the Gedro group sang as they entered the shelter at Douélé Doumba ("I have come for a reason/it is because they have called me"). Performers thus use texts to reaffirm the authority of Ge by claiming its roots in ancestral times and by asserting its relevance today; even in the pluralistic climate of contemporary Man, people "call" upon Ge in times of need. Gueu Gbe Alphonse expressed this sentiment when we discussed the issue of competition for adherents among the practitioners of the various religions in Man. Responding to the proselytizing of local Muslim and Christian factions, Gueu Gbe said:

> The *ge*, he cannot complain. He has time. He is in his sacred hut. . . . The *ge*, he is not aggressive. . . . He is patient. Ge, it's the fundamental truth. Ge, it *is* time. It is yesterday, it is today, it is tomorrow. It has time. People can leave, but they always return [to Ge]. (Gueu Gbe 1997a)

Many of my consultants expressed similar views. It was often a point of pride to portray Ge as above the fracas, as unconcerned about the increasing popularity of other religions. Ge will always be there, waiting in the sacred house, knowing that if people temporarily go elsewhere to meet their religious needs they will eventually return. *Genu* are too proud to manifest if they are not called upon. They will not push themselves on people or seek out converts. But when they are summoned in the appropriate manner and for good reason, they do come, with confidence and authority.

Some *getan* texts express notions about the system or school of Ge in a humorous way. The following song plays on the physical/metaphysical ambiguity surrounding Ge performance. Many Dan consider a *ge* in performance to be a manifestation of spirit, not a human in costume, even though everyone (except, perhaps, uninitiated children) knows that a person is in fact wearing the *ge* attire. At one point in Gedro's performance at Douélé Doumba, the following song was sung by Lien Sati Yvonne and Tiemoko Christine—who as women are technically not supposed to know that a man is behind the mask—to playfully provoke and jest the male performers in Gedro's group:

Example 5.8. Text of *getan "Dɛ pö ge baa ye?"*

| *Dɛ pö ge baa ye?* | Who, then, arranges [dresses, prepares] the *ge*? |
| refrain: *Ge nin ge baa.* | It's the *ge* who arranges the *ge*. |

As they sang, Yvonne and Christine smiled mischievously at the men who sang the response, occasionally making eye contact with them as they danced playfully toward them. The men at times returned their own knowing smiles, as if to acknowledge that they understood an inside joke.

As we later interpreted this moment in the performance, Jacques emphasized the importance of taking into account context when interpreting the meaning of *getan.* Outside of the context in which it was performed, this song does have a general meaning. The question, "Who, then, arranges the *ge*?" is clearly rhetorical in any context in which Dan are present. Everyone knows that the belief system holds that *no one* arranges the *ge.* The *ge* arrives from the spiritual dimension in exactly the same form that people see; the clothes, facial mask, and other physical characteristics are simply how that particular *ge* manifests among humans. The answer, "It's the *ge* who arranges the *ge*" upholds this belief. While there is perhaps a bit of humor in the rhetorical question itself, in this context, asked by women of men, the question became clearly humorous and full of jest. And the answer, coming from the men, became playfully evasive.

TEXTS AND CONTEXTS

The context in which a song is sung becomes even more important when considering songs specific to certain circumstances and songs associated with specific *genu.* Jean-Claude and Gba Ernest taught me that these more specific songs are the oldest and most powerful songs. While many *getannu* can be sung to spiritually animate a particular *ge,* these older songs get to a *ge*'s roots. These older *getannu* tend to inspire profound, nostalgic, and ecstatic feelings in people, while they inspire individual *genu* to act, to actualize the specific powers and functions accorded them. These songs thus tend to be sung in contexts in which the specific powers of a particular *ge* are required.

Songs that are associated with particular activities usually fulfill specific functions. Compared to the general pool of *getan,* these songs tend to be used for specific purposes, toward specific ends. Jean-Claude taught me that certain songs are used to comment on the fact that someone who is not "clear" is present at the Ge performance. The use of the word "clear" in this context refers to a person's spiritual disposition. A person who engages in socially destructive spiritual be- havior called *duyaa* (sorcery) is considered not "clear." As Jean-Claude said:

[handwritten margin note: Relates to the development of consciousness in rasa (Becker)]

> If, for example, the *ge* is in the process of dancing, and someone arrives who is not clear, he is in the crowd, and he looks at the *ge,* and the *ge,* well, the person's image passes by him. But to really verify his face, to freeze the per- son's image in his mind [we play] . . . a song that is directly in connection with the person who has arrived. And that is in direct connection with those *yinannu* who can effectively freeze his image [in the *ge*'s mind]. (Goueu 1997b)

As Jean-Claude went on to explain, once the *ge* has the "unclear" person's face clearly fixed in his mind and he is certain of the person's malevolence, he will confront the person, accusing him of wrongdoing. But it is only with the aid of specific *yinannu,* who come after being called by a specific song, that the *ge* is able to engage the spiritual vision that enables him to see the spirit of the person in question.

After he finished the above description, Jean-Claude went on to tell a story of an experience of this kind that he witnessed. The *ge* who was manifest was a *gegblɛɛn* (stilt *ge*) who was not a *zu ge.* Confronted with the presence of a *du- yaami* (sorcerer), the *gegblɛɛn* decided to elicit the aid of certain *yinannu* who can only be summoned with a song associated with a *zu ge.* The *gegblɛɛn* thus initiated a *zu ge* song specific to the circumstance in which he found himself.

This story is an example of an acceptable intertextual leap, of a context in which a *ge* in need of another's *yinannu* is permitted to use a *getan* to contact them. Such a move is not always permissible, however. Even though it is possible for one *ge* to perform another's *getan,* it does not follow that any *ge* at any time may sing any other *ge*'s *getan.* There are rules—times when such a move is appropriate and times when it is not. To cite a crude example, Gedro, in the middle of a joyous moment and for no particular reason, could not dance to a Gegbadë song that deals with a problem of sorcery. Moreover, certain songs can never be sung outside of their context. The *getan* of the head *ge* of the Déoulé Yam Festival, who manifests only on the seventh and final night of the semiannual festival, cannot be performed at other times or by other *genu.* The haunting unusual sound of this *ge* is heard only during his tour of the village to bless the inhabitants for their hard work in sustaining the village.

Still, there are many examples of acceptable exchanges of *getannu* that are associated with specific contexts. Jacques explained the general principle behind this use of songs: "There are songs that have a mystical relationship with [stages of] the ceremony. It's not all the songs that have this mystical relationship. There are certain songs which are very mystically powerful." Jacques compared these songs to the use of prayers in other religions to call certain spirits (Biemi in Biemi and Goueu 1997a). Just as Catholics meet specific needs by intoning specific prayers to specific saints, *genu* and *gedëmɛn* sing particular songs for particular functions to draw the appropriate *yinannu.* In many cases, if one *ge* is in need of the *yinannu* associated with another *ge,* he may sing the necessary *getan* to call the spirits to his aid.

The context in which a song is initiated is extremely significant and can affect the song's meaning. As I mentioned above, it is unacceptable to fight or argue in the presence of a *ge.* On one occasion, I witnessed Gegbadë invoke a song to quell a dispute among his drummers. Master drummer Goueu Tia Jean-Claude was yelling at one of his accompanying drummers for losing the rhythm at a critical moment of the event. Jean-Claude, preoccupied by this dispute, failed to remain focused on the *ge* (one of his most fundamental responsibilities as master drummer), even speaking at the same time as the *ge.* To restore order and comment on this breach of proper conduct, Gegbadë intoned the following song:

Example 5.9. Text of *getan "Mɛngɓan yaa dɔ gewon gu"*

Mɛngɓan yaa dɔ gewon gu	No one places himself within a *ge* affair
refrain: *Kö ye ɗianyaazë*	in order to speak in a negative way

In this context, this song had a specific meaning and function. This same song could be sung in another context as a reminder of one of the rules of Ge performance, but still it would index a circumstance like that described above—a time when someone is behaving improperly and needs to be put back in his or her place. In the intertextual flow of *getan* performance, performers use *getannu* toward specific ends, affecting the meanings of the songs.

Getan generally plays more specific roles and fulfills more specific functions for Gegbadë than for Gedro. Because he is primarily a rejoicing *ge,* Gedro can dance to a wider variety of songs. Gedro's songs, like the *ge* himself, are primarily for rejoicing and uplifting a crowd. Gba Ernest, who sings for both Gegbadë and Gedro, told me that Gedro's songs are generally "weaker," meaning less spiritually potent, because his performances are more "peaceful." Gegbadë, on the other hand, often must provoke and challenge sorcerers, so his *getannu* are accordingly more powerful. Still, not every *getan* sung during a Gegbadë manifestation fulfills specific functions. Gba Ernest explained that some of the same "weaker" songs sung during Gedro performances can be sung for Gegbadë as well, but only after he has finished "working" and is heading back into his sacred house. Similarly, a song that is very powerful in the context of a Gegbadë manifestation might be sung during a Gedro manifestation merely for the purpose of exciting and entertaining the crowd. The song in Figure 5.3, *"Ge nin nu ba"* ("The *ge* has arrived") will strike fear in the hearts of people if sung when Gegbadë is arriving in a village to combat sorcerers. This same song, in the context of a Gedro performance, might be sung merely to "heat up the crowd" (Gba Ernest 1997a). But generally, *getannu* sung in the context of a Gegbadë manifestation are extremely powerful and are used toward very specific spiritual ends to meet very specific goals.

One of Gegbadë's primary roles is divination. He uses *getan* toward this end. Jean-Claude explained:

> If the *ge* is doing a divination, for the *ge* to tell you what he sees in the mystical images, images of your spirit . . . there are songs. . . . To have these visions, he is helped by spirits [*yinan*]. He collaborates with those spirits, with that power. So [for the *ge*] to really be inspired, so that those spirits come, to really do the

divination well, there are specific songs that we sing to excite the *ge*. (Goueu 1997d)

Below is an example of a song that Gegbadë can initiate in order to read someone's destiny:

Example 5.10. Text of *getan "Ðɛga yong gu yi nin dɛ"*

Ðɛga yong gu yi nin dɛ	This is the day for looking into the television.
refrain: *(a-ɓoo) Yi nin dɛ*	(vocables) This is the day.

Singing the above song is one of the ways that the *ge*'s sight into the spiritual dimension is activated when he looks into his hourglass-shaped *télévision*.

GETAN LANGUAGE AND HISTORY

By far the majority of *getannu* I heard and recorded were entirely in the Dan language, although I did encounter *getannu* sung in other languages. As is generally true, local history—of individuals and of groups—is reflected in language use. *Getan* texts evidence the mobility of western Côte d'Ivoire, a region where people and ideas have been, and continue to be, in near-constant flow. Considering the dramatic immigration of northern Mande speakers to the Man region that has occurred since the advent of the colonial period and the fact that Jula is used as a trade language in Man and throughout the country, it is not surprising that Jula words occasionally show up in Dan speech. As in speech, so in song. In certain *getannu,* my consultants integrated Jula words or phrases into Dan texts, much as they do occasionally in speech. The following Kong song makes use of the Jula modifier "*nyuman,*" or "good":

Example 5.11. Text of *getan "Më ö man kë Kong dɛ dian nyuman"*

Më ö man kë Kong—dɛ dian nyuman	What will I do for the Kong—good word
Deɓonu ɓa ge	Women's *ge*
refrain: *(ii-yo) Ðian nyuman*	(vocables) Good word

In the following *getan,* the boys of the Biélé youth *gbage* combine Dan with Jula *and* French. In fact, the boundaries between Jula and Dan are blurry when one considers certain words. My consultants unanimously identified "*barika*" (thank you) as being of Jula origin; yet this word is one of the most common ways of saying "thank you" in everyday Dan speech today. On the other hand, the uses in Example 5.12 below of "*a ni cɛ*" (a greeting, also meaning "thank you" in Jula) and *chérie* (French for "darling" or "dearest") demonstrate the incorporation of other languages into Dan *getan* text. This is evidence of linguistic fluidity in Côte d'Ivoire, where most people are multilingual. Ivorians frequently switch linguistic codes in conversation, at times fusing more than one language into a single sentence:

Example 5.12. Text of *getan* "*Ba i nwe ɓo ma chérie nwe ɓo*"

Ba i nwe ɓo ma chérie nwe ɓo	I thank you, dearest—thank you
refrain: *A ni cɛ, a ni cɛ barika—o*	Thank you, thank you, thank you—o
Ge ɓa pö nin ɓa a ni cɛ	This is a *ge* thing—thank you

I encountered many instances in which history can be traced in *getan* texts. Gua ta ge is a rejoicing *ge* from the Goh village of Déoulé. The Goh are a very small subgroup of Dan who consider themselves to be a mixture of Dan and Toura—an ethnic group who live just to their northeast. Yet certain families who live in Déoulé identify as Dan due to their origins. Gua ta Ge is from the sacred hut of one such family—the Gbongues. Like all Dan *genu,* most of Gua ta ge's *getannu* are sung in Dan. During Gua ta Ge performances, however, Jacques and I noted a number of *getannu* that we were unable to translate and that we later learned were sung in Mau, the language of the southern Maninka (Malinké) population who live just north of the Dan. Later, I asked the *gedëmɛn* of Gua ta ge's sacred hut why they sing songs in Mau during Gua ta ge manifestations. They responded with a historical explanation, claiming that this *ge* predates their southerly migration to their present location from the north hundreds of years ago.[8] Accordingly, some of Gua ta ge's *getannu* are sung in northern languages. Moreover, since this particular family has in more recent times migrated to a Goh village, Gua ta ge's manifestations also include songs in Goh. Both the distant history of the Dan ethnic group and the more recent past of the Gbongue family are evidenced in the fact that this *ge*'s performances feature *getannu* sung in Dan, Goh, and Mau.

Oulai Théodore, who is in charge of the sacred hut that includes the *zu ge* Gegbadë, told me that many *zu genu* sing songs in Mau. Théodore and others explained to me that the Mau are renowned for their *genu* who deal with problems of sorcery.[9] More than one *zumi* told me that all Dan *zuminu* and *zu genu* trace some historical connection to their neighbors to the north (Mli 1997a; Oulai 1997a). This is the case for Théodore, whose training included a lengthy apprenticeship with a Mau *zumi.*

Gegbadë is remarkable, however, in that he sings in *many* languages, reflecting the extent to which he travels. Gegbadë has a national and, to some extent, international reputation as an effective prosecutor of sorcery-related crimes. While he works steadily for Dan clients in the Man area, he also travels extensively, working in many non–Dan-speaking settings. Frequently, Gegbadë sings in the language of the area where he is working. He does not translate *getannu* into other languages but rather creates new *getannu* in the local language that are appropriate to the situation at hand. As a result, the *getan* repertoire of Gegbadë includes songs not only in Dan and Mau but also in Guéré, Bété, Dida, Mano (a Liberian ethnic group), Guérzé (a Guinean ethnic group), and even Jula (Oulai 1997b). Because he is such a highly mobile *ge,* Gegbadë has become extraordinarily multilingual. Gegbadë's multilingual ability illustrates the extent to which Ge is intertwined with the broader social and cultural landscape, not only of contemporary Côte d'Ivoire but also of the West African region.

BOUNDARIES OF *GETAN*

Performers in Ge manifestations, with very few exceptions, are initiated Dan adults. In initiation, and even more so through experience, people learn the rules of Ge performance. Perhaps because the rudiments are taught in initiation, I noted a high degree of uniformity among my consultants regarding the boundaries of what is and what is not appropriate to sing during Ge performances, or what is and is not *getan.* However, not everyone agrees about where the boundaries of *getan* lie. No culture group, of any size, is completely homogeneous. Like all cultural mores, musical and religious rules are constantly in the process of being negotiated. A relatively recent innovation, and one that can cause disagreement and controversy in the communities in which I have studied, has been the incorporation of references to popular music into certain Ge performances.

I am not arguing that *getan* was until recently a closed and static body of music whose boundaries were unanimously agreed upon by all practitioners. For centuries, performers of *getan* have encountered and interacted with performers of styles of music different from their own. While mobility and ethnic integration have certainly increased in recent times, the Dan throughout their history have been in contact with peoples of many other ethnicities. The decision, therefore, about what "outside" influences might be permitted to be incorporated into *getan* did not first arise with the mass introduction of non-Dan peoples and mass media into the region. The incorporation of elements of popular culture into *getan* that I witnessed in 1997 was, rather, just one contemporary example of the negotiation of the boundaries of this sacred phenomenon.

Today, popular music from many parts of the world form a part of the everyday soundscape of all the *getan* performers from whom I learned. My consultants have regular access to radio. The state-run Fréquence 2, which is produced in Abidjan and broadcast nationally, was extremely popular in the Man region in 1997. Fréquence 2 features a broad range of pop music by artists from Côte d'Ivoire, other African nations, the Caribbean, Europe, and North America. The biggest hits of 1997 included songs by artists from Algeria, the Democratic Republic of Congo, and various regions of Côte d'Ivoire. Many of my consultants also frequently listen to cassettes. Though many of them do not own cassette players themselves, in open-air bars and restaurants, in buses and taxis, and in many other public locations they are exposed to Ivorian "cassette culture" (Manual 1993).

My consultants generally label the music they hear from these mediated sources as "popular" or "modern," which they contrast with music such as *getan,* which they call "traditional." While my consultants hold "traditional music" and "modern music" to be separate categories, they are not mutually exclusive, because boundaries between these categories are permeable. Much Ivorian popular music draws upon (emically-defined) traditional rhythms of Côte d'Ivoire's diverse ethnic populations, and traditional musicians incorporate influences from popular culture. These boundaries, however, can become a matter of great importance for Ge performers, because only the traditional music of *getan* will attract the *yinan* necessary to manifest a *ge.* The issue of musical boundaries extends beyond this utilitarian argument, however; it also involves paying musical and religious respect to the ancestors and "the tradition" of Ge. But, whether *ge* performers decide to incorporate or reject popular-music influences, they are interacting with these influences, acting as agents selecting and rejecting influences present in their daily lives as they continually negotiate and (re)define this sacred phenomenon.

Rejoicing *genu* are the only genre that incorporates references to popular music or culture into Ge performance. But the practice is controversial among the Dan even when only the genre of *tankë ge* is considered. Those *genu* who do appropriate popular-culture references are frequently called *masques ye ye* in French, a term which indicates their fashionability among youth, though many older Dan consider such *genu* to be lacking seriousness. I observed three different ways in which *ge* performers made popular-culture references during *ge* manifestations: 1) references to popular-music rhythms in the rhythmic interaction between a dancing *ge* and a master drummer's solos; 2) gestural and dance imitations by comedic *genu* (*trukë ge*) of characters in American and European movies and television and of Ivorian political figures; and 3) singing of popular songs, not by a *ge* himself, but by members of his group. Since I am presently discussing the boundaries of the sung aspect of *getan,* I will here deal only with the actual singing of popular songs.

Singing of popular songs during Ge performance is by far the most controversial of the three ways of referencing popular culture listed above. I experienced this occasionally but found no support for such behavior when I discussed the matter with performers. The first time I witnessed the singing of a pop song was during a manifestation of one of the warrior *genu* of the Déoulé Yam Festival called Zaclo.[10] Zaclo has two primary roles—that of a policeman who keeps order during the festival and that of a messenger who announces the date of the festival to people in other villages, effectively delivering a traditional "card of invitation" (Village of Déoulé 1988, 4). It was in this latter capacity that one Sunday in March 1997, Zaclo and his group of young men made the 20-kilometer journey from Déoulé to Man to announce the date of the Yam Festival to dignitaries and the general populace. Since I had spent quite a bit of time in Déoulé in 1994 and had informed them of my interest in the Yam Festival in 1997, the group visited our house on their journey through town, which also included stops at the homes of local politicians and a tour through the Man market.

The sonic elements of a Zaclo manifestation are generally as follows: Zaclo himself does not sing or speak but emits guttural, grunt-like sounds throughout the course of any manifestation. A single musical instrument accompanies him—a small, single-pitched trumpet made of a goat horn. The trumpet player blows his instrument sporadically, its high-pitched bursts interspersing with cries of "Zaclo" by other members of the group. Two men sing improvised unaccompanied vocal lines, one leading and the second following in parallel thirds below.[11] Occasionally these two men, or perhaps the *gekia,* will break out into a more standard, call-and-response–style *getan,* the other members of the group singing the response to their call. The shouts, singing, and trumpet-playing combine to create the necessary sonic environment for the appropriate *yinan* to come, empowering the spirit of Zaclo.

While Zaclo and his group were dancing on our porch, members of the group began singing "A Sec Kotoko"—a pop song of the *zouglou*[12] genre by the Ivorian band Les Poissons Choc. They did not sing the whole song, but rather just repeated the catchy refrain *"On sera se voir"* (We will see each other again) for a minute or so. Several months later, Gbongue Félix, a member of the Zaclo group, stopped by our house. After we chatted for a while, I asked him if he would help me translate some of the Goh songs I had recorded the day Zaclo toured Man. When our conversation turned to "A Sec Kotoko," I asked him why they had sung that song. He smiled sheepishly and looked away. "Singing that song during a Zaclo manifestation was not right. We did this because of the amount of beer we had drunk," he admitted. Gbongue, who had not initiated the song but did sing along, continued, "This happened only because we were in the city, away from our elders and ancestors." He explained that they would never have been so frivolous at home in Déoulé, where expectations for Ge performance are strictly enforced by elders and ancestors. So the combination of drink and the feeling of abandon of being in Man inspired the group to break the rules and sing a song that he later felt was an inappropriate choice for the *getan* of Zaclo (Gbongue 1997).

Another occasion when performers incorporated a popular song into *getan* singing was during the final match of the Gebia Final, or Ge Racing Final, held in the Man soccer stadium on June 21, 1997. *Gebia* is a traditional sport that pits human runners against the least sacred genre of *ge*—the *biansëge,* or racing *ge.* The rules of the game are slightly different in the village context, but in the setting of the soccer stadium, two teams representing different local villages compete, each of which has a cadre of runners and at least one *biansëge.* Each team takes turns choosing a runner from the other team to compete against their *biansëge.* The runner gets a 2-meter handicap and must run the length of the soccer field and back without being caught by the pursuing *ge.* Generally, the music at *gebia* events consists of a specific genre of *getan* called *giantan,* which, like most *getan,* is accompanied by three to four drummers and a gourd rattle. *Giantannu* are old war songs, which, played at rapid tempos, incite feelings of intensity and competition to inspire both the *genu* and human runners. At the 1997 *gebia* events held in the soccer stadium, three musical groups performed: a neutral group charged with impartially inspiring both teams that was positioned just behind the goalpost where the races begin, and one group for each team, consisting of people from that team's village, that was positioned on the sidelines next to their respective teams.

I was invited to attend and document this event by Gba Gama and his team from Petit Gbapleu, who were thrilled and proud to have made it through the weeks of competition to the final. In the moments leading up to the race, when Petit Gbapleu's *giantan* group was ecstatically drumming and singing to draw the *yinannu* to their *biansëge,* they sang a reggae song by the Jamaican artist U-Roy, "Go There Natty Dread." Rather than being sung to a reggae beat, the melody was layered over a standard rapid *getan* rhythm. In fact, the singers themselves, though familiar with the song, which had been a hit years earlier in Côte d'Ivoire, did not know the words (not surprisingly, as they are in Jamaican English), and sang something like "Go ze natty de." This sounded to me very much like Dan vocables and without Jacques' prompting, I would have mistaken this for just another typical *getan* with a vocable refrain.

I used this incident as a way of exploring the boundaries of *getan.* To be sure, this was not a terribly powerful *ge,* but it was a *ge* nonetheless, and a reggae song had been sung to inspire him. Was this permissible? I unfortunately never did get the opportunity to ask the performers of this song their opinions regarding what they had done. But everyone with whom I did discuss this, including Petit Gbapleu's leading master drummer Goueu Tia Jean-Claude, found the singing of this song inappropriate. Jean-Claude argued that singing "Go There Natty Dread" was a mistake, a violation of the rules. Vehemently, he explained:

> That is joking around. If you are going to inspire a mask, you have to sing a song that pleases him. . . . But a reggae song? What mask will that inspire? . . . The mask has come with a goal, and he must complete his mission. For ex-

ample, you have to go work in the fields. You know that to work the rice in the fields, you need a hoe. But you arrive in the fields, and you take out your machete. In the end, you will be discouraged! A machete cannot cover a grain of rice. . . . You have to take your hoe, dig up the dirt, and hide the grain underground so the birds can't eat it. . . . But if you take your machete, and you are there—that's joking around! So if you want to achieve a goal, you must do what you must do. You cannot do otherwise. . . . That's why I won't play with that group. Because it is a joke. . . . When the mask comes out and enters your dance group, it's to find strength! It's to inspire him! It's to rid himself of fear, before going out onto the field. . . . And you joke around. That discourages him! (Goueu 1997h)

Jean-Claude ardently argued that one cannot sing reggae or funk or any popular music during the manifestation of a *ge* (although quoting popular-music *rhythms* can be acceptable). What the *giantan* group was playing had nothing to do with the *ge,* Jean-Claude insisted, but was *woyo*—a cross-ethnic, loose genre played by young men that has become popular nationwide. That Jean-Claude refuses to play with the Petit Gbapleu *giantan* group, which includes many of his closest friends, is testimony to the depth of his conviction about the importance of playing the appropriate music when a *ge* is manifest. He blamed the ineffectiveness of Petit Gbapleu's *biansëge* on the irresponsible behavior of this group (Goueu 1997h).[13] Exasperated, Jean-Claude completed his thoughts with a proverb: "*Sieu ya pëu ye blii pia ye zi mo ë wouai maa*" (For a fire to burn a whole forest down, it must begin in its place).

Based on these two incidents and many conversations with consultants, it seems to be generally the case that singing popular songs when a *ge* is out is not acceptable. New songs can be created and considered *getan,* but nearly all of my consultants assert a boundary between *getan* and popular song. These incidents serve as examples, however, that *ge* performers do sometimes challenge these boundaries. Patrick McNaughton asks, "Which is more important to know, the rules or the ways people live them?" (1993, 83). Yet it would be an exaggeration to state that these two examples render *getan* rules meaningless. At this point in time, it appears that these were mistakes and that exploring these mistakes helped me to confirm generally held rules regarding *getan* boundaries (Blacking 1967). Peoples' reactions to these incidents affirm those rules even as the performers challenge them. The dynamic of cultural change is thus—innovation, criticism, gradual change. Whether it will become acceptable at some later point to sing popular songs at Ge performances is irrelevant, but the fact that conflict exists regarding the performance of this tradition is terribly relevant. It serves as one more example of the process of tradition, in which individuals and communities communicate in a dialectic manner, through expressive forms, in a perpetual ne-gotiation of what they consider to be right and good in their art and religion (Glassie 1982, 1995). These examples also underscore the importance of music in the performance of Ge. In these examples, music is the primary mediating factor between practitioners of Ge and the diversifying world around them. Some *ge* performers choose to challenge the boundaries around *getan* by incorporating popular songs into their performances. Others chastise them for doing so, en-forcing clearer boundaries around Ge in an effort to protect that which is most fundamental to their ethnic and religious identity. Music thus is central to the negotiation of identity through Ge performance.

PERFORMANCE OF *GETAN*

Just as *getan* tends to follow a standard structure, there are also standard roles for performers in both Gedro and Gegbadë performances. The *ge* is always in charge of all aspects of his performance, including the music. Second in command is the *ɓaakpizëmɛn* or *ɓaadezëmɛn* (master drummer). When the *ge* is not yet physically present, the master drummer leads not only the *ɓaazëmɛn* (other drummers) but the *geatankëmɛn* (singers) as well. Goueu Tia Jean-Claude generally serves as master drummer for both Gedro and Gegbadë. In the beginning stages of events, before Gedro or Gegbadë emerge from their sacred houses, Jean-Claude initiates some of the songs and sets the tempo of every song by playing the rhythms of the accompanying drums on his *ɓaade* (mother drum) until the repeating parts are established to his satisfaction. Once each song is proceeding well, Jean-Claude begins soloing on his *ɓaade*. Even as he solos, though, he continues to lead the ensemble. A *ɓaakpizëmɛn* must remain ever alert to any problems and move to correct them swiftly. If an accompanying drummer is dragging the tempo, for example, Jean-Claude will begin playing that person's pattern to bring the accompanying drummer up to speed. At this stage of the event, before the *ge* is visibly present, Jean-Claude also determines the length of each song by using drummed signals. Using the different pitches of his three-headed drum, Jean-Claude can mimic the tonal patterns of several Dan sentences, each of which essentially means, "Stop."[14] During early parts of a performance, before the *ge* has emerged from the sacred house, the master drummer is clearly in charge. He retains that authority to some extent when Gegbadë and Gedro physically emerge.

Among the singers, there are generally one or two leaders called *geatanɓomɛn,* who initiate songs and sing solo parts. *Geatanɓomɛnnu* are virtuoso singers who have developed keen improvisational ability and masterful knowledge of *getan* repertoire. Singing the call of a *getan* requires not only musical ability but also a quick mind. As a song progresses, the *geatanɓomɛn* improvises, extemporizing words and varying the melody. Singers "supporting" the soloists by following a fourth below frequently lag slightly behind the soloists, since they cannot always predict what the improvising soloist will sing. Over time, however, singers develop repertoires of common textual and melodic motifs that they can draw upon while improvising. When soloists sing one of these recognizable motifs, supporting singers are able to follow more easily. In any case, supporting singers must vigilantly follow the soloists they accompany, remaining ever alert and quick to adjust to any and every improvisation thrown their way. Song leaders and supporting singers can be either male or female, and the chorus of accompanying singers and dancers is often mostly female. Singing, dancing, and clapping are ways in which women participate directly in the manifestations of both Gedro and Gegbadë. Women are vital to the performance of both *genu.*

The rules regarding who sings the call and who responds are in fact flexible. For example, if someone in the chorus initiates a song, she or he might continue to sing every other "A" call. Alternatively, someone in the chorus might initiate a song but then the principal singer might take over singing the "A" call, leaving the initiator either to sing the secondary "A" call or to simply sing the refrain with the rest of the chorus.

Song selection at a Ge performance operates according to rules learned primarily through experience. The rules differ in different contexts and for different *genu.* During performances of sacred *genu* who sing, such as Gegbadë, the principal singer primarily tunes his attention to the *ge,* who initiates most songs. The principal singer then repeats the initial call initiated by the *ge,* and the *geatankëmɛn* (chorus)[15] picks up the song by singing the refrain. At performances of *genu* who do not sing, the performers most likely to initiate a song are the principal singer and the master drummer. Any initiated person present, however, may intone a song, as long as it is a *getan* of the proper genre, although people who are not members of the performing group cannot come out of nowhere and haphazardly initiate a song. Such a person must first present a "kola"—a small monetary gift—to the *ge* to ask permission to initiate a song, and the song must be of the appropriate genre (Goueu 1997f).

Anyone singing in the chorus—or for that matter, any initiated person present—may intone a song during a manifestation of many *genu* who sing, but only during certain stages of the event.[16] At more serious stages of a performance, such as during a benediction, a divination, or pursuit of a sorcerer, it would be inappropriate for just anyone to intone a song. At such moments, people recognize that control of the event needs to rest with the *ge.* In fact, it can be dangerous for a person to initiate an inappropriate song during the manifestation of a powerful *ge.* Less powerful *genu* might fine a person for making such an error, but a *zu ge,* for example, would consider such behavior an attack and would return fire with a mystical attack of his own.[17] At *zu ge* manifestations, people usually remain quiet to avoid making a mistake and offending the *ge* (Goueu 1997f). But at any stage of a manifestation of a singing *ge,* the *ge,* the master drummer, and the principal singer are more likely to initiate songs than others present.

Gegbadë and Gedro performances flow very differently through time. Gedro's primary function is to dance, and he rarely speaks or sings. Songs go on for long periods—five to ten minutes—to permit Gedro plenty of opportunity to thrill the crowd with his fleet-footed virtuosity. During Gegbadë performances, in contrast, *getannu* tend to be much shorter in duration, sometimes lasting as little as thirty seconds and rarely exceeding two minutes. Gegbadë starts and stops the music frequently to speak or sing to the crowd, because Gegbadë does not manifest merely to entertain. The primary focus of his performances is the communication of important information in the form of divinations, sacrifices, and sorcery accusations. Gegbadë initiates songs in part based on their texts in order to communicate specific things. Gegbadë performances tend to flow as follows: the *ge* speaks in proverbs, initiating a song which continues for up to two minutes; the *ge* gestures, stopping the song in order to speak a little more; then the *ge* initiates another song, which he soon stops again in order to speak, and so forth. As such, Gegbadë performances are segmented into brief musical and verbal passages, woven together by the will of the *ge* to accomplish the goals of his manifestation. While the master drummer and principal singer retain important roles while Gegbadë is physically present, the *ge* clearly directs the flow of the event.

The leadership roles of master drummer and principal singer tend to be played by elder musicians, though this is not always the case—Jean-Claude, who is in his mid-20s, being a case in point. More typically, master drummers are older men who have, through many years of experience, developed not only the musical and directorial skills required for this role but also the reputation that allows them to command the respect and deference accorded to them by others present at a performance. Likewise, principal singers are often elder women or men—masters in terms of their encyclopedic knowledge of *getan* repertoires and their improvisational ability.

There are exceptions. On several occasions, including the performance at Douélé Doumba narrated at the beginning of this chapter, I witnessed the young woman Lien Sati Yvonne play the role of principal singer for Gedro. Yvonne is exceptional in many ways. Although only in her 20s, she already is initiated to the highest level in the women's Kong society—a distinction usually reserved for postmenopausal women. Yvonne is viewed as an extraordinary musical and spiritual talent in Petit Gbapleu; I would not be at all surprised to return in a couple of decades to find her leading the Kong society as *zuďe* of Petit Gbapleu.

The fact that both Jean-Claude and Yvonne play leading roles in Petit Gbapleu Ge performance might also have to do with the general youth-oriented nature of Ge performance today in their neighborhood. Since so many of the leaders in Petit Gbapleu Ge affairs have died in the past two decades and since so many elders favor Islam to Dan religion, even leadership roles in Ge performance are being played by younger people. While the youth orientation of Ge performance is particularly pronounced in Petit Gbapleu, it might not be only in this old village turned urban neighborhood that Ge performers are typically younger than in times past. Several elders told me that as rejoicing *genu* have become more and more important, younger people are more frequently performing Ge. This, some elders argue, is the reason that *ye ye* attitudes are becoming more prevalent in Ge performances at the end of the twentieth century.

[handwritten: RESPECT for ELDERS, but a YOUTH-ORIENTED NATURE]

TANKWI

It is unusual for a person or a *ge* to launch immediately into a *getan* without warning. Usually, a performer will first initiate a *tankwi,* which is a brief musical interlude like the "*wɛɓoo wɛnze*" sung by a Gedro performer at the funeral described at the beginning of this chapter. Performers sing *tankwinu* for several reasons: to cue people that someone is about to initiate a *getan,* to pass the time between *getannu,* and/or to make sure everyone remains focused and inspired. Like *getannu,* a *tankwi* can be created on the spot, in which case probably only the person initiating the song will sing. More commonly, performers will sing one of many popular *tankwinu* that everyone knows, enabling everyone to join in. Also, just like *getan,* certain genres of *tankwi* are associated with certain *genu.* Racing *genu* (*biansëge*) and war *genu* (*gbage*), for instance, each have their own distinctive *tankwi,* which differs from that of the *genu* I studied more closely— Gedro and Gegbadë. Gedro *tankwi* tends to be playful, full of jest and mockery. *Tankwi* for Gegbadë, on the other hand, consists primarily of sung proverbs, which are generally more serious in nature.

Figure 5.4. *Tankwi "Wɛɓoo wɛnze."* Transcribed by Daniel B. Reed.

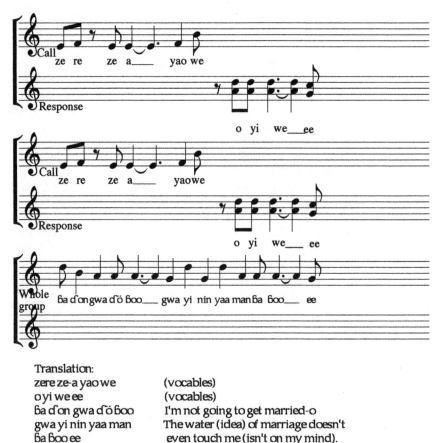

Translation:

zere ze-a yao we   (vocables)
o yi we ee   (vocables)
ɓa ɗon gwa ɗö ɓoo   I'm not going to get married-o
gwa yi nin yaa man   The water (idea) of marriage doesn't
ɓa ɓoo ee   even touch me (isn't on my mind).

Figure 5.5. *Tankwi "Zere ze-a yao-we."* Transcribed by Daniel B. Reed.

Before beginning a *getan,* a singer often sings a *tankwi* as a cue that he or she is about to intone a *getan,* to focus everyone's attention on the person singing. It is essentially a way of asking, "Excuse me, I would like to start a song—are you all ready?" As Jean-Claude said, "In the traditional context, you cannot just get up and sing like that—you have to see if the chorus is ready to respond. If they are not, you don't sing" (Goueu 1997g). "Wɛɓoo wɛnze" is the *tankwi* most commonly used in this way during Gedro and Gegbadë performances. As in the opening narrative, the person planning to initiate a song sings the vocable line, "*wɛɓoo wɛnze,*" to which others respond in kind or with another vocable line—"*ee-a-ee-a.*" Usually both the initiator and the rest of the group together repeat the line "*wɛɓoo wɛnze,*" after which the person who initiated the *tankwi* begins a *getan.*

During performances of rejoicing *genu* such as Gedro, performers often use *tankwinu* to pass the time and amuse themselves between *getannu.* Since *tankwinu* are accompanied only by the gourd rattle, these breaks permit the drummers to rest and get a drink of water or palm wine. Jacques compared this use of *tankwi* to instrumentalists in a band recreating between songs. One musician may quote a song, for fun, and another may join in, while others are tuning or otherwise preparing for the next number. Figure 5.4 demonstrates a common *tankwi* form often used for this purpose. One person usually sings the beginning call, to which the chorus responds, while the latter phrases are sung by everyone together. Singers singing *tankwi* melodies are almost always "supported" by others harmonizing in parallel fourths below the melody, just as they are when singing *getannu.* There are no rules regarding who should sing which part. Often during the latter part of a *tankwi,* the chorus will split—those with higher voices singing the melody, others supporting a fourth below.

The playful *tankwi* transcribed in Figure 5.5 mocks young girls who, unlike in times past when arranged marriages were the norm, want to make up their own minds about marriage. Even when they are playful in nature, *tankwi* texts sometimes comment on social issues. I encountered several *tankwinu,* in fact, that dealt with the behavior of young women, reinforcing societal norms such as fidelity and bearing children only in wedlock. As with *getan* texts, context is again critical to consider when interpreting a *tankwi.* When I heard this *tankwi* sung it was always by men, who use this *tankwi,* according to Jacques, to mock young women who want to think for themselves.

A *tankwi* can also be used "to look for inspiration" (Goueu 1997g). Sometimes a *ge* or a human will sing "*wɛɓoo wɛnze*" with no intention of then initiating a *getan* but merely to be sure everyone in the group is remaining focused on the matter at hand. I often witnessed Gegbadë use "*wɛɓoo wɛnze*" for this purpose, to keep his musicians alert during long tedious stretches of sorcerer interrogations. Similarly, performers may sing a *tankwi* to ensure that everyone, musicians and the *ge* alike, remain inspired, so that the energy of the performance remains high and the necessary *yinannu* remain present. Gba Ernest explained to me that while it is very common to use *tankwinu* in this way, it is not always necessary. "If the *ge* is really hot, you don't need the *tankwi,* you just jump right in and sing a song itself" (Gba Ernest 1997c).

GETAN AESTHETICS AND *GBAKWI*

To be "hot" (*wɔsi*) is the aim of every *ge* in performance. The desire to be hot is one of many of my consultants' aesthetic preferences that cannot be properly understood in isolation from the specific goals they are trying to attain through a given Ge performance. In other words, some of my consultants' aesthetic decisions are also practical decisions. They play *getan* in such a way as to maximize its effect in realizing the task at hand, in manifesting the power of a *ge* to accomplish what it is that he does. Patrick McNaughton argues that aesthetics are "strategies for organizing the resources that become form" (1998, 15). Considered in this way, aesthetics are inseparable from the idea of strategy—the idea of accomplishing something. Art is expressed with goals in mind, to achieve certain things. This does not remove or eliminate art's capacity to express feeling or beauty or horror, or anything for that matter. Rather, self-expression is one motivation that can lead to choosing certain strategies for organizing resources in particular ways.

My *getan* teachers accomplish more than particular strategic goals through their aesthetic choices. These aesthetic decisions also are fundamentally linked to Dan-ness, to their idea of what it means to be Dan. One aspect of Ge is the notion of proper behavior for adults in Dan society. Since it is music sound that makes manifest these social ideals, then music sound is a fundamental expression of Dan identity for the *getan* performers with whom I studied. Christopher Waterman describes a similar multifaceted concept of aesthetics as he understood it to be constituted in juju performance. Advocating for the value of attempting to understand our consultants' concepts of aesthetics, Waterman complains that too often Western musicological approaches

> presume a radical distinction between abstracted musical "structures" (forms, scales, melodic and rhythmic modes) and expressive "qualities" (timbre, texture, rhythmic flow). This is not a useful distinction for Yoruba musicians and listeners. The experiential impact of the metaphor "good music is society writ small" depends upon the generation of sensuous textures. An effective performance of juju predicates not only the structure of the ideal society, but also its "feel": intense, vibrant, loud, buzzing, and fluid. (1990a, 220)

Likewise, my consultants' aesthetic choices manifest their ideals of Dan-ness while enabling them to accomplish more immediate goals by attracting an appropriate *yinan* to do so.

Singers use various methods to heat up a performance, including singing loudly with a buzzing edgy timbre in high registers and performing songs at fast tempos. During one lesson with Gba Ernest, Jacques mocked me for singing "soprano." My comparatively light round tone, developed in vocal training in the United States, sounded "ordinary" to them (Gba Ernest 1997d). From that point on, my lessons began focusing as much on timbre as on getting the right notes. A timbre that will make a Ge performance hot is one that is somewhat tense and tight, with an edge and intensity that cuts through the volume of the drums. Likewise, singing a song in a high register adds a kind of urgency that makes it "hot." *Getan* can be sung in any comfortable register, but, as Gba Ernest told me, singing in the high part of his range "makes it hotter" (Gba Ernest 1997c). He cautioned, though, that if he sings this way too often he becomes hoarse. Even though singers put a secret powder into their palm wine to keep them from losing their voices, Gba still must pace himself by singing some songs in a lower register in order to make it through an entire performance, which often lasts all night (Gba Ernest 1997e). Tempo also plays an important role in making a performance hot. Gedro dances nearly every *getan* at an extremely quick tempo. These same songs may be sung in other contexts—for Gegbadë, for example, at slower tempos—but for Gedro, who is known for rapid dancing to blisteringly fast rhythms, songs must be played fast for the *ge* to be hot.

Especially at certain moments in his performance, to be hot is also crucial for Gegbadë. I noticed over time that singers sang songs differently with Gegbadë when he was en route to and first arriving at a performance space than they generally do throughout Gegbadë's performance. I later learned that what I was noticing was an approach to singing *getan* called *gbakwi*. Gba Ernest explained to me why *ge* performers use the technique of *gbakwi* at these beginning stages of a manifestation. When performers are walking to a performance site, drummers cannot play, since they must carry their drums. Singing in *gbakwi* style fills in rhythmic spaces left by the drums, which keeps the energy of the *getan* high until the group is once again stationary and the drumming can resume. Yet singers do not sing *gbakwi* in this context just because it sounds good. Keeping the energy of a performance high when a *ge* is en route is imperative, as this is a moment when the *ge* is particularly vulnerable to malevolent spiritual acts. Keeping the musical energy high attracts the *yinannu* who can protect the *ge,* warding off such attacks (Gba Ernest 1997f).

In *gbakwi,* singers gradually unravel the standard structure of *getan.* One by one, singers abandon the call or response and begin improvising in a freer manner.

Singers may begin *gbakwi* by eliminating or adding a note to the refrain. For example, the refrain, "*ɗo n ka/ɗo n ka*" might become "*ɗo/ɗo*" or "*ɗo n ka/ɗo n ka-o.*" Or this same melody that had been previously sung in unison or in parallel-fourth harmonies might be broken up into segments and sung hocket style, individual singers or groups of singers forming a melodic pattern by the coordination of their unique parts (see Figure 5.6b). Singers might also break away to form completely new parts, usually vocable lines, which interlock with the other parts, forming a rhythmically complex whole. This is a fluid improvised process, in which a group of three might break off from the whole, then two of the three leave to create something else new while one remains—any grouping and any number of groups is possible.

In the passage that follows, Jean-Claude explained how and why singers in Gegbadë's group split off from the main singing group (*tankëmɛn*) to form groups of *gbakwimɛn* (those who sing *gbakwi*):

> Usually in a song . . . the principal singer sings, but . . . the chorus, we can divide up. Jacques and I, we are together, then you two, you are together, then two others are together. . . . The manner that your group responds to the music, it's not like that that Jacques and I are going to respond. Also, we can change. . . . We can make noises, [sings] "*ee-a, o-a, ee-a*" . . . but it must go with the music. When we divide up, you two, you can respond, but in your own way. Either you respond directly to the dance, to the song [that is, sing the refrain], or you create something [else] that could go with the music. . . . Often, when we sing, the whole chorus responds together. Everyone responds with the same words. Then the *ge* stops and makes a signal with his hand, he puts his hand like that [gestures]. That's to say, "Don't respond all together with the same words. You others, divide yourselves up." . . . Some continue responding normally to the dance [singing the refrain], while another group can create something like for example, "*Ee-a, o-a, o-a*" so that the dance may be a little better. It's like that. (Goueu 1997g)

Jean-Claude went on to say that Gegbadë cues the switch to *gbakwi* "because when he stands where we sing, and all of us are responding with the same words, . . . for him, it's not sweet to hear. . . . When we are all singing the same thing, it's not sweet for him to hear" (1997g). While this most frequently occurs while the group is en route to or arriving at a performance space, Gegbadë can make such a cue at any time. Ultimately, the decision to sing *gbakwi* is made according to the aesthetics—that is, the strategic goals—of the *ge*.

In Figures 5.6a and b, I use James Koetting's Time Unit Box System to represent the rhythmic aspects of how Gegbadë's singers used *gbakwi* to heighten the intensity of the *getan* "*ɗo n ka*" while en route to the performance space in Yokoboué. Figure 5.6a shows how the singers began singing the song, while Figure 5.6b demonstrates how the song was eventually sung after having evolved through various stages.

Call	ɗo	n	ka	o--	---o-	--o							
Refrain							ɗon	ka		ɗon	ka		

Figure 5.6a. *Do n ka* at beginning of performance at Yokoboué, August 2, 1997. Transcribed by Daniel B. Reed.

Call	ɗo	n	ka	o---	---o-	--o	ɗon	ka				
gbawi				ɗon	ka				ɗon	ka		
gbawi						ɗon	ka					
gbawi	o											

Figure 5.6b. Gbakwi six minutes into performance of *ɗo n ka* at Yokoboué, August 2, 1997. Transcribed by Daniel B. Reed.

These examples are like snapshots, freezing just two instants of a complex process in time. *Gbakwi* is an improvisational process; this song went through many phases between what I have above represented as Figures 5.6a and b. At least a dozen of the above charts would be required to accurately represent the complete and complex evolution of this performance. Using the sophisticated and subtle technique of *gbakwi,* performers created perhaps my favorite musical moments of any Ge performances I experienced.

My experience also bears out the idea, expressed to me over and over by my teachers Jean-Claude and Gba Ernest, that improvisation and variation are at the heart of *getan* aesthetics. When observing performances, the times when people were most elated, the times when the energy felt ecstatic and *genu* and people danced with abandon, were times when fine improvisation was occurring, when the repetition of the call-and-response form was varied in artful ways. In my singing lessons, when I accurately reproduced the melody that Gba Ernest taught me, he would smile encouragingly and say, "That's it." But when I would attempt to move beyond mere imitation, when I would take risks and vary the melody, Gba and Jacques would clap, howl, laugh, and congratulate me. The depth of *getan,* its richness, the thing that my consultants seemed to most value, was variation. *Gbakwi* is the extreme of that, but even more moderate improvisation excited and inspired my consultants. Repetition is central to *getan* singing, but it is nothing without variation. Performers and *genu* value vocal improvisation and use it effectively as a resource to accomplish their goals. The same can be said of drumming in *getan* performance.

Making hot music (*tan wɔsi*) is yet another strategy *ge* performers use to achieve their goals. They make aesthetic choices—including repetition and skillful variation, playing songs at quick tempos, and (most important) improvising in innovative ways—to enable them to achieve specific goals, such as the attraction of powerful spirits who manifest Ge, who enable *genu* to accomplish tasks, and who protect *genu* and other performers by augmenting their spiritual defenses. Being hot is furthermore to demonstrate excellence, to be good. Performing in a hot manner, along with singing an appropriate text at an opportune moment, means that one is behaving properly, that one is participating in the manifestation of Ge. In sum, the sonic aspect of Ge performance is essential, not only to the spiritual and technical unfolding of the performance, but also to the overall communicative and affective power of Ge in peoples' lives. In the diversifying context in which they live, Gedro performers sing "I choose Ge," positioning themselves vis-à-vis the world around them and accomplishing tasks that help them deal with the challenges their world presents.

SIX

Drums as Instruments of Social and Religious Action

In 1997, one of the young people who was most active in Ge performance in the Man neighborhood of Petit Gbapleu was Goueu Tia Jean-Claude (Figure 6.1). Jean-Claude already had walked down several other religious paths, having spent time as a Muslim, a Catholic, a Baptist, and a member of the Celestine Church before he decided "to live within the tradition" (Goueu 1997e). At the informal gatherings of youth at Gba Gama's bar, Jean-Claude picked up drumming and astonished everyone with his natural skill at playing drums and singing. People immediately began talking about the musical "gift" that he had obviously been given from Zlan. When Petit Gbapleu's most highly sought-after master drummer died in the mid-1990s, Jean-Claude was called upon to fill the void.

Most of what I learned about drumming in Ge performance I learned in lessons with Jean-Claude. Once or twice a week, Jean-Claude would arrive at our house in the Man neighborhood of Domoraud from his home in Petit Gbapleu. Often he would bring along one of his apprentices so that we had enough hands to play several parts at once. I tape-recorded these sessions, during which we drummed and talked about *getan* and related issues. We also conducted a number of interviews and spent a fair amount of informal time together just relaxing. My brief apprenticeship with Jean-Claude was like an intensive version of the kind of specialized training undertaken by Dan men who pursue drumming beyond what is learned in the first stage of initiation. I assisted Jean-Claude as he built my drums. I learned the basic drum and gourd rattle rhythmic patterns, variations of these patterns, and a handful of master-drum solos. Finally, I experienced as many Ge performances as possible, usually as a conspicuous audience member. On a few occasions I drummed in public, though only once with a *ge*—Gedro. It was in these lessons that I began to deepen my understanding of the ways aesthetics merge with religious and social action in Gegbadë and Gedro perform-

Figure 6.1. Goueu Tia Jean-Claude. Photograph by Daniel B. Reed.

ances.[1] I began to comprehend the ways *ge* performers use drums as a means to communicate—with each other, with their audiences, and with the spirit world—to accomplish goals. Drumming is even more central to Ge performance than the sung aspect of *getan*. In the rhythmic interactions between a *ge* and a master drummer, the most powerful communication occurs; performers establish relationship both with the spiritual domain and with the pluralistic world in which they live.

LEARNING TO DRUM

Most young men are introduced to drumming in initiation. Only those who show a particular talent for and attraction to drumming will continue furthering their drumming education. Advanced study of drumming is an example of a "specialized" initiation in which young men informally apprentice themselves to older masters. Drumming education includes learning the rhythms and techniques of Dan drumming and how to build drums. Drummers also learn special techniques for maintaining endurance and stamina, including massaging the hands with a liquid made of medicinal plants. This training, along with endurance built up through experience and the animation that comes from palm wine and from the performance of the music itself, enables drummers to sustain the substantial amount of energy necessary to make it through long performances (Gba Ernest 1997e). While drumming education begins in the first stages of initiation, it is primarily through experience that drummers learn the musical techniques, the rules and norms—in short, all the specialized technical knowledge required to drum for *ge* performances.

Drumming for a sacred *ge* such as Gegbadë requires even more special training and knowledge. Combating sorcery is serious and dangerous business, and drummers must learn both how to protect themselves against sorcery attacks and how to play in order to call the *yinannu* to activate the *ge*'s powers. While Jean-Claude learned much of this "on the job," a certain amount of training with Oulai Théodore was also necessary. Because of the critical nature of his role in Gegbadë performance, Jean-Claude has undergone a specialized education with Théodore.

Singers and drummers who are part of a particular *ge*'s performing group gather in sacred locales—in a sacred house or a sacred forest—to learn the *getan* associated with that *ge*. But they also learn a great deal about how to perform, including repertoire and behavioral norms of performance, through the experience of performing. Training—in initiation, in rehearsal, and in performance—is only one factor that influences a drummer's musical development. My teachers explained to me that talent also plays a major role. Talent is one of those mysterious notions, as much in my own society as in that of my Dan teachers. In my musical experiences in the United States, people have explained the idea of talent in different ways, sometimes attributing it to genetics, other times to environmental factors or to some combination of "nature and nurture." Yet many people I have known also assign a kind of mystical or spiritual quality to the idea of exceptional talent, sometimes describing it as a "gift" originating from God or from some unknown near-magical source. My consultants also attributed virtuosic musical ability to spiritual sources—"gifts" from God or inheritance of ability from either an exceptionally talented living elder or a deceased ancestor. Musicians who come from a musically talented family are considered to have inherited their talent, whereas others, such as Jean-Claude, possess skills that are not traceable to familial predecessors. In such cases, people shake their heads and identify the talent as a "gift." In either case, though, individual musicians, like all people, have their own personal *yinan,* from whom they find inspiration. Not everyone has a *yinan* that can inspire brilliant drumming. Thus, the skills and talent that make for great drumming are far from universal in Dan society.

THE INSTRUMENTS

While there are different types of *getan* for different sorts of *genu,* the *getan* for Gebgadë, Gedro, and many other *genu* typically features three to four drums (pl. *ɓaanu*) and a gourd rattle (*gle*). All of the drums (see Figure 6.2) are played with the hands. The most important of these instruments is the drum played by the master drummer, the *ɓaadе* (mother drum), which plays many roles. Musically, the *ɓaadе* serves as the focal point much of the time during Ge performances, as the master drummer's solos, coordinated with the dancing *ge,* layer over the top of the interlocking patterns of the rest of the ensemble. Furthermore, the master drummer uses the *ɓaadе* to communicate in many ways with various participants. Using the *ɓaadе* to signal text, the master drummer communicates with his fellow drummers and other people who are not part of the performing nucleus. To accompany the *ɓaadе,* two drums—the *zikri* and the *ɓaanëyak-wade*—are required, while a third—the *lökö'së*—is optional.[2] These drums, along with the *gle,* form a rich interlocking polyrhythm, each instrumentalist playing a set pattern for each of the three rhythms they play—*zi-k-ri, di-pi-tin,* and *ti-ti-din.*[3] Gegbadë's group adds a rather unique element—a musician playing two bells (*dɔɔganu;* sing. *dɔɔga*), one in each hand. Of all the *genu* I have seen who make use of this instrumental ensemble, only Gegbadë's performances featured

Figure 6.2. Drummers at a Gedro performance. Drums pictured (L to R) are: ɓaanëyakwade, ɓaaɖe (played by Jean-Claude), and zikri. Oulai Théodore is second from right. Photograph by Daniel B. Reed.

the *dɔɔganu.* Many *genu* attach bells to their ankles, which add another layer of percussion when they dance, as does the swishing sound of the *ge*'s raffia skirt. Rounding out the percussive aspect of these performances is the improvisational clapping, mostly performed by women singers, which artfully accents the rhythm. Ethnomusicologist Steven Friedson complains that the word "clapping" is woefully inadequate to describe the music women do with their hands in spirit-possession performances in Malawi (1996, 110). Likewise, I find no word in the English language that adequately captures the fabulously complex hand percussion that women improvise in Ge performance.

The drums which *ge* performers use to contribute to the sonic aspect of the manifestation of Ge are those most commonly associated with Dan peoples. These same drums are used in many types of Dan dance settings. The instruments and the rhythms drummers play on them are recognized by many Ivorians as distinctly Dan and are a clear expression of Dan identity, both locally and nationally. As Gueu Gbe Alphonse and others taught me, these rhythms and the techniques for playing the drums are learned in "the Mask school," or men's initiation. *Gedëmɛn* assert that these rhythms express a sense of Dan ethnic identity because at the core of Dan ethnic identity is the notion of Ge (Gueu Gbe 1997a).

The drums are all constructed out of more or less the same materials. Each of the drums has a goblet-shaped wooden body, though the drums vary in size. Generally, the smallest is the *lökö'së,* measuring around twenty inches in height and approximately seven inches in diameter. The largest, the *zikri,* is usually about twenty-three inches high and ten inches in diameter. While the relative pitch and timbre of each drum is affected by its size, this is not the most important factor in determining the drum's sound. The degree to which the interior of each drum is hollowed out significantly influences its timbre and pitch. The greater the

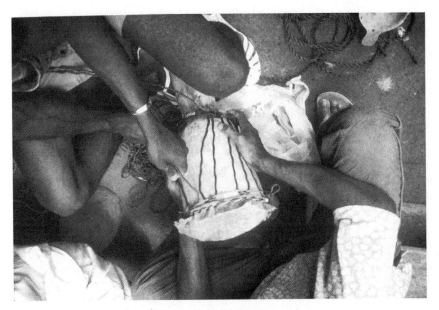

Figure 6.3. Drum-making. Photograph by Daniel B. Reed.

hollowed-out circumference of a drum, the more *gbin* (heavy) the drum will sound. Conversely, a *kpɛɛ* (dry) sound is produced by a drum whose inner circumference is smaller because its walls are thicker.

Antelope or red-deer leather is used for the drum's skin. This skin is held onto the drum with durable nylon rope threaded through holes punctured in the skin and around a rope ring circling the drum's body roughly ½" to 1" from the top rim (see Figure 6.3). This rope is laced tightly around the body of the drum and is tied to either a metal ring or another rope ring, tightly wrapped in fabric, which circles the base of the "cup" part of the goblet. Rope tension is thus held between the top and bottom rings, ensuring that the skin remains taut. Prior to a performance, drummers pound the top rope ring with a wooden mallet, forcing the ring to move slightly lower on the outer circumference of the drum, tightening the skin. From time to time, more substantial maintenance is required, as the skin begins to stretch and loosen to the point that drummers must disassemble the entire drum in order to retie the ropes more tightly.

An unusual aspect of these instruments is that two types—the *ɓaad̗e* and *ɓaanëyakwade*—are actually multiple-headed drums, consisting of two or more drum bodies tied together. Only the *zikri* and *lökö'së* are single-headed, single-bodied drums. *Baad̗enu* and *ɓaanëyakwadenu* consist of one central larger drum, to which is tied a variable number of additional smaller drums.[4] The actual number of heads varies, but a total of between three and five is common. Occasionally, exceptional drummers play drums which exceed the more typical three to five heads; legendary drummer Zingbe Martin reportedly played a nine-headed *ɓaad̗e*. Drummers generally agree that only virtuoso flashy drummers can effectively make use of a drum with more than the average number of heads. Many excellent drummers choose to remain with three to five heads, which seems to be the norm. The smaller drum bodies are attached to the largest drum's body using the same kind of nylon rope that tightens each drum's head. The arrangement of the drums varies—some drummers prefer to place the smaller heads on the sides

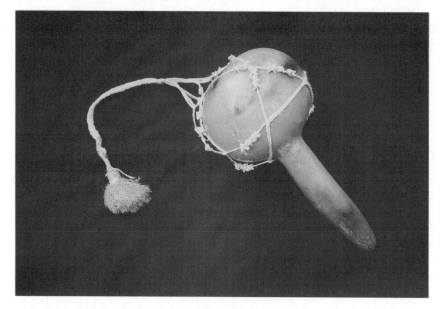

Figure 6.4. *Gle.* Photograph by Daniel B. Reed.

of the main larger drum, just to its right and left. Other drummers tie the smaller drums behind the main drum's body, raising them up higher so that their heads can be more readily accessed. There was no single common look for either of these two types of drums. They vary rather dramatically, the only constant being the single larger head and a variable number of smaller heads attached. *Baaɗe* players also frequently attach metal resonators called *ɓaasɛ* to their drums. *Baasɛnu,* which vary in shape and size, consist of relatively thin strips of metal with holes perforated along their edges, through which small metal rings are attached which vibrate when the drum is struck. At the base of the *ɓaasɛ* are thin posts, which drummers fix beneath the nylon ropes on the drum.

In addition to the drums, a rattle of some sort is always present in this kind of Ge performance ensemble. Most common is the gourd rattle called *gle* (Figure 6.4). The body of the *gle* is a dried, hollowed-out gourd. Durable string, preferably strung with snake bones (although small seeds or beads can substitute) is tied loosely around the rounded portion of the gourd. The string gathers together in a braided end, which *gle* players generally hold in the left hand. The straight end of the gourd is held in the right hand and used as a handle. By flexing the wrist of the right hand while the left hand holds the braided end of the string loose but steady, *gle* players produce a loud percussive sound as the snake bones scrape and strike against the hard wood-like surface of the dried gourd. The hole cut into the gourd when it is hollowed out also serves as a sound hole, amplifying the attack of the bones on the gourd. The *gle* struck me as being rather easy to play at first, but this was deceptive. It is, in fact, a very difficult instrument to master. Virtuoso *gle* players excel in subtle and rapid flicks of the wrist necessary to produce intricate rhythmic patterns. Like the accompanying drums, the *gle* is used to play specific patterns for each of the three rhythms. *Gle* players interlock their patterns with the accompanying drums, adding a distinctive sonic layer to the repeating polyrhythmic foundation of *getan.* On occasion, when no *gle* or proficient *gle* player is available, performers substitute a *sekpe.* A small rattle consisting of a basket-like chamber woven from dried plants and filled with tiny pebbles, the *sekpe* is relatively easy to play, as performers hold it by a small handle and shake it up and down, approximating (or even dramatically simplifying) the more complex *gle* patterns. The youthful Gedro group frequently substituted a *sekpe* for a *gle,* but for Gegbadë, performers always played a *gle.*

Performers in Gegbadë manifestations include another instrument, the iron bell called *dɔɔga.* Measuring approximately six inches, the *dɔɔga* is a cup-shaped bell with an iron clapper, which is manufactured by local blacksmiths. *Dɔɔga* players hold one bell in each hand, alternating them, playing either a constant, symmetrical duple pattern (for the rhythm *zi-k-ri*) or a three beats on, one beat off pattern (for the rhythm *di-pi-tin*) that interlocks with the patterns played on the drums and *gle.* Jean-Claude and Jacques explained to me why Gegbadë performances feature this instrument. The *dɔɔga* is quite loud and is used to draw attention to the fact that a powerful *ge* has arrived. They explained:

(JC): When arriving in a village, to alert people that we are arriving, it's the *dɔɔga* that sounds. (J): . . . When a man who has no fear of what he wants to do, when he arrives, people must be informed that he is arriving. It's only someone who is afraid of his adversary (JC): who hides himself, (J): who sneaks up on someone. But when you are not afraid of your adversary, you stand before him. So when [Oulai] Théodore wants to enter a village. . . . When his *ge* must appear, since his *ge* is afraid of no one, it is necessary that people know that his *ge* is out. . . . So they play the *dɔɔga.* Then *everyone* knows that the *ge* is coming. . . . Even before the *ge* comes out, we play the *dɔɔga.* For example, when Gegbadë went to Bofesso [a village where a sorcery conflict took place in 1997], Dominique took the *dɔɔga* and did a tour of the whole village. . . . And then Dominique came back to tell the *ge* that he was finished with the warning. After that, he took up position walking in advance of the *ge* and the rest of the group [as they entered the village]. That is an attitude of someone who has no fear of his adversaries. (Biemi and Goueu 1997b)

The *dɔɔga* is also incorporated into the performance of Gegbadë's *getan,* to serve as a constant reminder of his warrior-like powers. To emphasize this point to me, Jean-Claude invoked a proverb: "*dɔɔga ye wi klumi ta, yaa wi dwamɛn ta*" (The *dɔɔga* speaks [plays] for a courageous man, it does not speak [play] for a fugitive) (Goueu in Biemi and Goueu 1997b).

Gegbadë himself occasionally plays a factory-manufactured bell, called a *sraman,* that is attached to the end of one of his many power objects (*geɓɔga*). The *sraman* is about ten inches long and about two inches in diameter. I was never permitted to touch it, but the part to which the bell is attached looks to be made of leather. Like many power objects, it is covered with the buildup of years of animal blood and kola-nut sacrifices. Cowrie shells are attached to its body. The *sraman* spontaneously rings of its own accord when Gegbadë points it at a sorcerer or a sorcerer's power object. It also sometimes rings when Gegbadë has received a message from the *yinannu* identifying a sacrifice that is required of someone who has sought his help to solve a problem. While Gegbadë holds the *sraman* in his hand, it rings side to side in a free rhythm. This usually occurs between songs, when no other instruments are playing and no one is singing.

Dancing *genu* themselves add percussive layers to the sound of *getan.* All *genu* who manifest visibly wear raffia skirts, which they toss around as they dance, creating a rhythmic, swishing sound. More powerful *genu* such as Gegbadë wear larger, heavier skirts, which create an especially loud sound as they are tossed about by the body of the dancing *ge*. Also very common, especially for rejoicing *genu* such as Gedro, are ankle bells, or *gbuŋ*. The *gbuŋ* are particularly important for Gedro, because their sounds follow the patterns of his dance steps. As the master drummer finesses solo rhythms from his *ɓaadɛ*, the *ge* "plays" his *gbuŋ*. These rehearsed patterns are the sonic and visual focal points of Gedro performances; the *gbuŋ* and the *ɓaadɛ* match each other's rapid rhythms beat for beat.

THE RHYTHMIC FOUNDATION

As I learned from Jean-Claude, performers create the rhythmic foundation of Gegbadë and Gedro manifestations by playing specific patterns on each of the accompanying instruments for each of the three rhythms. The names of all three of the rhythms played in these kinds of Ge performances are taken from the mnemonic syllables used to teach the patterns played on the *zikri*. Known as the "timekeeper" drum, the *zikri* serves a role similar to that of the bell line in some parts of West Africa; the other musicians in a Ge performance orient the patterns they play or sing to the pattern of the *zikri*. Zikri drummers thus bear the primary responsibility for maintaining the tempo of a *getan*. The first and most common of the three *getan* rhythms shares the same name with the drum—*zi-k-ri* (Figure 6.5).[5]

The patterns of mnemonic syllables for all three accompanying drums loosely correlate with the sounds they imitate. Drummers can produce up to three different sounds on each drum (with the exception of the *lökö'së*—see below): open, closed, and slap. An open sound is achieved by striking the drum and immediately releasing the hand from the skin, maximizing the drum's resonance. Drummers produce the closed sound by striking the drum and leaving the hand in contact with the skin. By maintaining contact, the hand reduces the resonance of the drum while stretching the skin slightly, producing a sound pitched almost a half-step higher. Drummers achieve the slap sound by moving the hand forward toward the center of the drum, resting the palm on the drum's rim and slapping. The slap technique produces a sound that is louder, has a sharper attack, and is lower pitched than the other two sounds. In the case of the *zi-k-ri* pattern above, *zi* is a closed sound, while *k* and *ri* represent open sounds. In Figure 6.6, I have adapted the Time Unit Box System to represent the rhythm and relative pitch of the *zi-k-ri* pattern played on the *zikri* drum. Absolute pitch does not apply in the tuning of *getan* drums, but relative pitch is essential. The difference between the higher and lower pitches is almost a half-step. The resultant rhythmic and pitched pattern—the most popular rhythm not only in *getan* but for all Dan dances—is the most common of all Dan musical signatures.

Since the *ɓaanëyakwade* consists of multiple drums, beginning players must

Zikri	zi		k	ri				zi		k	ri		
ɓaanë...	zi	ki	ni	li	kpa			zi	ki	ni	li	kpa	
Gle					x	x	x	x		x			
Lökö'së*	së				kö	'së			lö		kö		

Figure 6.5. TUBS transcription of the rhythm *zi-k-ri* (* = optional). Transcribed by Daniel B. Reed.

Zikri high (closed)	zi			
Zikri low (open)			k	ri

Figure 6.6. *Zikri* drum pattern for the rhythm *zi-k-ri*. Transcribed by Daniel B. Reed.

memorize the rhythmic patterns as well as which drums to play the patterns on. The basic patterns are taught assuming a three-headed instrument—the most common instrument that all beginning drummers play. The *ɓaanëyakwade* pattern for the rhythm *zi-k-ri* is played as shown in Figure 6.7.

This pattern can be reversed for drummers who prefer to begin the pattern with the left hand. Drummers tune the multiple drums of the *ɓaanëyakwade* to different pitches. The smaller drums of the *ɓaanëyakwade,* called children, are tuned to higher pitches than the largest drum. The smaller children drums are all tuned to different pitches as well. Value is placed upon the fact that the pitches vary so that the sound of each drum is distinct; the exact pitch of each drum and the exact intervals between the drums can vary. Because of the difference in pitch of the multiple drums, *ɓaanëyakwade* patterns are quite melodic. Dan frequently compare the sound of the *ɓaanëyakwade* to that of the xylophone (*bala*) played by northern Mande peoples in their midst. Because of the multiple tuning options, these melodic patterns vary from instrument to instrument and from performance to performance.

Drummers use slightly different techniques when playing the *lökö'së.* They make use of just two sounds: the resonant tone produced by the open stroke and a lower-pitched sound produced by striking the center of the drum with the palm. For the *zi-k-ri* rhythm (see Figure 6.5), the lower-pitched sound is represented by the " *'së*" syllable, while "*lö*" and "*kö*" refer to open strokes with the right and left hands, respectively. Like the *zikri* drum, the *lökö'së* drum takes its name from the mnemonic syllables used to describe the pattern it plays for the rhythm *zi-k-ri.*

Jean-Claude taught me the *gle* rhythms by mimicking the instrument's sound with his tongue and the back of his front teeth, making a kind of "dzzt" sound. This, he said, is the way *gle* rhythms are taught and remembered; no mnemonic syllables are used. In my transcriptions, I have chosen to represent the sound of the *gle* with a simple "x" which does not imitate the sound but merely identifies the pattern. Accented strikes are represented by a capitalized "X."

Syllable	Drum	Hand	Type of sound
zi	right	right	open
ki	center	left	open
ni	center	right	open
li	left	left	open
kpa	center	right	slap

Figure 6.7. *Ɓaanëyakwade* pattern for the rhythm *zi-k-ri*. Transcribed by Daniel B. Reed.

	di	pi	tin		di	pi	tin		di	pi	tin		di	pi	tin		di
Zikri	di	pi	tin		di	pi	tin		di	pi	tin		di	pi	tin		di
Baanë			zi	ki	li	ki	zi	ki	kpa		zi	ki	li	ki	zi	ki	kpa
Gle			X	x	x	X	x	x	X		X	x	x	X	x	x	X
Lök...*	kö	lö	lö						kö	lö	lö						kö

Figure 6.8. The rhythm *di-pi-tin* with pattern *kö-lö-lö* (* = optional). Transcribed by Daniel B. Reed.

	di	pi	tin		di	pi	tin		di	pi	tin		di	pi	tin		di
Zikri	di	pi	tin		di	pi	tin		di	pi	tin		di	pi	tin		di
Baanë			zi	ki	li	ki	zi	ki	kpa		zi	ki	li	ki	zi	ki	kpa
Gle			X	x	x	X	x	x	X		X	x	x	X	x	x	X
Lök...*					kö	se		lö	kö	se			kö	se			lö

Figure 6.9. The rhythm *di-pi-tin* with pattern *lö-kö-'së* (* = optional). Transcribed by Daniel B. Reed.

Syllable	Drum	Hand	Type of sound
zi	right	right	open
ki	center	left	open
li	center	right	open
ki	left	left	open
zi	right	right	open
ki	center	left	open
kpa	center	right	slap

Figure 6.10. *Baanëyakwade* pattern for the rhythm *di-pi-tin*. Transcribed by Daniel B. Reed.

Drummers use the other two rhythms less frequently in Ge performance, because the great majority of *getannu* are sung to the *zi-k-ri* rhythm. Still, nearly every Ge performance features at least one *getan* that is accompanied by each of the other two rhythms. The name of the rhythm *di-pi-tin* mimics the sound the *zikri* plays (see Figures 6.8 and 6.9). The *zikri* drum's pattern for *di-pi-tin* begins with two closed strokes ("*di*" and "*pi*") followed by an open stroke ("*tin*"). The *lökö'së* player can choose from two different patterns: the pattern *kö-lö-lö* (Figure 6.8), which consists of three consecutive open strokes that rhythmically match every other of the *zikri*'s *dipitin* patterns (typically used at faster tempos), and the pattern *lö-kö-'së* (Figure 6.9), which is identical to the pattern played for the rhythm *zi-k-ri*. Open strokes on the *lökö'së* are much higher pitched than the *zikri* and resemble the sound of a large woodblock, so the pitches and timbres of the two drums' parts are quite distinct.

The *baanëyakwade* drum's pattern in *di-pi-tin* is played as shown in Figure 6.10.

Zikiri	ti		ti			din			ti		ti			din			ti		ti			din	
Baanëya..						kpi	ki	li	kpi		gblin		kpa*	kpi	ki	li	kpi		gblin		kpa*	kpi	ki
Gle					x	x		x	x		x		x	x		x	x		x		x	x	
Lökö'së*	kö	lö	lö						kö	lö	lö						kö	lö	lö				

Figure 6.11. The rhythm *ti-ti-din* (* = optional). Transcribed by Daniel B. Reed.

Syllable	Drum	Hand	Type of sound
kpi	left	left	open
ki	center	right	open
li	center	left	open
kpi	right	right	open
(REST)			
gblin	center and right	both	open
(REST)			
kpa	center	right	slap

Figure 6.12. *Baanëyakwade* pattern for the rhythm *ti-ti-din*. Transcribed by Daniel B. Reed.

Zikri	zi		k	ri				zi		k	ri		
Baanëya..	zi	ki	ni	li	kpa			zi	ki	ni	li	kpa	
Gle					x	x	x	x		x			
Dɔɔga	hi			lo				hi			lo		

Figure 6.13. The rhythm *zi-k-ri* as played for Gegbadë (with *dɔɔganu*). Transcribed by Daniel B. Reed.

Like the first two rhythms, the name of the third rhythm—*ti-ti-din*—comes from the mnemonic syllables used to teach the *zi-k-ri* drum pattern. For *ti-ti-din*, *zikri* drummers play two open strokes ("*ti ti*") followed by one closed stroke ("*din*") in the rhythm shown in Figure 6.11.

The optional *lökö'së* drum's pattern is identical to one of those that can be played for the rhythm *di-pi-tin*: three open strokes (*kö-lö-lö*). Drummers play the *Baanëyakwade* drum's pattern as shown in Figure 6.12. This pattern features a different sound—"*gblin*"—created by playing the center and right drums simultaneously, or nearly simultaneously, in a flam.[6] Because the two heads are tuned to different pitches, two distinct pitches are simultaneously audible, creating the effect of harmony. But since the drums are tuned variously, the intervals between the two pitches of *gblin* also vary.

The iron bell adds another component to Gegbadë performance. Figure 6.13 shows the rhythm *zi-k-ri* with the addition of the *dɔɔga* pattern. Note that I have not included the *lökö'së* pattern; at no Gegbadë performance that I attended was this drum used. The interlocking foundation of Gegbadë performances was always provided by the *zikri, baanëyakwade, gle,* and *dɔɔga.* In Figures 6.13 and 6.14 I represent the *dɔɔga* pattern with the words "hi" and "lo," referring to the two bells, one of which is pitched higher than the other. As in the case of the tuning of the drums, the pitches of the *dɔɔganu* are relative.

	di	pi	tin		di	pi	tin		di	pi	tin		di	pi	tin		di
Zikri	di	pi	tin		di	pi	tin		di	pi	tin		di	pi	tin		di
'Baanë			zi	ki	li	ki	zi	ki	kpa		zi	ki	li	ki	zi	ki	kpa
Gle			X	x	x	X	x	x	X		X	x	x	X	x	x	X
'Dɔɔga			hi		lo		hi				hi		lo		hi		

Figure 6.14. The rhythm *di-pi-tin* as played for Gegbadë (with *dɔɔganu*). Transcribed by Daniel B. Reed.

Though the vast majority of Gegbadë's *getannu* are sung to the rhythm *zi-k-ri*, occasionally *getannu* with *di-pi-tin* are performed. Figure 6.14 shows the rhythm *di-pi-tin* with the *dɔɔga* pattern.

IMPROVISATION, VARIATION, AND MASTERY

During the early stages of my lessons with Jean-Claude, I was a bit confused when I attended Ge performances. I was studiously learning and practicing the basic rhythms outlined above, but when present at Ge performances, especially those of Gedro, I had trouble picking out some of the patterns I had learned. As time went on, I began to understand why: the mark of a great drummer is the ability to vary the basic patterns through improvisation. As Gba Ernest taught me, "Doing variations is a measure of your mastery. If you haven't mastered things yet, you stick to the standard" (1997b). I also began to understand why I was having the most trouble following the drumming at Gedro performances. For more powerful *genu* such as Gegbadë, each section of music is very short—thirty seconds or a minute. Gegbadë performances are segmented into small pieces. He invokes a proverb, talks a bit more, sings a little on his own, then initiates a song that the drummers and singers pick up, always for a particular purpose. For example, he might initiate a song that enables him to read a person's destiny. This takes just a minute or so; he then gestures to stop the music and announces what he has seen. Since his musical segments are so short, accompanying drummers tend to stick with the standard rhythmic patterns. In contrast, during performances of dance *genu* such as Gedro, songs often go on for a long time, and accompanying drummers are more likely to introduce variations (ibid.).

Key in this process of variation is maintaining some essential integrity of the pattern while varying strokes in artful ways. The *zikri* player has the least

Zikiri	zi		ki	ri		(ri)	zi		ki	ri		(ri)
'Baanëya..	zi	ki	ni	li	kpa		zi	ki	ni	li	kpa	
Gle					x	x	x	x		x		
Lökö'së*	'së					kö	' së			lö		kö

Figure 6.15. Common variation for the pattern *zi-k-ri*. Transcribed by Daniel B. Reed.

	di	pi	tin		di	pi	tin		di	pi	tin		di	pi	tin		di
Zikri																	
ƁaanëÌ			zi	ki	li	ki	zi	ki	kpa	ki*	zi	ki	li	ki	zi	ki	kpa
Gle			X	x	x	X	x	x	X		X	x	x	X	x	x	X
Lök...*	kö	lö	lö					kö	lö	lö							kö

Figure 6.16. The rhythm *di-pi-tin* with common variation of *ɓaanëyakwade* pattern (* = optional). Transcribed by Daniel B. Reed.

flexibility. Still, when playing the *zi-k-ri* pattern, drummers frequently add the variation transcribed in Figure 6.15.

Of the accompanying drums, the *ɓaanëyakwade* is the instrument whose patterns are varied the most, in part because this multiheaded drum offers so many possibilities to imaginative players. In the later stages of my lessons with Jean-Claude, he began teaching me a repertoire of common *ɓaanëyakwade* variations. One of these variations is shown in Figure 6.16, in which Jean-Claude varies the standard *ɓaanëyakwade* pattern for *di-pi-tin* by adding a stroke at the end of the pattern, which I emphasize in bold. *Ɓaanëyakwade* players frequently alter the sound of their patterns by simply selecting different heads for the individual strokes of the pattern. Since the heads are pitched, the resulting melodic patterns change rather dramatically.

Yet another common variation is shown in Figure 6.17. In this example, not only is the extra beat added at the end of the pattern, but also the slap on the central drum disappears and the final three strokes are all played on the left drum (the variations from the standard pattern are in bold).

The variations presented here are common but elementary examples. Great *ɓaanëyakwade* players are master improvisers who follow the inspiration of the moment in deciding exactly what to play. Improvisation for *ɓaanëyakwade* players is analogous to improvisation for principal singers: a common repertoire of possible variations exist, but truly great artists improvise more freely, creating and incorporating new ideas on the spot.

Syllable	Drum	Hand	Type of sound
zi	right	right	open
ki	center	left	open
li	center	right	open
ki	left	left	open
zi	right	right	open
ki	**left**	**left**	**open**
ki	**left**	**right**	**open**
ki	**left**	**left**	**open**

Figure 6.17. Variation of *ɓaanëyakwade* pattern for the rhythm *di-pi-tin*. Transcribed by Daniel B. Reed.

Gba Ernest, who is renowned in the Man region for his skill on the *ɓaanë-yakwade,* varies the basic patterns constantly, accenting certain strokes, adding or subtracting strokes, and, as I mentioned above, varying which heads he uses to play the patterns. Musicians such as Gba Ernest are highly valued in the community of *gedëmɛn* not only because their virtuosity is impressive musically but also because it is effective spiritually. The skill with which Gba Ernest plays raises the intensity of a performance, inspiring both people and *genu* to the highest level of their abilities.

→ VIRTVOSITY as a facilitator for spiritual performance/etc.

TEMPO

Each of the three *getan* rhythms can be played at three different tempos. Tempo is a marker that associates a performance of a song with a certain genre of *ge.* The elder *ge* of the sacred hut, a *gegɔn* such as Gegbadë, generally dances to *getannu* played at the slowest tempo. Gedro and other dance *genu* generally dance to the medium tempo. The fastest tempo is associated with *giantan,* or war music—which is today most commonly played for the racing *ge.* In fact, both the medium and fast tempos are extremely quick. The *giantan* tempo is so fast that drummers are forced to simplify and minimize the patterns they play to keep up.

Genu can dance, however, to tempos other than the one most associated with them. For example, Jean-Claude told me "Gedro can be dancing, and everyone is tired, then someone can initiate a song that is always sung slowly, like a *gegɔn* song, to give everybody a break" (Goueu 1997b). Whoever then dances, be it a person or Gedro, will dance more slowly and gracefully, blending a Gedro style with that of a *gegɔn.* Conversely, a *gegɔn* might initiate a faster song, such as one associated with Gedro, to pick up the energy during a slow point in his performance. In this case, the *gegɔn* might dance a bit more rapidly than usual. But more likely, a person will ask for the *gegɔn's bisa* (flywhisk), which permits him or her to dance in the *ge's* stead. Because a *ge* of wisdom is old and wears a long heavy raffia skirt, a *gegɔn* cannot dance in the style of a rejoicing *ge.* In each case, the context dictates how the song will be performed.

Layering over top of the interlocking accompanying instruments is the sound of the *ɓaade. Baade* players are soloists. There is no way for me to represent in a simple distilled way what *ɓaade* players play, as I have for the accompanying instruments for each of the three standard rhythms. The *ɓaade,* however, is by far the most important instrument in the ensemble. The importance of the *ɓaade* lies in the role it plays in interactions between the master drummer and the *ge.*

THE AESTHETICS OF POWER: *BAADE* DRUMMING AS MEDIATION BETWEEN THE WORLDS

It is through the interaction between a *ge* and his master drummer that much communication takes place in Ge performance—between the worlds of humans and spirit, between performers and audience members, between and among performers themselves. In the process, *ge* performers negotiate boundaries between their religious identity and many other factors in their worlds. Overall, in Ge performance, music is *the* most fundamental instrumental force in manifesting power—the capacity to make things happen (cf. Arens and Karp 1989). Manifesting of power is achieved through the mediation through music of the mystical and corporeal realms. This functional capacity is inextricably linked to ideas about, and characteristics of, music sound in Ge performance.

No element of Ge performance is more important in this regard than the interactions that take place between the master drummer and the *ge*. This inter-action is the most important aspect of the performances of both Gedro and Geg-badë. However, the communication that takes place between the master drummer and *ge* during Gedro performance is quite different from that which takes place in performances of Gegbadë. Jean-Claude taught me much about similarities and differences between his roles with each *ge*.

One day in 1997, in the courtyard of Théodore's sacred house, Jacques and I sat with members of the Gegbadë group—Jean-Claude, Théodore, and others—waiting for a performance to begin. On a bench under the shade of a mango tree, we talked, joked, drummed, and drank palm wine. After a while, Théodore brought the drums out of the sacred house for tuning. Jean-Claude began tapping the nylon-rope rings that surround the head of each drum with the wooden club designed specially for this purpose. As he pounded each ring, the heads of each drum tightened, rising in pitch to the desired high and resonant ringing tone. Théodore casually tapped his hand on each drum, evaluating their sounds. Jean-Claude had brought along his own *ɓaaɗe* from the sacred house in Petit Gbapleu. When Théodore tapped this instrument, his brow furrowed and he exclaimed, "That's not Ge." He went on to say that this drum was better suited for dances than for the manifestation of a *zu ge*. Only later, in my lessons with Gba Ernest and Jean-Claude, would I learn what Théodore had meant.

In my music lessons, I learned that the master drumming for a *zu ge* mani-festation must be *gbin* (heavy). A *ɓaaɗe* for any Ge performance, but especially a more serious and more sacred *ge* such as a *zu ge*, must be more *gbin* than one used for other purposes such as dances where no *ge* is present. As has been noted elsewhere in West Africa (Stone 1982; Waterman 1990a) indigenous West African aesthetic terms sometimes do not directly correlate to aesthetic terms used com-monly in Western musicological discourse. This term, "*gbin*," and the term to which it contrasts, "*kpɛɛ*" (dry), bring together, in single terms, aesthetic pref-erences that many North American musicians would describe using three different words: pitch, timbre, and volume.[7]

As its translation "heavy" suggests, *gbin* means deeper, or lower in pitch. Yet it also has timbral qualities, including a certain resonance that is produced by a *ɓaaɗe* tuned so that it is lower in pitch. Also contributing to the heaviness of the sound are metal resonators called *ɓaasɛ* (sing.), which are often attached to the *ɓaaɗe* to add what Jean-Claude calls *ziing* (Goueu 1997h). I found this point especially interesting. The addition of *ɓaasɛnu* to the drum adds a sound that is common in much African music—a buzzing or rattling timbre. Shona musicians in Zimbabwe add bottle caps to their *mbiras* to create this effect (Berliner 1978). Mande harp and jembe players attach metal resonators very similar to *ɓaasɛnu* to their instruments to produce the same rattling effect (Charry 2000, 217). Many other examples could be provided, as this is one of the aesthetic characteristics most common in music of Africa. Yet I had never before considered this "rattling" effect anything remotely like "heavy." To my ears, this sound is unpitched. But if I had to discuss it in terms of pitch, I would say that it adds a kind of high-frequency brilliance, something I would sooner call "high" than "low" or "heavy." *Gbin,* however, is a rich concept which exceeds the limitations my musical vo-cabulary placed upon my own my previous experience of sound. *Gbin* might also refer to a sense of density in which multiple sounds interact to create layers of different timbres, which is another effect achieved by the addition of *ɓaasɛnu* to drums. For Jean-Claude, and those who initiated him, the addition of the *ɓaasɛ* makes the sound heavier, which is preferred for *ge*—and especially highly sacred *ge*—performance.

A certain drumming technique is also used to make the sound more *gbin*. When a drummer uses more of his hand—all the fingers, even the palm—and strikes the drum closer to the center of its head, lower frequencies are produced, resulting in a heavier sound. In contrast, a drummer achieves a *kpɛɛ* sound by using less of his hand, striking the head of the drum closer to the rim and with only a few fingers or even a single finger. This produces a sound more appropriate for a dance or entertainment *ge*, but is not at all desired for a highly sacred *ge* such as a *zu ge*.

My consultants also used the terms "*gbin*" and "*lourd*" ("heavy" in French) to describe *genu* who are considered to be more sacred in the power hierarchy of Ge. To emphasize just how serious, potentially dangerous, or powerful a particular *ge* is, one might say, "But that *ge*, now he is *gbin!*" This last use of the term "*gbin*" reiterates my point that this term, and the preference for heavier-sounding drums in *zu ge* performance—indeed, *getan* aesthetics overall—conceptually extend beyond what is merely pleasant to the ear. Creating a heavy sound enables Jean-Claude to accomplish specific goals. *Zu ge* drums must be heavier sounding—resonant, deeper in pitch, and louder—so they can be heard from great distances. People everywhere, even those farthest away, must be able to hear the drum clearly so that they know that a powerful *ge* is present. Even more important, the sound must be *gbin* so that the appropriate *yinannu* hear it and are attracted by it to the performance space to empower the *ge*. The more *gbin* a *ge* is, the more *gbin* the drumming must be; there is a direct correlation between the relative spiritual power of each *ge* and the desired sound of the drums in Ge performance. This is what Théodore was referring to when he complained that Jean-Claude's *ɓaaɗe* was "not Ge" (Goueu 1997f).[8]

While heavier-sounding master drumming is generally preferred for Gegbadë, Jean-Claude taught me that aesthetics, along with tempo and pacing, change according to Gegbadë's needs during the course of a performance. There are three different modes of master drumming for a *ge* such as Gegbadë. Each of these three modes corresponds with one of the three different types of *yinan*: *yinannu* of joy, *yinannu* of destiny, and *yinannu* of war.

The *yinannu* of joy are called at the beginning of a performance—to manifest the *ge*—and at other times throughout the performance when Gegbadë simply wants to dance for joy (in contrast to dancing for other purposes). At these moments, Jean-Claude plays mostly on just two drums—the large central drum and the smaller one on the left. He plays fairly rapid patterns and draws a *kpɛɛ* sound out of his instrument. The tempo and sound of the drums inspire feelings of joy in Gegbadë, and he dances joyously. Jean-Claude's drummed solos synchronize with Gegbadë's choreographed dance routines, which range in duration from around five to twenty seconds. When Jean-Claude taught me about this in our lessons, he called this musical/dance interaction "*ɓaagen*" (drum's feet) or "*pas de danse*" (dance steps). That is, he did not use separate words to describe what the *ge* does and what he himself plays. He was not playing rhythms or rhythmic patterns or anything else that I might describe using musical terminology; rather, he played dance steps on his drum. There is no separate word in Jean-Claude's dialect of Dan that means simply "music." "*Tan*" means music and dance simultaneously. That Jean-Claude called the rehearsed solos he plays while Gedro dances "dance steps" reinforces the idea that music and dance are deeply connected ideas in the minds of some Dan people.

When calling the *yinannu* of joy, Jean-Claude and Gegbadë have fun, challenging each other through music and dance. Usually, Gegbadë leads and Jean-Claude must play along with the dance steps the *ge* has chosen. If a performance has lasted a long time, Gegbadë might run out of rehearsed dance steps. In such cases, both Gegbadë and Jean-Claude are free to spontaneously create dance steps that the other must try to follow. Jean-Claude told me that this is a competition of sorts. If Jean-Claude plays a dance step that the *ge* has trouble matching in movement, he wins one point. Likewise, if Gegbadë spontaneously creates a dance step that throws off Jean-Claude, chalk up one point for the *ge*. In the spirit of joy, the two principal players in this performance challenge one another to create increasingly more difficult, more interesting dance steps, which the other will later be required to practice so that he is not bested again at a future performance. There are multiple levels of communication occurring during the time that the *yinannu* of joy are being called. Performers weave moments of levity into the generally serious performances.

The second approach to drumming relates to one of Gegbadë's primary roles—his ability to read peoples' destinies. As in the narrative in Chapter 1 in which Djomande hired Gegbadë to find a cure for his wife's illness, people frequently hire Gegbadë to look into their futures and divine what they should do to solve problems. Gegbadë performs this task by using music to communicate with the *yinannu* of destiny. One of the ways Gegbadë receives messages from the *yinannu* is through his *téléphone*—a power object that he holds to his ear. For the message to come through the *téléphone,* however, Jean-Claude must drum in a *gbin* style, using only the two children drums—those smaller drums attached to the larger central drum. Figure 6.18 shows one of the patterns Jean-Claude frequently plays to draw the *yinan*'s message through the *téléphone.*

Another divination method Gegbadë uses is to initiate a song specific to this purpose, after which he sits down to wait for the *yinannu* to arrive with their message. Nothing will happen without the aid of the master drummer. While the song progresses, at the moment when Gegbadë senses the potential message, Jean-Claude plays only the two children drums toward the centers of their heads and using his whole hand to produce a particularly *gbin* sound. Jean-Claude must be careful not to overplay at this moment. He told me:

> You play a little, you stop. You do a step, you stop. You do one, you stop. Because the *ge* can let the music continue to sound, and at the same time, speak the destiny, at the same time, talk . . . to the person whom he is addressing. If you play too much, the person will not understand what the *ge* says. (Goueu 1997i)

Figure 6.18. Rhythm to activate *téléphone.* Transcribed by Daniel B. Reed.

The accompanying drummers remain especially attentive to the master drummer during this time, as he might cue them to slow the tempo a bit or lower their volume. So in this instance, the master drummer must first enable the communication between the *ge* and the *yinannu* and then direct the ensemble in the moments immediately thereafter so that the communication between the *ge* and his client is effective.

(3) The third mode of master drumming for Gegbadë is reserved for those moments when the *ge* is ready to combat sorcerers by chasing away their negative spiritual power (*duyaa*). In such instances, Jean-Claude must play rapidly and constantly. He does not stop and start, as he does when the *ge* wants to read someone's destiny. Rather, he plays loud and fast solos in order to draw the *yinannu* of war to the *ge,* to make him "ferocious." Jean-Claude distinguishes what he plays at these moments from dance steps. In other words, these are not rehearsed *kpɛɛ*-sounding patterns. To call the *yinannu* of war, Jean-Claude plays wildly, in a less smooth and controlled way than he does to call the *yinannu* of joy. And Gegbadë dances accordingly—turning and turning wildly with frightening quick gestures. Most commonly, the *yinannu* of war are called during what performers called "war songs" played in the rhythm *di-pi-tin* at a fast tempo.

Frequently, at these moments, Gegbadë's energetic dancing takes him far away from the group of drummers and singers and toward, for example, someone he suspects of wrongdoing. No longer is he tranquil, like when he is reading someone's destiny. He now moves wildly around within the circle of the performance space. Jean-Claude must remain alert for this, because when the *ge* moves away, he must follow, playing his drum in such a way as to keep the *yinannu* of war present. When he leaves the group and enters into the circle of the performance space to follow the *ge,* Jean-Claude uses his drum to communicate to the rest of the group what is happening. Figure 6.19 shows the pattern he plays to inform the other drummers that he is about to leave to follow the *ge.* The accompanying drummers then know that they must play even more loudly themselves, so that Jean-Claude, who will be far away and playing loudly next to the *ge,* can hear the repeating rhythmic patterns well and stay with the group.

Drumming empowers Gegbadë to receive spiritual messages, the drummers using music, as Friedson writes, to "make translucent the boundary between human and spirit" (Friedson 1996, 100). The interaction between the master drummer and Gegbadë is critical in linking the *zu ge* to the mystical realm. Drumming furthermore is crucial as a means of communication, helping performers and audience members understand what is going on at important moments of Gegbadë performances.

As in Gegbadë performances, the communication that takes place between the *ge* and the master drummer is the visual and aural focal point during performances of Gedro. But the type of communication differs. Gedro has no need

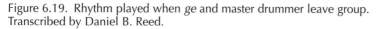

Figure 6.19. Rhythm played when *ge* and master drummer leave group. Transcribed by Daniel B. Reed.

of the *yinan* of destiny or war. His sole purpose is to dance for joy. While Jean-Claude does use his drum to call the *yinan* of joy for Gedro, equally important is his use of the drum to incorporate influences from traditional and popular dances in their midst and posit relationship to the world around them. Jean-Claude's responsibilities as master drummer for Gedro thus differ from what is expected of him when he drums for Gegbadë. For both *genu,* however, the master drummer serves the crucial role of mediator—between performers and the contemporary corporeal world in which they live (the focus of drumming for Gedro) and between performers and *geɓɔ,* the world of the spirits (the focus of drumming for Gegbadë). I was able to understand this only in music lessons, where I learned the importance of the interactions between the master drum and the *ge.* Drums, as one of the primary means of communication which make these mediations possible, are instruments in more than one sense of the word. Drums in Ge performance are instruments of social and religious action.

SEVEN

Gedro at Gueheva

By far the majority of our field experiences never see the light of day, remaining tucked away in notebooks full of illegible field notes and in the corners of our minds full of competing and fading memories. Yet contained within these oft-forgotten pages are often found the crucial moments of transformation that make fieldwork what it is. Metamorphoses, the changes that take place in our understanding and in our own consciousness as we learn about another culture, are rarely included in our epistemologies, yet they are the basis of our analytical constructs. Up to this point in the book I have led the reader down a path that might seem to represent Ge and my understanding of Ge as a contained and containable phenomenon. Yet the reality of fieldwork is not so simple. In doing fieldwork we remain in our own cultural skin, even as we live and breathe in, and attempt to understand, a wholly different world. We move back and forth between our worldview and those of others and become amphibious in a sense (Gottlieb and Graham 1993, 254). We are in two worlds at once, an experience Gottlieb and Graham call "parallel worlds" (1993). When we then return home from the field and begin writing based on our field experiences, we remain somewhat betwixt and between. Bodily, we are back home, and yet, as if dreaming, our consciousness floats back and forth between here and now and the people and events in the field that so profoundly transformed our thinking.

In this chapter and Chapter 8, I present narratives constructed from the interweaving of two voices: my voice from Côte d'Ivoire, 1997, represented by original field notes which appear in italics, and my voice from back home in the United States, which is in roman typeface. These voices have much in common and yet are distinct in certain key ways. One way in which these voices differ is in their relative degrees of removal from the ethnographic experience. The original field notes are themselves removed from the experiences they describe, but far less so than the writing I have done since returning home. The voice from home has been written after a great deal more reflection and consultation—with Jacques, other consultants in feedback interviews, Nicole, and other colleagues, students, and mentors—and after repeated listening to field recordings, viewing of field videos, and reading of interview transcripts, field notes, and field video indexes. Sometimes, then, despite its greater distance from my field experiences, this voice offers greater descriptive detail than do my field notes.

These two voices, however, also have much in common. Both voices include narrative description and preliminary analysis. Both voices include input from others. In some cases, detailed conversations with people occurred between my original experiences of events and the moment when I committed these experiences to paper in the form of field notes. Thus, both voices are, to greater or lesser extents, polyvocal creations. By incorporating field notes into this text I lay open my research process, exposing strengths and weaknesses, smooth roads and rough edges, things I am proud of and things I am not. In so doing, I invite the reader one step closer to a direct look at how I know what I know about Ge performance.

GEDRO AT GUEHEVA

On March 28th and 29th, 1997, I attended the first annual Gueheva Festival of Masks and Traditional Dance at the Leon Robert Stadium in the center of Man. For two full days, several thousand locals, tourists from other parts of Côte d'Ivoire and neighboring countries, and a small number of Europeans, Asians, and North Americans attended this controversial though popular event. The centerpiece of the Gueheva Festival (from the organizers' standpoint) was a stage set near the center of the soccer field, where speeches and performances occurred (though much action took place in other locations as well). Journalists from all the major Ivorian newspapers and television stations, the French Press Agency, and other media organizations were present to cover this rare event.

This was one of a handful of times in Ivorian history that masks have been gathered together to perform in a large-scale, government-sponsored festival in a stadium.[1] Twice before, in 1979 and 1983, the Ivorian government produced mask festivals in Man to promote tourism and advance the idea of the mask as a unifying symbol for Côte d'Ivoire (Steiner 1994, 96). Then, in 1987, the Ivorian Ministries of Tourism and Culture took the idea of a mask festival to a new, more explicitly national (and nationalistic) level by producing Festimask in the administrative capital (and home of President Félix Houphouet-Boigny) of Yamoussoukro. As Christopher Steiner has observed, Festimask, which featured mask performances by ethnic groups from all over Côte d'Ivoire, represented a kind of paradoxical effort on the part of the national government to both spotlight the nation's ethnic heterogeneity and bring "disparate ethnic groups together into a single, united cause" (1994, 97). Gueheva, like these previous festivals and many other smaller-scale government-sponsored events (such as the hairdresser's party discussed in Chapter 3) was clearly an effort by the Ivorian government to accomplish several goals, including promoting the ruling party (PDCI) through association with, if not appropriation of, locally and nationally popular masks.

Like the previous large-scale mask festivals, Gueheva was a controversial event. Some Ivorians deplored Gueheva, considering the festival to be a defamation of sacred traditions. Gueu Gbe Alphonse remonstrated that at Gueheva, "the mask was like an object of the circus" (Gueu Gbe 1997d). In an editorial in the national daily *Fraternité-Matin* just days after the festival, Zio Moussa blasted Gueheva as a "profanation of the sacred" and asked if the death of masks would not be better than their "folklorization" (a strong pejorative in French) (Zio 1997). Yet for the youthful Gedro group from Petit Gbapleu, the Gueheva Festival was an ideal setting in which to dance and drum complex identities that are both rooted in Dan history and related to the contemporary world in which they live. This was a chance to demonstrate to the diverse crowd of thousands that despite the fact that many of their elders had embraced Islam and abandoned Ge, despite the growing influence of Christianity, despite the ubiquitous presence on the streets of Man of mediated popular musics and expressive traditions of other ethnic groups, Ge was still central to their lives.

31 March 1997, Man. We arrived early—8:00—Fri. morning. The event was scheduled to begin at 9:30 with a "Cérémonie d'ouverture" and "Allocutions"— speeches. When we arrived, there was practically no one there. We tried to decide where to set up, over the din of a CRANKED-UP P.A. Gradually, people began filling the stands of the stadium. At one point, the blasting P.A. was turned off, which was a relief in and of itself, and a group of women sitting waiting in the stands began passing the time by singing, entertaining themselves. This was so refreshing, and I wished they would turn the damn P.A. off for good. This brought to mind the contrast I see here between, say, Déoulé [one of the villages where I conducted research], *where people still entertain themselves, and Domoraud* [the neighborhood where we lived in Man], *where that happens to a lesser extent and people listen to the radio, cassettes, etc. more. . . . a theme running through the whole event—the P.A. drowned out the women singing just as the police and organizers dominated the authority of the masks.*

Eventually, masks [Dan *genu*, along with masks of Wobé, Guéré, Mau, and other peoples] *began to arrive through the same gate as the spectators—the main gate into the stadium. Some walked in, complete with their ensembles of musicians, etc. Others arrived in gbarkas. Some arrived in big city-owned work trucks, sitting flamboyantly on top of the cab, or perched on a seat in the back, towering above the steadily increasing crowds. . . .*

Not a single group arrived out of performance mode. Each group came through the gate as if it was a grand entrance onto the public square of a village, with much pomp and circumstance. This was no entrance, in street clothes, through a backstage door. Always, it was at least a processional, if not a full-out performance—singing, dancing, etc. [Elder women's groups danced through the gates shaking iron-pellet rattles and singing. Young girls' groups entered dancing Temate to the sound of rapid drum rhythms. Dan jugglers strutted in, performing gymnastic moves with little girls wearing headdresses and white face paint.] *Other musical groups arrived as well . . . including a huge group of dozow* [members of the multiethnic hunters' society] *who had evidently been hired as a special security force.* [Not true—they came of their own volition as part of their campaign to make an impression on the Ivorian public that they are a security force superior to the state police and army (Bakoyoko 1997).] *The dozo entrance took me by surprise, partially because their dress, their demeanor and their music was so contrasting to the other groups. They came in single file, like soldiers holding their guns on their shoulders, very calm, subdued, and dignified, wearing leather skins. Arrogant, poised. And with a dozongoni* [hunter's harp] *player, an iron rasp, and some kind of shaman-like figure. They circled the whole field, then formed a circle together near the gate, before breaking apart, forming a kind of security line around the soccer field. . . .*

As each mask and dance group arrived, they did so in grand style—the masks, especially the stilt genu, immediately dancing and drawing a crowd. Thus, before the festival actually "began," it began despite itself, despite the plans of the organizers. Spread out all over the field, in bleachers, on the racetrack around the field, were groups of people in constantly shifting circles—masks would move, and spectators would follow them, something hot would occur, people would flock. Masks of different ethnic groups danced together (some had attendants carrying signs identifying mask and village). [This was a true interethnic celebration. Perhaps the most extreme and wonderful example was when Jacques and I saw a Mau stilt mask (from northwest Côte d'Ivoire) dance a Gouro mask rhythm (from the center of the country) to the drumming of a local Jula ensemble.] *Some danced to pop music rhythms.* [I saw a Dan stilt *ge* drink soda pop from a bottle. All the while, pop music blasted from the stage.] *It was a veritable fête. Thus, the festival began as it would continue—resisting the kind of structure the officials had intended, spontaneously exploding[,] like when masks come out in the village.*

Eventually, long after the printed 9:30 start time (11:30–12:00?), the MC started asking the mask group leaders (on behalf of the organizers) to take all masks into the stadium annex—a smaller, walled-off area connected by a gate to one end of the stadium. Since the MC had been sound-checking and then gabbing through the P.A. (over the loud music) the whole morning, it was kind of a boy-who-cried-wolf situation in that it was not a clear "beginning," at least not to me, and it took a very long time for it to have an impact; he had to repeat it over and over. Slowly, the masks began obeying, dancing and performing, of course, the whole way there, and thus taking crowds with them.

Eventually, the "ouverture" and "allocutions" began. Speeches by the mayor, the préfet, etc. This was interesting to a point, but after a while my attention began drifting toward the main gate where masks continued arriving in grand style. I ran into Tia [Mameri Tia Thomas—my main consultant from Déoulé], *and we went there* [to the main gate] *together. I then asked him (he had some kind of loose role of authority at the festival* [working for the mayor's office]) *if he thought I would be permitted to go into the annex to see what was going on there. I was curious because it seemed like hordes of people were curious, and trying to catch glimpses in, each time the gate would open a bit. He said that, with my authorization, it was no problem.* [I had purchased badges from the mayor's office granting me permission to move freely to film and photograph the event. Journalists had these same badges.]

So, we fought our way through a mildly dangerous crowd to the gate, glanced in past the police violently preventing people from entering [flogging them with leather straps], *and saw . . . not a backstage scene of performers seated, waiting to be called, but rather a performance, a fête de manifestations in full swing, again resisting the structure of the program. They were willing to be corralled into the annex (reluctantly willing), but they damn sure weren't going to stop the party. They were out, after all—masks don't tend to sit still—these types anyway— in public (others do—think of the one that oversaw the excisée dance in Dompleu in '94).*

After many, many speeches (which Nicole audio recorded), they finally announced that the "défilé" [parade] was set to begin. Kinesthetically and proxemically, the procession was fascinating. First of all, it was a line, leading from the annex gate up the running track in-between the stage and the main bleachers after which it dissolved into a kind of continuing dance/party spread out around the soccer field [where people formed circles around each group, returning to this more familiar spatial organization]. *Again, both the masks and the audience con-*

stantly resisted the linear approach. Masks kept breaking out of the line, to go dance "naturally" in the grassy/dirt area in front of the stands, wowing the crowds[,] who would cheer in approval. And people were constantly spilling over the lines demarcating the "performance" space, either kids sneaking out from beneath the stands or people curling out toward the action; police and soldiers kept beating them back with leather straps.

Certain masks really took the limelight and were seemingly permitted to "break the rules," leave the line[,] and give a solo performance. My impression was that the authorities were simply giving in spontaneously, reacting to the moment, realizing how unpopular a move it would be to halt something that really pleased the crowd. Every mask that did this, though, was eventually given the boot.

The procession, and for that matter the whole festival, was fascinating from a power or authority point of view. Perhaps at the top of the pyramid were the organizers—represented at the event by the two MCs who constantly tried to keep things moving and cut masks off (especially during the next part—the stage performances) and by others in plain clothes with "Comité d'organisation" badges who were ushering and directing people and masks constantly. Then were the police and army folks—beating back crowds and keeping masks and their attendants from transgressing spatially [.] There were throughout the event lines that were not to be crossed but were constantly challenged, and it was mostly the police and army who took control of this. But the dozo, discussed earlier, had a similar role. Finally, a Sakpe [a *ge* who manifests to keep order, usually during performances of other *genu*] *was directing people around as well, as he would do in a "traditional" event.*

Somewhere near the bottom of this heap were the masks themselves and their gekianu, musicians, etc., and the directors of the groups, at least one of which seemed to be present from each village. Yet the masks, mask group directors, etc., who are accustomed to being in charge, constantly resisted this positioning— defying, sometimes very directly and deliberately, the authority assumed by the organizers (refusing to quit the stage "on time," for example), and the police (see, especially, video footage of the stilt ge defiantly dancing toward the police zone, across a line beyond which he was not supposed to be). Then over top of all, completely hands-off and ceremonial, were the officials like the Préfet, Minister of Culture and, especially, the Mayor [all representing the ultimate power of the PDCI, which was behind the organization of the event]. *These overlaying, different systems of authority were fascinating.*

Thus, overall, the masks et al. were resisting both the spatial and temporal ordering of the event. Actually, it wasn't just the masks and dancers who resisted the temporal structure—the pre-printed program was almost completely abandoned by the authorities as well. Friday the 28th both the opening ceremonies and the procession began hours late, and the "animation populaire" in town was limited, and certainly didn't "begin" at any particular hour (20:00—the program said). Both days, the masks seem to have for the most part danced home to their sacred houses improvised in local schools, entertaining folks a little at that location (according to at least one report in Libreville [a neighborhood of Man]*), before retiring for the night (the schedule had stated that there would be a break and that things would begin again at predetermined times).*

The conference, most unfortunately, on "Place et Rôle de Masque dans la Société d'Aujourd'hui" didn't even happen [though a similar one did occur a few weeks later]—*a grave disappointment for me. The 10:30 "exhibition" of masks* [the stage show] *may have started by 12 or 1 on Saturday, even though they had announced a 9 A.M. start the previous night when they had run out of time to exhibit all the dances then. The "Dîner-Gala" was also cancelled.*

[Beginning late in the afternoon on the 27th, and continuing on the 28th, performing groups took the stage, one at a time, for very brief "exhibitions." At least thirty-eight masks and more than thirty dance groups each were given between two and ten minutes to perform before they were hurried off the stage.] *The presentation of the masks on stage was somewhat ludicrous. The masks that obeyed and stayed on stage (and there were many that didn't) obviously felt constrained by the space, and the musicians all were forced to stay put on a platform at the back of the stage, fixed as they never are in a village. Then came the ostensibly polite "Merci's" from the MCs that were often euphemisms for "Get the fuck off the stage, you stage hog—your time is up!!"*

By the midafternoon of the second day of the festival, time had begun to drag. I was exhausted, having spent two days straight under the oppressive dry-season sun, trading off photographing and videotaping with Jacques. I had made the mistake the first day of wearing a sleeveless Dan *bubu*, and I cursed my foolishness, knowing that sunburn and mild heatstroke were partially to blame for my utter weariness. Yet I was also frankly tired of masks and of the whole festival. Early on the day before it had been fascinating, but by this point I found my attention drifting, watching as group after group spent a brief moment on stage before being rudely ferried off by the MCs. Masks were all starting to look the same.

Judging by the behavior of the crowd, I was not alone in my increasing malaise. The audience had become smaller. The first day, the stage was surrounded by spectators and journalists with camcorders and cameras. Now the crowd under the sun had thinned out, though the grandstand remained packed beyond capacity. Fewer spontaneous dances were occurring around the soccer field. I noticed many people socializing, paying little attention to the stage. It began to feel as if the whole affair had gone on long enough and people were just riding it out to the end. Some people were getting tired and impatient. Directors of groups began approaching the MCs and organizers, pleading for their groups to be the next called to the stage. The MCs grew weary of this, and arguments broke out. It seemed that many group directors worried that they were losing the moment—that by the time they got on stage, no one would care.

It was in this context that Gedro of Petit Gbapleu was called to the stage. I recognized the name of the neighborhood, since people had told me that it was well known for *genu*. But this was the first time I had heard of this *ge* who would become so important to my research. I immediately perked up when the crowd began cheering as soon as Gedro took the stage and his group began singing a song to the rhythm *zi-k-ri* played at a typically Gedro rapid tempo. MCs positioned themselves just in front of Jean-Claude's *ɓaaɗe* and the *zikri* with microphones, so that the master drumming patterns and the primary underlying rhythm were clearly audible over the other instruments and the call-and-response singing of the men and women who crowded the high platform at the back of the stage. This brief performance consisted of segments; like all Gedro performances, the *ge* and master drummer Jean-Claude layered short dance-step routines over the continual percussive polyrhythm. Gedro and Jean-Claude began with several traditional dance-step routines. After each, the crowd responded with cheers. Gedro danced using short, sharp movements, isolating his feet and legs. For the most part, his upper body remained still, though he accented his leg movements with large sweeping movements of his arms. His raffia skirt exaggerated movements of his hips. About one minute into the performance, the *ye ye* began. Following an aural cue from Jean-Claude, they launched into two successive routines of the popular Zaouli mask from the Gouro region. At the end of the first Zaouli segment, the crowd exploded into cheers that continued on as they began the best-known Zaouli rhythmic pattern. Gedro's feet moved almost too quickly for my eyes to follow, perfectly in sync with the sound of the *ɓaadɛ*. Gedro marked the Zaouli segment's completion by dropping to his knees and thrusting his pelvis repeatedly in time with the rhythm, as if making love with an imaginary partner. In response, the crowd broke out into an uproar of screaming applause. An envoy was sent from the grandstand to invite Gedro to come greet Mayor Bouys Philippe of Man and the visiting Ivorian minister of culture.

As the crowd cheered and the *zi-k-ri* rhythm continued, Gedro and his *gekia* hopped off the stage to follow the envoy to the mayor's seat in the font row of the stands. Milking this moment, Gedro stopped midway for a traditional routine, which ended with him cocking his head side to side in time with each exaggerated long step toward the Mayor's seat in the stands. The applause continued to increase in volume and intensity. Once Gedro arrived on the grandstand, first the mayor, then the minister of culture rose to greet him and shake his hand. [They probably also offered monetary gifts, though I was not in a good position to see if they did.] Then Gedro turned toward the stage and gestured a cue to Jean-Claude. They proceeded to do three short routines, Gedro dancing immediately in front of the politicians, before he ran down the grandstand stairs.

As Gedro ran back toward the stage, Jean-Claude played the aural cue that signals the beginning of *zigblithy*—the dance step associated with the popular-music style of the same name. Responding to this cue, the *ge* again stopped midway between the stands and the stage and without missing a beat joined Jean-Claude in the elaborate *zigblithy* routine. After he finished this with a characteristic pelvic thrust, Gedro ran back to the stage to the sound of uproarious applause. Spontaneously, the crowd began chanting *"Bissez! Bissez! Bissez!"* (Encore!). The minister of culture again stood, stepped over to Mayor Bouys, grabbed his hand, and lifted his arm in the air in a congratulatory gesture, as if to say, "The festival has been a grand success!" An MC initiated a popular Ivorian call-and-response chant which is used "to heat up a crowd" (Biemi Gba Jacques), shouting over and over *"Ye-i!"* into the mike, the crowd responding in kind. Gedro gladly honored their request by taking the stage to dance some more.

All in all, this was extraordinary, given that just a few minutes earlier the feeling in the air was that everyone was sick and tired and ready to go home. During the whole festival, only two other masks had been invited to greet Mayor Buoys. Only one other mask had received anything close to the reception accorded to Gedro, and that was the featured guest of the festival, the only mask who was not from the western region of the country—the Gouro mask Zaouli himself. The reaction to Gedro reflected the fact that this *ge* had become a local superstar, a *ge* popular across a wide spectrum of religious and ethnic lines.

In this context, Gedro's performance held multiple meanings. For many Muslims and Christians and members of other ethnic groups in the audience, this was entertainment, not a religious experience. But for the performers, this was sacred.

By incorporating popular music and dance, Gedro performers made the enactment of their religious identity relevant to their contemporary context and attempted to make a living doing so. Through Gedro performance, performers enacted their dynamic and fluid notion of tradition that is perfectly suited to their desires to adapt their identities to changing circumstances. Their incorporation of popular influences appealed to a broad cross-section of Man residents, many of whom were more familiar with the latest hits than with deep Dan culture. And with their very presence on stage performing a *ge,* Gedro performers deliberately distinguished themselves from their Muslim elders who had abandoned "the tradition." If Ge performance is the manifestation of Dan ideals, then an idealization of Dan identity for Gedro performers in 1997 was both rooted in the ways of the ancestors and cunningly cosmopolitan.

Like the performers, some local governmental officials viewed this festival as meaningful and profitable. Mayor Buoys and his first assistant, Deputy Mayor Oulai Siaba, are both Dan men who sincerely wished both to promote local cultural practice and to generate tourist revenues for the community. And yet, similar to what happened at the PDCI hairdresser's party, the visiting minister of culture, the mayor's office, and all local offices representing the national ruling party also used this occasion to shore up their political power in the region, benefiting by association with the popular masks.

The controversy over the very idea of this festival exemplifies changing and heterogeneous notions of what Ge is and what kinds of performance contexts are appropriate for even a less sacred dance *ge.* For some, Gueheva was a natural extension of the boundaries of Ge in a contemporary, increasingly more diverse social and religious context. For others, this event went beyond the limits of acceptability; it was sacrilege. All in all, this event clearly demonstrated the negotiation of religious, ethnic, and power boundaries that occurred through Ge performance in late twentieth-century Côte d'Ivoire.

EIGHT

Gegbadë at Yokoboué

Generally speaking, in Côte d'Ivoire, younger people are expected to obey the wishes of elders. Elder males regularly make "requests" which the young feel strong social pressure to honor. Such was the case when, in the summer of 1997, Jacques began getting "requests" from *zumi* Oulai Théodore to use our phone. As a result, Jacques became a middleman in the negotiations for Gegbadë to embark on a major business trip. Through a series of phone calls, Jacques helped set up a job for Gegbadë's group more than 400 kilometers away in Yokoboué—a village in the Dida ethnic region on the south-central coast of Côte d'Ivoire. In the process, we became acquainted with the woman who hired the *ge* for this trip: Madame Amso Edomtchi.[1] Through numerous phone calls, visits by Edomtchi and her family to Man, and our own trips to Yokoboué and her present home in Abidjan, we grew to know and befriend Edomtchi. And we learned her story about why she had sought out Gegbadë.

Madame Amso Edomtchi had tried everything. Having grown up in Yokoboué, a predominantly Christian town situated 120 kilometers west of the capital city of Abidjan, Edomtchi had been taught that prayer was the solution to problems. Her faith in Jesus and regular attendance at church had always been successful strategies in dealing with life's challenges. A friend of hers told me, "Before, when you said 'church,' it was Madame Edomtchi!" When Edomtchi began seeking for solutions to her sorcery-related problems outside the Church, it was astounding to those around her.

Things that are extraordinary, unexplainable, that are, as Edomtchi said, "beyond" her, she attributes to sorcery. Rampant crop failure, consistent inability of children to succeed in school, failure to complete what should otherwise be a simple task such as building a home, medically unexplainable health problems often leading to death—these are some common complaints which lead to accusations of sorcery crimes. And they are crimes; the practice of sorcery is illegal in Côte d'Ivoire. Prior to 1981, the Ivorian judiciary used the French legal code, which did not recognize the existence of sorcery. Ivorian officials created the Ivorian Penal Code in 1981 (Aggrey 1981) in an effort to adapt the French judicial system to the Ivorian social and cultural context. One such adaptation was the introduction of anti-sorcery legislation, which criminalized the practice of sorcery.[2] Many Ivorians I know hold that the spiritual power behind sorcery is neutral and that only the positive use of this power can effectively combat its negative use. Still, the word itself—"*sorcellerie*" or "sorcery"—is generally used to refer solely to negative sorcery. For the purposes of this narrative, I will likewise use the term "sorcery" to refer only to socially destructive spiritual action—what my Dan consultants called *duyaa*—and "sorcerer" to refer to practitioners of such action.[3]

When Edomtchi's father died an untimely and unexplainable death several years ago, no one in her devoutly Christian family believed that sorcerers could have been responsible. But death continued to haunt the family. One of Edomtchi's brothers, a powerful magistrate who, like Edomtchi, lived in Abidjan, fell ill. Edomtchi told me that her family

> did everything. We went everywhere with him. Zero. We could find nothing wrong . . . and at the last moment . . . before his death, one of his daughters also died, who was only three years old. She died. Fourth, another brother, a professor, he died of the same illness. You go to the hospital, they examine you, they find nothing at all, you return to the house, you suffer. You see? It's then that we began to ask ourselves the question—people talk about sorcery—does it exist? (Amso 1997)

In more recent years, misfortune spread through the family, even reaching Edomtchi herself. Edomtchi was a rather typical victim of sorcery. Born into a privileged, relatively wealthy family, Edomtchi moved from Yokoboué to Abidjan, founded a successful bakery business, and built a fine, rather lavish home. But troubles followed her. All the equipment in her bakery stopped working at once. She was in three car accidents over a short period of time. Her theory about why she has been mystically attacked: she kept her financial success to herself, unacceptable in Ivorian society where wealthier people are often expected to provide for their less fortunate family members.[4] Her problems started when, she says, a fellow native of Yokoboué living in Abidjan spread news of her success to people back home in the village.

But it was not her own ill fortune that finally inspired Edomtchi to seek for solutions outside the church. Watching family members suffer and die became too much for Edomtchi to bear. This, she and other members of her family decided, was a matter that was not approachable through the Church. Because she was dealing with sorcery—something created not by God but by the devil—the only defense was to call upon people and spiritual powers familiar with this domain.

In late 1996, Edomtchi's family heard about a successful anti-sorcery campaign in the nearby town of Guitri and decided to seek out the party responsible for solving Guitri's problems. Guitri, though in the Dida ethnic region, is home to a small population of Dan migrant workers. Twice, these Dan migrant workers had hired Gegbadë and his group, who journeyed by bus from Man to the migrant community in the Dida region. The indigenous Dida population took notice of the effectiveness with which Gegbadë dealt with sorcery among the Dan population. Word spread to Madame Edomtchi's family, and they made the decision to call Oulai Théodore, head of the sacred hut that houses this powerful and renowned *zu ge*.

The call to Oulai Théodore was not the only call that needed to be made in this situation. Because sorcery is illegal, the process of prosecuting sorcery crimes legally must involve the federal government.[5] For the first several years of the anti-sorcery law's existence, the Ivorian judiciary attempted to handle this problem themselves. But, as federal prosecutor Kone Seydou told me, they found it difficult to handle this mystical problem with a system of justice based on the French model, which requires the presentation of objectifiable evidence in a courtroom setting. Frustrated, in the mid-1980s, the judiciary changed strategies and began relying on traditional experts to identify guilty parties and hand them over to the courts. Edomtchi followed the standard legal procedure, procuring a legal certificate from the General Secretary (a federal official) of her region authorizing Gegbadë to go to work in Yokoboué.

In December 1996, Edomtchi hired Théodore to make an initial trip to Yokoboué. This first trip was merely diagnostic in nature. Gegbadë performed, confirming that sorcery was the cause of the family's problems, but stated that a return trip would be necessary for him to begin actually solving the problem. In the meantime, things kept getting worse. In the summer of 1997, her family began experiencing unprecedented tragedy. Seven people died in just a few months—young and old—most in medically unexplainable ways. Then an eighth, a young girl just ten years old. Edomtchi's prayers were not working, and she decided to go back to Théodore.

Many opposed Edomtchi's continued interest in the *zu ge*. Rumors about which villagers were responsible for the sorcery began to circulate in Yokoboué, and debate and controversy raged. Edomtchi's Christian friends objected to the idea of seeking for a solution outside the church. They told her that sorcery is a falsehood and urged her simply to trust in God's power. But she argued that they were not looking at the situation realistically. She told me:

> We trust in the Lord, and despite the fact that we are in the Church, in the prayer, people die. And who dies? It's the doctors, the *sous-préfets,* the *préfets,* the lawyers who die. And after that, the young. . . . I have tried everything. Those who say go only to church, it's false! I believe in God, but sorcery *exists*! . . . It's now that I have noticed that it's two different things. Do you understand? Here, sorcerers are attacking us. The Lord is there, he is there for us all. But he has no way to crush sorcerers. Nothing at all! So if there is a fetisher or someone who has that power, you go and have that person wash you [in sorcery-repellant medicine], and then you go pray! But if you say, yes, I am going to pray and then, two to three days of the sickness continues, and [the Lord] has not taken it away, you get the idea? I prefer to go to . . . someone who can save me. You see? And then afterwards, if I have regained my strength, I will go see God. . . . Really, this is a situation you cannot neglect. If you neglect it, it's as if you have sold your life to the sorcerers. Sorcerers do not fear God. They are not afraid of the men of God. They kill them as they wish. That's all—it's true! They are not afraid! . . . This is the reality that one cannot flee. (Amso 1997)

In early August, 1997, Edomtchi's family again hired Oulai Théodore and his troupe of ten musicians, ritual specialists, and assistants to travel by bus from Man to Yokoboué. Edomtchi and her family timed the *zu ge* group's arrival to coincide with the funeral for the latest sorcery victim. They did so because they knew that their whole family would be present for the funeral, and they suspected certain members of their family.[6] The *zu ge* troupe was being housed in a half-finished California-style villa being built in the village by Edomtchi's family. The day after the official Catholic funeral mass, the *zu ge*'s work began.

Jacques made the trip to Yokoboué with the *zu ge* group. Nicole and I went first by bus to Abidjan to meet several American friends who had expressed an interest in joining us. They had heard a great deal about our experiences with *genu* (some had come out to visit us in Man) and wanted to explore the possibility of attending the event. I was leery of this—arriving with an entourage of Americans at this conflict-ridden event. Though by this time I had long since abandoned my initial apprehension toward studying sorcery-catching *genu*, I remained sensitive to the fact that my presence at these performances could be viewed as an intrusion. I was afraid that if I brought along several American friends, the people involved might have the impression that I saw this as no more than a tourist masquerade. But both Théodore and Edomtchi had insisted that bringing my friends to the event would be fine, so we went ahead. Besides, I thought later, though these events are grave and full of deep social discord, they are public rituals, and virtually anyone is free to attend. So attend we did, arriving in Yokoboué in our friend Leslie's American Embassy car—a gleaming fancy Toyota.

3 August 1997, Grand Lahou. We arrived on Friday afternoon from Abidjan— Nicole, Leah, Susanna, Leslie and I packed into Leslie's sleek WHITE of all colors Celica. . . . As we anticipated, we felt like extraterrestrials, elite extraterrestrials, arriving in the gleaming WHITE spaceship Celica. After spending our first seven months arriving at places like locals do—in taxis, bush taxis, buses, or gbarkas, Nicole and I were keenly aware of how odd and obvious we felt. How much of a difference it made to the villagers I don't know; perhaps it was mitigated by the fact that we had contacts there. As soon as I got out of the car to ask for info, a young man approached me, described Jacques and asked if I was there to meet him. I breathed a sigh of relief—it's always so great—those moments of feeling welcome here [in Africa] due to contacts. He instructed us to wait in his maquis [an open-air bar] while he sent a petit [a young boy] off to find Jacques. We had a drink and waited. Eventually two young men arrived who were part of the funeral organizing party and had been sent by Théodore to accompany us to meet him. Since we weren't yet done with our drinks, we invited them to sit down and finish our beer with us. While we were drinking, Jacques arrived, so we got the news.

The body had yet to arrive, so nothing had begun: the funeral party, those who had hired the ge, were not even yet in town. Since it was already 5:00ish, and it was clear that if anything were to happen that day, it would not be for hours, we opted to go to Grand Lahou and find a hotel, eat dinner, and come back later. I was immediately intrigued by the villagers' speculation that the ge might come out at night: Gegbadë always comes out only during the day—Théodore has a different gbɛnge [night ge] that comes out at night. At this point, the predictions, however, included [the following]: late in the evening, after the body has arrived; even later, during the wake; after midnight when everyone would be there (the chief and others had "fled" according to the young men [the chief and other elders were alleged suspects]); or, the next morning at 7:30 A.M. This I have come to expect, especially with this ge: there are always a bevy of predictions. While things with entertainment genu are always unpredictable, they seem ordered and predictable compared with events of a zu ge. There is so much conflict surrounding every manifestation that things never go "as planned," and there are usually several forecasts of possible times [for events to begin]. . . .

[We came back later that night, and were led to the compound where Théodore and his staff were being housed.] *We followed paths through the town for about ten minutes before arriving at a huge, gated courtyard on the outskirts. We entered the driveway and approached a huge, California-style villa, typical of the kind that village noteworthies who live in Abidjan are building in their home villages all over the country. This, like many, was not completely finished* [I later learned that this was attributed to the work of sorcerers as well], *and the huge rooms opening onto the expansive, L-shaped porch suggested less an unfinished U.S. home than some mix of a U.S. house and a large Roman meeting house. I continue to be fascinated by the ways Ivorians appropriate and reshape Western architectural ideas. Like our Attie neighbors* [in Man] *who have transformed the "garage" into their kitchen, this house had space for a yard, which was filled with 5-ft. high flowering weeds, and the distinction between "inside" and "outside" was largely erased.*

There, we met and greeted the Man folks, who we later learned were prisoners of sorts in this lavish villa. Now having waited 24 hours, they felt safer remaining quarantined in the compound's walls, since many there [in the village] *were not in support of their presence. Reluctantly, Théodore had granted Dominique and Jean-Claude permission to wander around a bit, so they weren't there, but we greeted everyone else and sat down to talk with Théodore, who did not rise to greet us but remained planted in a chair on the porch in a long, blue and cream Dan bubu. This did not seem unfriendly, but rather, dignified; Susanna later pointed out that she knew immediately who he was by his demeanor. He thanked us for coming, but told us that nothing would happen that night, and that we should return in the morning.*

[Late the next morning, we returned to the villa, wondering whether the family would have worked things out yet to the point that the group could begin working.] . . . *Jacques wasn't there. Théodore was either asleep or "preparing." People were sitting around, looking either edgy, bored, or both as a result of their continuing confinement and inactivity. Eventually, both Théodore and Jacques arrived. I was really concerned for Jacques, who said he was panicked about getting to his friend's wedding, slated for 3:00 in Abidjan. I tried to convince him to leave immediately, but he refused. We had constantly interrupted conversations, and, through Jacques, Théodore and I discussed things as well. I convinced Jacques to leave with us* [to get him to his wedding—one of the many things I was feeling was guilt, as Jacques' employer, that he was about to miss his friend's wedding (he was in the wedding party) because of work with me], *and explained to Théodore in a halted dialogue, interrupted by angry words between Théodore and his hosts about the continuing delays, that we were going to leave, that since it was already getting late, and nothing appeared to be happening soon, the situation was messy, and the last thing he needed was us around. Plus, we had left our friend* [Leslie] *on the beach, and had to be sure we got back to her before the last departing ferry* [she was at old Grand Lahou—which is accessible only by a boat ride across a lagoon; she would have been stranded alone had we not made the last "ferry" (actually just a small outboard boat) to join her]. *He understood.*

This all took a really long time, though. In the U.S. this would have been a ten-minute conversation and we would have been out of there. But we couldn't leave without formally addressing Théodore, through a mediator—Jacques—and this was slowed by the constant interruptions to deal with the problematic ar-rangements [between the warring family members and between Théodore and those who had hired him]. *But at no point did I have the feeling that anything was changing, just that everything remained unsure . . . we were trying to extri-cate ourselves from an event that, as rumor had it at the moment, might not occur at all.*

Sometime in the midst of all this, several middle-aged people—Madame Edomtchi, another woman[,] and a man—arrived and summoned Théodore. Théodore then called me over, asked why I had to leave, and began beseeching Jacques to stay to film. I resisted, explaining that I would love to [stay] *but I would keep my friends idly waiting, and that I believed Jacques should get out of* there pronto [to get to his wedding]. *Théodore relented with me but insisted that Jacques stay. Jacques accepted* [acquiescing to the authority of the "grand" or elder], *thereby missing his friend's wedding. I began to feel terribly guilty, and offered to stay in his stead, etc. But they wouldn't have it.*

Returning to my friends, I learned that Susanna and Leah now really wanted to stay—a switch from their earlier positions. [This was an extremely complicated moment for me—worried about Jacques on one hand; worried that I was keeping Leah, Susanna, and Nicole at this potentially dangerous event unwisely; worried what negative effects our presence could have on this conflict-ridden event. . . . Frankly, relaxing on the beach with Leslie at that moment seemed a very ap-pealing alternative to the mess we were in.] *Suddenly, I saw drums appear on the terrace, and the ge folks vanish into the house. Jacques said things would begin in an hour, but I respected no such predictions. Nevertheless, it suddenly dawned on me that the atmosphere had shifted and that things were happening—prepa-rations were underway and moving quickly. This was an "expandable moment"* [Stone 1988, 82]—*after things had seemed to be running in place, people were frustrated, ready to give up, etc., all of the sudden things had shifted to a different level of intensity, to a qualitatively different "feel." I was invited back into a room where Jean-Claude, Dominique, et al. were changing into their protective, dyed brown bubus, and decided things were definitely happening, and we all decided to stay.*

It was decided for us that to leave WHITE-mobile there during the event would be unsafe as it would be unprotected; there was continued fear that folks associated with the ge could be targeted for misdeeds. So we drove the car to the site of the event [the afflicted family's compound], *and walked back. Shortly thereafter, the musicians emerged onto the terrace, and the first "wɛɓoo wɛnze" was intoned.*

It was fun to experience this vicariously through Susanna and Leah's ex-citement. The atmosphere was joyous and intense, as if all the waiting and dis-puting had only made the debut that much sweeter, buoyed by a feeling of relief combined with the intense joy that I notice marks the calling of these spirits. Dominique danced before the drummers, Jean-Claude played like fire, Boni char-acteristically punctuating his zi-k-ris with occasional bursts of louder volume. I explained to Leah and Susanna that this was all to draw the spirits down, to inspire the ge to emerge. Leah later commented that before I had said this she had had the impression that they were simply getting warmed up, and I remem-

bered that not so long ago I had thought the same. At moments like that I realize that I now understand these events, that I can "read" them, from an informed point of view.

SIDEBAR: all of the following description is heavily influenced by a fascinating "debriefing" from later that night, wherein, to share with Leslie what she had missed, the four of us [Nicole, Susanna, Leah, and I] *took turns recounting different periods of time during the event. I wish I could have recorded this! Hearing peoples' different impressions,* how *they chose to describe* what *they chose to describe, was fabulous.* . . .

At the musicians' request, I began filming, even though it had been agreed upon, at a meeting in Man between Jacques, Théodore, Paul (of the family hiring the mask), Seri and me that Jacques should film because he could be accepted [by others] *as part of their group, while I could not. Interesting, the identity thing again—in this context, I am the outsider, because of my skin color.* [In some other contexts, I had felt less this way—for example, when drumming, I often felt 'inside' by virtue of my identity as a musician in a way Jacques did not. My feelings of my own identity were constantly shifting and were different in every context.] *Nevertheless, I filmed the debut, as the musicians raised the energy, and they approached the suburban hallway where one room had been transformed into a sacred house. At one earlier moment in the preparations, Théodore had invited me in* . . . [this part I cannot reproduce here, as I am not authorized to report on the goings-on inside sacred houses].[7]

[At this moment, Théodore and Gegbadë emerged from the sacred space created in the bedroom. Prior to their emergence, and throughout the manifestation, music plays vital and specific roles. As Zemp has observed, the Dan frequently use music to draw power to themselves while simultaneously chasing away fatigue and fear (1971, 175). The first song's refrain, "*do n ka,*" states simply "Send me," implying "send me to the battle." The musicians, wearing sorcery-deflecting shirts, augmented their invulnerability by singing this song, inspiring the courage, fervor, and confidence that protected them as they engaged in this dangerous work. Their faces alternatively betrayed a fiercely serious determination and joy. *Zu ge* music is intended to be joyous, as is the whole affair of combating sorcery, which is a celebration of the superior power of good over evil. The music draws to the members of the group not only joy, protection, and the power to prevail but also, and more fundamentally, the will to give themselves over to good, to act properly even in the face of great adversity. In short, by playing this music, the musicians draw to themselves the power of Ge.

The *ge* physically manifested only when the musicians had raised the spiritual intensity to the necessarily high level. On this day in Yokoboué, the musicians played for about twenty-five minutes before Gegbadë emerged from the sacred space created in the bedroom.

At this event, Jean-Claude was in his familiar role as master drummer, playing the *ɓaadɛ* and leading the musical ensemble. Accompanying musicians that day were Boniface on *zikri*, Gedegba on *ɓaanëyakwade*, Seri on *dɔɔga*, Santa on *gle*, and a small all-male chorus (the women who frequently perform with the group back in Man did not come along on this long journey). Dominique and Jerome served as *gekianu*, though at the performance site, each would also take on more specific roles: Jerome as *gewodïöyɔrɔmɛn*—intermediary for the *ge* (lit., "the person who repeats the words of the *ge*")—and Dominique as *zumiwodïöyɔrɔmɛn*—intermediary for the *zumi*.

The role of *zumiwodïöyɔrɔmɛn* was required at this event because Théodore worked alongside Gegbadë, taking on the role of *geazumi*—or the *ge*'s *zumi*. Théodore later explained to me that before any manifestation, he consults the *yinannu* in his sacred house, asking them how he should approach the particular situation he has been hired to resolve. Sometimes the visibly present *ge* himself directs the performance. In other contexts, however, Théodore himself is present alongside Gegbadë. A third possibility is that Théodore alone goes to tackle a problem without any *ge* physically present. However, and this is a crucial point, a *ge* need not be *visually* present to be a participant in the event. Théodore himself can channel the power of his *genu*. The faces of the *ge* need not be worn for their power to manifest (Vandenhoute 1989 [1952], 29). And some *genu* have no physical manifestation at all and are manifest only in the combination of certain musical sounds or in particular behaviors. This is the case for Théodore, who, through his behavior, and with the aid of music, has the capability to draw on the power of *genu* to do his work. This is one reason he is such an effective *zumi*.]

Gegbadë danced briefly, and as everyone prepared to walk to the event site, I passed the camcorder to Jacques. As we began walking to the site, accompanied only by the gle and dɔɔga. [The singers sang in *gbakwi* style, to keep the energy high, to protect both the *ge* and themselves during the vulnerable time spent en route.]

Susanna later described this early part of the event really well, . . . but when she mentioned how quickly we had all walked toward the site, it struck me how unusual this was. This ge usually walks along slowly, hands on hips, showing age, wisdom. We were speeding along at a healthy clip, as if to show determination and resolve to act quickly and now. [The look on Théodore's face was one of concentrated anger and determination.] *Théodore walked alongside the ge, dressed in jeans, an anti-sorcery bubu, and a Nike "Just Do It" cap on his head.* [Another member of the family of the deceased—Francois—walked in front of the entire entourage carrying a shotgun. This was later used to shoot into the air when the sorcerer's fetishes were being discovered.[8] To me, this added to the feeling of tension, to the feeling that they were heading into a battle. Somehow I had become a reporter of this conflict. Alain, Edomtchi, Paul, Francois, and other members of the immediate family were distinguishable by their clothing, made of a special commemorative cloth in a light blue and white pattern that was worn for the funeral].[9]

Along the way we aroused much interest[,] and many people, kids especially, joined, following the ge marching to the compound. [This happens in Dan country as well but was more pronounced here—perhaps because the Dida do not practice mask performance, so this was a novelty.]. *Susanna asked a woman about the suspicions; this woman told her that many people thought it was the mask himself who was responsible for the continuing deaths.* [Since the situation had worsened so much since Théodore's first visit, many in the village were now placing the blame on him and what they were calling his "magic."]

SIDEBAR: The day before, talking with the young men in the maquis, we learned that seven members of the family had been killed, the latest being a young girl. These young guys expressed great resolve to act—they want to develop and modernize Yokoboué, and expressed disdain for the older folks whom they said were keeping the village mired in old ways and despair with this relentless, stubborn sorcery. Later on in the event, while following Théodore into the forest, Paul told me they have a suspect or suspects. So there is much conflict surrounding

*this thing: some villagers blaming the mask, others members of their own family,
some embracing sorcery, some rejecting it, others fighting it.*

*We arrived in the compound, and a crowd packed into the small space be-
tween buildings, forming a tight circle under and around a palm shelter the family
had constructed to block the sun during the funeral.* [To our surprise, another
man was already filming the scene in the compound. Edomtchi later told us that
she had hired this man to film, using her video camera, so she would have a record
of the day's events.] *The people within and near the middle of the circle were
asked to remove their shoes.*

*It became immediately clear that it would be Théodore and not Gegbadë
who would be the star of this show.* [Théodore stood tall and imposing, holding
two items in his right hand: a *bisa* and what looked like a miniature bamboo mat
which he later used to locate the sorcerers' fetishes.] *He began by complaining
to Edomtchi's family about their poor treatment of his group—having to wait two
days* [to work] *when Jean-Claude's wife was ready to give birth any moment, etc.*
[and here he was hundreds of kilometers away]. *He addressed everything to a
middle-aged man named Alain, though not directly. Rather, the two men interacted through the intermediary of Dominique.* [Théodore spoke in Dan, which
probably no one understood, it being a local language of an area far away, one
of roughly sixty local languages in Côte d'Ivoire. Since he was speaking the words
of the *ge,* though, he had to speak in Dan. At a performance in the Dan region,
the person charged with passing on Théodore's words would have done so in Dan.
Here, Dominique repeated Théodore's words in French, so that the predominantly
Dida public would understand. Dominique's role was not just one of translator,
though. As *zumiwoɗiöyɔrɔmɛn,* he served as an intermediary between the powerful *zumi* and all people with whom he interacted. Théodore did not speak directly to nor did he receive words directly from Alain. Dominique also repeated
everything Alain said, translating it into Dan for Théodore, though Théodore is,
of course, a perfectly fluent French speaker. As he transmitted Théodore's words,
Dominique held the *sraman* bell in one hand and in the other a fetish I had never
before seen: it had the shape of the kind of ice scooper found in hotel ice ma-
chines, and, like the *télévision,* appeared to be leather on the outside with mirrors
and cowrie shells attached.] *Off to the side rested the ge on the ground, while the
musicians framed one end of the courtyard.*

*For about the first thirty minutes, after airing his complaints, Théodore introduced
himself and his presence. Much of* [his opening speech] *centered around boasting,
though not in an arrogant way—it was like the beginning of a rap album. . . .
Occasionally, at dramatic moments, he initiated a song. For example, at one point,
he shouted, "ɓa nu!" (I have arrived!),* then turned, threw his arms into the air,
and sang the same phrase to the musicians, who re-launched into a gbakwi-full
"ɗo n ka." Théodore walked toward Jean-Claude and stood facing him, his arms
open wide.* [Jean-Claude responded by drumming a rapid-fire roll using just his
two smaller children drums, creating a *gbin* sound to draw the power into Théodore's body.] *After thirty seconds or so, Théodore silenced them and began speaking again.*

At Gegbadë events, the high art of oratory plays an instrumental role. It is
the visually manifest Gegbadë himself who speaks at many events, weaving together proverbs with persuasive arguments like a fine lawyer and a priest wrapped
into one. At this event, Gegbadë said little, mostly resting on the ground, while

Théodore did the talking. Using our videotape of the event, Jacques transcribed, and I translated, the following excerpt from Théodore's opening speech:

> Alain, thank you. You know, things that are said behind a man's back, no one says in front of me. Do you understand? It's me, when that happens, I circumcise sorcerers. I have come! Those who were talking about me, may they come speak in front of me, so that they can give themselves a deadline. Again, I am here in this village! And we are going to see each other [those who can "see"—sorcerers and those who can combat them]. You know, I have been here once before in this village. What goes on in this village, I know it all! You know [sarcastically], the magic that I do—I have come! The *true* things that I do—I have arrived! They [the sorcerers] must leave the young alone! All that they have made [sorcery-wise], they need only muster it all and try to throw that stuff at me! Everything that they have, let them muster it. They should not be saying, "It's *me* who was not here in the village [when an act of sorcery took place]! That's why I give you this proverb: "I have eaten the head of an owl; thus, what is the head of a millet-eater?" [Owls are associated with sorcery, while a millet-eater is a small pesky bird that destroys millet crops.] *I* respect men, but the *sorcerer* remains directionless. It was sorcerers who killed Jesus. The sorcerer knows no good. When God created Jesus, people, we did not trust in him. And they went and they killed him! Will they now trust in Théodore? It's God who sent Jesus. He sent him as his messenger, and he said that he came to watch over the people of the earth. But it was we who live on the earth, we did not trust in Jesus. And then they killed him! That's why we ask forgiveness. Is this like that—Théodore, it's him whom we will trust? So calm yourselves, cool your hearts. Alain, you and your family have had words here [are in conflict]. So I have arrived!

This, in my mind, served two purposes: it obviously linked Théodore to Christ—a self-glorifying comparison, but [it] also associated the sorcerers there with those who killed Christ. This seems to be a "Don't kill the messenger" strategy, fending off attacks on himself, which he also addressed directly, saying "People say here I just do magic. Let them come forward now" . . . etc. [I also was intrigued by the fact that Théodore chose a Christian analogy here, given that this was such a predominantly Christian town. When working for the Mau man in Grand Gbapleu, Gegbadë sang many songs in Mau, including one that referred to Allah. Here, Dominique was translating Théodore's words into French. Yokoboué residents are also conversant in the language of the Bible. Thus, choosing a Christian analogy was a communicative strategy. Since 1989, when Gegbadë made his first long-distance journey to work (in San Pedro, on the southwest coast), his reputation and geographic range has continually widened. He adapts his performance to the context at hand. Just as Gedro now dances popular-music rhythms, Gegbadë chooses new communicative strategies to match his increasingly diverse clientele.]

At one point, he called a young boy out of the crowd to come forward, saying, "Don't be afraid" (which his body language and face definitely suggested that he was), and instructed him to lift the komo, or television, which the boy did. During the minute or so he held it aloft, Théodore looked into the television very intently, from different angles, clearly killing two birds with one stone, doing some "reading" while also demonstrating that it was not at all heavy (setting the sit-

uation up in case later an accused person would be asked to lift it—sorcerers cannot lift it).

Another early spoken motif was "I'm here—you have called—what do you want me to do?" [He stated several options—that he could find the sorcerer's fetishes and destroy them or he could "plant" something in the family compound which would compel the guilty to eventually come forward—either of these options would require him to return another time to finish the work of confronting the accused.] *After several repetitions of this, Edomtchi, who had hired him, spoke up, loud and clear, that people were dying and that finding those responsible was what they were asking him to do. She spoke forcefully, and afterwards the crowd applauded heartily, releasing some of the palpable tension in the air. One woman near me said, "That's Madame Edomtchi! When she talks, even men are quiet!"* [Nicole and I really enjoyed this moment, after so many months living in an extremely patriarchal area where strong public statements from women like this were very rare.]

Throughout, maybe it's even banal to say, but just so I don't start taking things for granted: he uses his bisa like a phone [the one he actually calls his telephone], *his komo he calls his television, he wears a Nike hat, makes references to Jesus, stays in a villa, a bedroom becomes a sacred house. These things exist, these Ge manifestations, very much in the context of modernity.*

When Théodore would sense sorcery's presence, he would smile, a big, toothy ear-to-ear smile. This is joyous for them—the music is uplifting, and the whole event designed to welcome and make use of positive spirits in battling negative forces. It's a battle, but in waging it they don't forget, in fact they need, forces of joy.

Eventually, Théodore began looking over the heads of people behind us and saying that he saw something in a tree. (He did this after leaving the center to tour the compound, so that he knew the family compound's exact limits). We all assumed he was referring to a tree we could see from the compound. But suddenly, he cleared a path through the circle of people and began marching with the musicians through the village, toward the forest. [Gegbadë stayed behind in the compound.] *The whole time, Seri marched alongside Théodore, playing an insistent, duple rhythm on the dɔɔga bells. Many of us present followed him for about 15 minutes down a trail, passing first a banana farm, a forest, more fields, yet more forest. . . . We were all instructed to pick leaves and carry them along the way, somehow in support of the ge.* [Dozens of people hurriedly followed Théodore as he marched quickly up the trail. At this moment, there was a near-festive feeling in the air, especially among children who rushed ahead, waving green leaves, chasing the sound of the dɔɔga through the forest. Yet many people seemed simultaneously excited and frightened. The slightest crack of a twig underfoot caused people to scurry back in nervous laughter.] [Finally, Théodore] *settled beneath a tree in a partially cleared area. Beneath the tree, Théodore spoke again, saying that he saw the family's compound there* [at the base of that tree], *meaning that this is where the sorcerers were holding their meetings. So he could see the negative compound replicated there* [in a mystical sense—sorcerers work in a parallel realm].

Théodore led everyone back from the forest and now began actively looking for the sorcerer's fetishes. Upon returning to the compound, the musicians began performing again. Unlike before, when Théodore had been directing them, they now initiated songs on their own, singing *tankwi* between the songs, as usual.

After everyone was back and things were settled, the musicians stopped playing, though Seri continued from time to time on the ɗɔɔga bells. Théodore asked the family to bring forward a bucket and to fill it with water. He took off his hat and washed his head in what he called the "medicated" water. (I am not sure if he placed a plant solution or something in the water—I assume he must have.) Théodore kept his attention fixed on one particular house in the compound—a rectangular thatched-roof building. Occasionally, he took the small bamboo mat and held it up, facing the house. This mat had two flaps, each of which was about four inches square, with a hinge connecting them in the middle. When he oriented this object toward something, if the two flaps opened up and remained open, this was a sign that sorcery was present (see Figure 4.3). When Théodore faced this object toward the house in question, it opened. Several times, Théodore entered the house, then returned to the courtyard. Finally, he came back out and talked with Alain. He asked Alain to direct everyone to cut leaves, from any tree, and hold them in their hands. Everyone began waving their leaves in the air. Then Alain led others in making a pile of leaves on the ground, so that they would be ready to be placed into the bucket when they had "caught" the fetish. Through this whole ordeal, Seri kept the ɗɔɔga bells ringing at a frenetic pace.

Théodore, Jerome, Seri, Jean-Claude, and Dominique then entered the house with two young Dida men and Alain and undressed in front of them. This was done to show that they had no fetishes hidden on their persons, to prove that this was not a magic act. While they all remained in the house, Guedegba (one of the drummers) shot the rifle into the air. The group inside the house dug a hole in the ground and waited. Fetishes are visible only to people with the power to see into this realm. Thus, at this moment, only Théodore could see the fetish. He grabbed it out of the air when it escaped from the hole they had dug in the ground floor of the house. Since the fetish becomes visible to others only when it comes into contact with sacred water, Théodore immediately placed it into the bucket. His aides covered the fetish with leaves, and they took it outside into the courtyard. Once back outside in front of the crowd, Théodore removed the fetish from the bucket and placed it on the ground for all to see.

As soon as the fetish appeared on the ground, many in the crowd covered their noses to stave off the stench. It stank like a cadaver or spoiled meat. It is much harder to describe what the fetish looked like. It was covered in a sticky, slimy black substance that made it difficult to identify its parts. According to Théodore, it consisted of some kind of container with three large snail shells attached to it and pens and locks inside. Théodore said that he had seen a snail in the forest at the place where the sorcerers met and that this snail shell had a role in the sorcerer's work. He had told Alain, while still there in the forest, that they would find a snail shell back in the compound. The pens were there, he said, to harm young students. The locks prevented the peoples' souls that the sorcerers had eaten from leaving.

Later that evening, Théodore found yet another fetish. At that point, he was satisfied that he had found the tools the sorcerers had been using to harm the family. He had not yet identified guilty parties. However, he later told me that he prefers to merely find the evidence and then let the guilty come forward of their own accord. When he accuses individuals himself, denials and fights break out (which I can attest to, having seen this occur at other Gegbadë manifestations). Although Edomtchi would have preferred that he settle the entire matter on that visit, Théodore and his group left several days later with plans to return at some later date to finish the work they had begun. When I left Côte d'Ivoire several months later, Théodore had not yet returned to Yokoboué to complete the work.

Shortly before I left Côte d'Ivoire, I met one last time with Edomtchi, who told me that one more person had died since Théodore's visit to Yokoboué, bringing the total to nine. She remained anxious for the whole affair to be settled, yet was unwavering in her belief in Théodore and his *zu ge*. She told me, "I like the mask because it's something that *cannot* be wrong!" (Amso 1997). Although Edomtchi had gone outside the church to seek a solution to her problems, she did not believe that calling upon a sorcery-seizing mask was inconsistent with her Christian faith. She told me

> Since the mask protects people, I think it comes from God. . . . [The mask] comes from the Lord. If he didn't have that power, he would not succeed. But [the mask] knows well, very well, that the devil exists. . . . I think that it comes from the Lord, that the spirit that is the mask comes from the Lord. (Amso 1997)

Edomtchi's statement of her beliefs indicates a creative, individually crafted synthesis of religious resources of disparate origins. Like Ge performers who strategically appropriate various outside sources into their performance, Edomtchi enacts her agency, integrating Ge into her own personal and syncretic version of Christianity that she believes is best suited to her pursuit of her goal: ending the rampant spread of death in her family.

Conflict is a central theme of this narrative. As I mentioned in the opening chapter, before my work with Gegbadë, I had never before been in the presence of people being accused of, and admitting to, murder. *Zu ge* performance deals with serious human discord. In my experience with sorcery, victims frequently seemed to have money. Edomtchi believed her wealth had something to do with her own victimization. Is sorcery an attempt to sanction those who do not respect the value of sharing resources, those who flaunt and hoard wealth? Are members of Edomtchi's family victims of "the leveling mechanism" of their jealous kin that C. F. Fisiy (1998) describes in his study of sorcery in Cameroon? Given that alleged suspects included the chief of Yokoboué (this was also the case in Bofesso—a case I alluded to in Chapter 1), might sorcery be at the center of power struggles between public authority figures and others (see Gottlieb 1989; Speed 1998)? How exactly does this ambiguous, secretive, mystical practice work? Gueu Gbe Alphonse contends that sorcery is a little-understood phenomenon, even among Dan people themselves. It was Gueu Gbe's hope that a future researcher would dedicate an entire ethnographic study to an exploration of sorcery among the Dan. For me, many questions remain around this topic.

What is clear, though, is that the Dan phenomenon of Ge is considered by many to be an effective sorcery combatant. The use of *getan* to bridge the mystical plane with that of humans and manifest Ge is distinctly Dan. Yet the power manifested by drums and songs of *getan* is not limited to Dan peoples. *Zu ge* music crosses both dimensional boundaries and ethnic boundaries when Théodore and his group enact Ge to solve sorcery problems of non-Dan people. As the efficacious aspect of the *zu ge* manifestation, music also brings together a Dan system of justice with that of the federal government of Côte d'Ivoire. And as

Edomtchi's words above show, *zu ge* performance, and specifically *zu ge* music, crosses religious boundaries as well.

Relationships between religions, between dimensions of existence, between ethnic groups, and between systems of justice are negotiated in this *zu ge* performance. The concept of Ge, which involves the embodiment in performance of fundamental notions of Dan religious and ethnic identity, expands at this moment in Ivorian history as Ge performers collaborate with the judiciary of the federal government. Likewise, federal governmental officials incorporate aspects of the traditional Dan system of justice, demonstrating that Ivorian judicial tradition, like all judicial traditions, is a dynamic interpretive process (Gadamer 1975). Meanwhile, through this performance Amso Edomtchi weaves aspects of Dan religion into her family's Christian tradition, thereby articulating her own unique Christian identity. And the *zu ge* performers apply their particularly Dan method of sorcery-detecting to the problems of this woman of another ethnicity and religious persuasion. All of this boundary negotiation transpires in this one performance, which centers around the most fundamental traversing of boundaries: the use of music sound to create what Paul Stoller calls a "fusion of the worlds" (1989, 31, 113) of the living and the dead, of human and spirit, of people and God. These are boundary negotiations with a purpose, boundaries crossed as people use *getan* to help them solve problems—maintenance of social order, reclamation of family health and peace, making a living, crafting identities, and finding the strength and courage to grapple with the challenges of a sometimes troublesome world.

In the beginning, there was a river. The river became a road
and the road branched out to the whole world. And because
the road was once a river it was always hungry.

—BEN OKRI, *THE FAMISHED ROAD*

NINE

Pathways of Communication and Transformation

This book began when I was on a road looking for a place to live in Man and crossed paths with a *ge*. Recently I traveled a different pathway, one of an intercontinental phone line to Abidjan. Through the distortion, delays, and echoes of a satellite connection, Jacques and I struggled to touch base, somehow weaving memories, present-day experiences, and future dreams into five minutes of conversation. I appealed to him to respond soon to a letter I had sent him including questions that had come up in the process of writing—a few translation clarifications, some content confirmations. Noting the sense of urgency in my voice (as my deadline was approaching), Jacques told me he would respond via a friend's e-mail account at the library of the Société Internationale de Linguistique. We asked each other to pass on greetings to family and friends. Then he proudly pronounced, "Goodbye." It being late evening in Abidjan, I responded "*i nyɛ së ɓo*"—sweet dreams. With my primary consultants, I am still walking this pathway of communication called fieldwork. Our ongoing conversations make up the core of this ethnography.

This book represents my experiences engaging in communication with various people about their experiences and interpretations of Ge and Ge performance. Ethnography, like life itself, is a field of interaction and intersubjectivity. I have researched Ge performances not in pursuit of a singular, bird's-eye perspective, but to explore, from multiple perspectives, why and how Ge performances mattered to Ivorians in the 1990s. For many of my consultants, their experiences with Ge have had profoundly transformative effects on their thinking and their lives. Let me offer just several of many possible examples.

For Jacques, the city-dweller from Abidjan, Ge had always been a connection to his roots and, along with Catholicism, a resource of moral and ethical guidelines. His initiation, directed by *genu* and with Ge as its guiding principle, had offered him invaluable experience in building character and learning proper behavior for Dan adults. Through his experiences with Ge during his participation in the fieldwork for this book, however, Jacques says he continued his initiation; as he said: "During the time that you did your research, I initiated myself." This statement speaks to both the inherent reciprocality of ethnography and the importance of Ge in Jacques' life. Through Ge, Jacques has deepened his knowledge of his identity as a Dan person, his sense of self. Moreover, for Jacques, Ge serves as a form of resistance. That the melodies, rhythms, and instruments of *getan*— themselves manifestations of Ge—are now used in Catholic worship services represents to Jacques a triumph of Ge, and Dan culture, over French colonial attempts to abolish local cultural practice and belief.

Oulai Théodore's life changed dramatically when he accepted what he views as his calling to work as a *zumi*. His reluctant acceptance of this calling forced him to recognize the power that spirits had over his life and that he could tap into this same power to help others and make a healthy living doing so. As a result, he crafted a new identity for himself. No longer a young Catholic intellectual training for a career as a hotelier, Théodore transformed himself, or he would say allowed himself to be transformed, into a master of Dan religious practice. In his work—a ritual involving traditional dance, music, and art and legal papers from the federal government—Théodore now naturally and comfortably combines elements of various traditions into a coherent syncretic whole that reflects and shapes his life as a contemporary Dan man.

Amso Edomtchi, one of Théodore's clients, experienced an equally transformative shift in understanding as a result of her involvement with Ge. No longer does she hold that all problems can be solved through the Catholic church. Edomtchi now believes in the power of the *zu ge,* who, she told me recently over the phone, finally succeeded in halting the killings in Yokoboué. Edomtchi's experiences have changed her beliefs, her religious practices, and her identity as a Christian. Music sound, the medium for the channeling of Ge to combat sorcery, is the operative force at the center of both Edomtchi's and Théodore's narratives.

Music was also at the center of Goueu Tia Jean-Claude's personal transformation through Ge. By choosing to be a master drummer for Ge performances, Jean-Claude achieved many goals, from earning much-needed cash to creating a complex identity for himself. By choosing Ge, Jean-Claude and his youthful comrades in the loosely organized rebellious Ge revival in Petit Gbapleu asserted identities in opposition to powerful Muslim elders in their community. Unlike in some other parts of West Africa, where Islam is eroding local cultural, artistic, and religious practice (see Monts 1998, 1984), in Petit Gbapleu young people revived local tradition, and rejected Islam, through performance. In an Ivorian context in which respect for elders is so highly valued that it is nearly absolute, these youth skipped over the power and authority of their elders to align themselves with what they saw as the more fundamental power and authority of the ultimate elders—the ancestors—and "the tradition." And yet Jean-Claude's choice of "the tradition" did not imply backwardness or conservatism. Through "the tradition," Jean-Claude drummed an identity that was worldly and aware, cosmopolitan and urbane. For Jean-Claude, Ge performance, a performance complex he defines as traditional, was a suitable expressive choice for a modern hip young Dan man. And not only was Ge performance a good fit for Jean-Claude, it was also in itself a vehicle for him to negotiate a complex modern identity in relationship to the pluralistic world around him.

Just as my consultants' experiences with Ge have transformed their lives and identities, my experiences studying Ge performance have shifted my perspective and understanding of the complexity, the processes, and the roles of a traditional performance complex in contemporary life. I have developed a deep appreciation for the ways people rely upon Ge to help them navigate their lives. When Ivorians are suffering, they have many options for relieving their pain. They can go to doctor's offices or hospitals. They can go to churches or mosques. They can consult priests or marabouts. Or they can call a *zumi* or a *zu ge*. People come to Théodore and Gegbadë when they are desperate for help. Their family members are sick or dying and they seek an end to their misery. Through performance, using music to activate powerful spirits, Gegbadë resolves their conflicts so their lives can return to normal. Gedro affects peoples' lives in ways that are different but no less meaningful. He dances for joy. When the rainy season ends and people harvest the fruits of their labor, when a loved one has died and her memory must be celebrated, when politicians seek to link themselves with powerful local symbols for public-relations purposes, when festival organizers need a form of entertainment that a diverse populace can appreciate, Gedro is called. The lives of many Ivorians are hard, marked by limited resources and unreachable dreams. Through their participation in the performances of Gedro and Gegbadë—as performers or audience members, as elder overseers of sacred houses, or as seekers of benedictions—they find meaning, hope, and the means to improve their lives.

I have studied these performances from multiple perspectives, with various people, to learn what meanings they generate in peoples' lives. At the center of my research was my work with performers and practitioners of Ge. They taught me how—through this complex phenomenon involving theory and action, ideas and behavior—they accomplished goals, from the mundane though imperative goal of earning a living to the profound work of creating meaning and identity for themselves. In relation to their changing and diversifying worlds, they negotiated religious and ethnic identity through their involvement with Ge. The musicians among them showed me how music was at the center of these negotiations. They taught me that the interaction between master drummers and dancing *genu* was the most important place to look for acts of communication that generate meaning in their lives. Both community and conflict, however, were created through Ge performance. By talking with others who were not performers and practitioners, I was able to see even more clearly how Ge performance held multiple meanings in 1990s Côte d'Ivoire. *Genu* were variously defined: as a part of a religious system, as a form of entertainment, as an economic industry, as a political tool, as an instrument of justice, as a form of resistance. Ge performance is an arena for communication of many kinds. It is a site for social action.

Ge performance integrates resources that originate outside of "the tradition" into a religious practice as cosmopolitan and dynamic as any that one might find around the world today. Like the road in the Ben Okri excerpt above, Ge performers branch out to the whole world through "the tradition." By making reference to Jesus and Allah, speaking and singing in numerous languages, and collaborating with the state judiciary, Théodore and Gegbadë demonstrate that the boundaries between Ge and the rest of the world are fluid and negotiable. Similarly, Jean-Claude and Gedro weave disparate rhythms and dances—some local, others from afar—into their performances, negotiating boundaries between the enactment of their religious and ethnic identity and the world in which they live. Both Gedro and Gegbadë performances exhibit negotiations between state and local power bases. As entertainment masks have done since the colonial era, Gedro dances to validate the state in numerous state-sponsored ceremonies and events. That state legal officials involve, indeed rely upon, Gegbadë to help enforce federal law indicates that local spiritual/religious authority can work to assert local autonomy in collaboration with hegemonic national power.[1] Ge performance metaphorically represents, in a single expressive form, contemporary African life, in which various traditions—some of local origin, others born anywhere from recording studios in Kinshasa to garment factories on other continents—coexist naturally and are interwoven by creative African agents (cf. Piot 1999). Like Okri's road, Ge performance is hungry. Ge performance shows that traditional arts can be a means through which performers ingest and digest the world, selecting new ideas and reshaping them to represent and shape their identities and feed their own needs.

Like many contemporary spirit-possession cults in Africa (see Behrend and Luig 1999), Ge performance is the farthest thing from a premodern practice; this manifestation of "the tradition" is not in opposition to, but rather is supportive of, modernity. What I find particularly interesting, though, is that performers themselves define Ge, this multifaceted concept and performance complex that is as much a part of their modern lives as buses and television, as traditional. This I see as my consultants' contribution to debates about the problematic terms of tradition and modernity. For Ge performers, Ge is absolutely traditional, and yet their notion of tradition, which is fluid, dynamic, and historically contingent, shows that the categories of tradition and modernity are not dichotomous and are relevant to their understanding of their lives.

My consultants taught me that their concept of theory and action called Ge— "the tradition"—is timeless and current, ahistorical and of the moment, eternal and in style. Glassie points out that although academics attempt to produce universally applicable definitions of the term "tradition," the many different local usages of this word are not *wrong* (Glassie 1995). An argument that only scholars understand the true definition of this word would be the height of academic arrogance, not to mention unethnographic. People use the term in various ways, such as, "This is our family tradition," or "Bluegrass is traditional music." These applications of the word can reveal subtle understandings of the concept that are real and true in peoples' experiences. Many of my consultants use this word strategically, locating themselves vis-à-vis the world around them; of all the options in their lives, it is Ge that is *their* tradition, that is most fundamental to their identities as residents of a pluralistic contemporary world.

Through Ge performance, agents interact with their worlds, sometimes forming clear boundaries by rejecting forces outside "the tradition," other times syncretically blending resources of differing origins. They make such choices strategically in order to accomplish tasks in relationship to new realities in their lives. And they make such choices musically, exploiting the effective pathway of communication called *getan*. Through Ge performance, my consultants act, engaging their worlds, positing relationship to their worlds. People and institutions collaborate, cooperate, and combat through Ge performance and discourse surrounding the topic. Multiple meanings are generated through the pathways of communication between performers and spirits, audience members, event organizers, and others. In the human and extrahuman interactions in sound at the center of the process of Ge performance, people get things done.

GLOSSARY

All glossed terms are in Dan unless otherwise noted.

biansë ge   racing *ge;* also sometimes called *gunyege*
Biélé   village in the northern Dan region, just south of Biankouma
bisa   general name for sacred objects which are held in the hand during Ge performances. Examples include the flywhisk and the object connected to the *sraman* bell.
bubu   robe-like shirt
bɛman (pl. *bɛmannu*)   ancestor spirit
ɓaa   drum
ɓaaɗe (pl. *ɓaaɗenu*)   (lit., "mother drum"); the master drum, played by the master
drummer in Ge performances
ɓaaɗezëmɛn   master drummer; person who plays the *ɓaaɗe*
ɓaagen   rhythm (lit., drum feet)
ɓaakpizëmɛmɛn   master drummer
ɓaanëyakwade (pl. *ɓaanëyakwadenu*)   one of the accompanying drums in Ge performances, consisting of three or more heads
ɓaasɛ   metal resonators attached to the *ɓaaɗe drum*
deɓo   to do a benediction
dɛɓo   divination; spiritual consultation
deɓo ge   a *ge* who does benedictions
dɛɓogenu   *genu* who do divination or spiritual consultation
dɛn   *ge* who directs boys' initiation
Déoulé   village northeast of Man, most of whose inhabitants identify as "Goh"—a
cross between the Dan and Tura ethnic groups
dian (pl.*diannu*)   a type of spirit who appeared among humans in former times ("during the time of the ancestors")
dipitin   one of the rhythms played on the drums and *gle* to manifest the sonic aspect of
certain genres of *genu*
dozo (pl. *dozow*)   panethnic hunting society which originated in the savanna among
northern Mande peoples and which today serves multiple functions, including that
of a private security force in Côte d'Ivoire
du   a neutral spiritual power, usually translated as "sorcery," which can be used toward
positive or negative ends
duga   (lit., "grain [*ga*] of *du*"); general name for any number of power objects (*fétiche*)
used by *dumi*
dumi   sorcerer
dusë   positive *du,* or the use of *du* toward positive ends
duyaa   negative *du,* or the use of *du* toward negative ends
duyaami   practitioner of *duyaa,* or negative sorcery
ɗiömɛn   ancestor
ɗɔɔga   an iron bell which is played during Gegbadë performances
ɗɔɔtan   music of the elder women's society Kong
fétiche   French word to describe various power objects, including *duga* and *geɓɔga*
gbage   war *ge* that formerly led warriors into battle and who today is primarily an entertainment or rejoicing *ge*

gbakwi a style of singing *getan* in which singers deconstruct the standard call-and-response pattern and begin improvising vocables in a freer manner

gbannë boys' initiation

gbarkas minibuses used for public transport

gbɛguwon sacred matter/affair

gbɛnge night *ge*—a genre of *ge* who manifests only during the night

gbin heavy

gbung iron pellets used as instruments, either shaken or worn as ankle bells

Ge the system, school, or institution of Ge

ge (pl. *genu*) individual performing manifestations of Ge

ge ɓasi "dressed *ge*"—a *ge* who can be seen by anyone, including women and noninitiates

ge ɗua gu a performing *ge* (lit., the *ge* is in the raffia)

ge kpesi "undressed *ge*"—a *ge* who can be seen only by initiates; alternatively, a *ge* who has no visual manifestation but who manifests only in sound

ge kpin the *ge* is performing (lit., the *ge* is outside)

geatanɓomɛn principal singer for a *ge* performance (lit., the *ge*'s singer)

geatankëmɛn the chorus of singers and dancers in a ge performance (lit., the ge's dancers)

gebia *ge* race, during which racing *genu* (*biansë ge*) are pitted against human runners

geɓɔ a spiritual plane whose various translations include "the beyond," "the spiritual dimension," "the mystical plane"; the dimension where ancestors (*bɛman*) and spirits (*yinan*) reside next to God (Zlan); The place where *genu* reside when not manifest in performance among humans.

geɓɔga (lit., "grain [*ga*] from/of *geɓɔ*"); power object (*fétiche*) used by *genu*

gedëmɛn (lit., "fathers of the *ge*"); general term which refers to all people initiated or involved in the performance in any way of a *ge*

Gedro frog *ge*—a subgenre of the genre of *genu* called *tankë ge* (rejoicing *ge*); the proper name of the *ge* from Petit Gbapleu who is central to this book

Gegbadë proper name of the *gegɔn/zu ge* from Grand Gbapleu who is central to this book

gegblɛɛn (lit., "long *ge*"); a genre of *ge* who dance on stilts

gegɔn (lit., "male *ge*"); a genre of *ge* whose face is characterized by a long beak who are generally high in the hierarchy of any sacred house

gekia (pl. *gekianu*) assistant or attendant to the *ge*

gekpenë (lit., "short *ge*"); generally refers to rejoicing *genu* who do not dance on stilts

getan *ge* song/dance; the musical aspect of a *ge* manifestation

gewëɗë (pl. *gewëɗënu*) (lit., "face of the *ge*"); mask

gewoɗiöyɔrɔmɛn person who transmits the word of the *ge*

Gewon (lit., affair/matter of Ge); tradition

giantan (pl. *giantannu*) war music; today often associated with racing *genu* (*biansë ge*)

gle gourd rattle with an external net laced with snake bones, seeds, or beads

Gouro southern Mande ethnic group who live in central Côte d'Ivoire

Grand Gbapleu village on the edge of Man, one of two founding villages of Man

Guéré subgroup of Wè peoples who live to the south of the Dan

gunɗiö sacred space; can refer to a sacred forest, a sacred house, or any other space designated as sacred

gunkɔ sacred house—village home of *genu*, where *ge* paraphernalia is housed

Jola ethnic group whose homeland is in the Casamance region of Senegal and Guinea Bissau

Jula northern Mande ethnic group whose homeland is north-central Côte d'Ivoire and southern Burkina Faso; also a general term that Ivorians use to describe all northerners/Muslims living in the south; the name of the common market or trade language in Côte d'Ivoire; "trader" in northern Mande languages such as Jula, Bamanakan, and Maninkakan

Julabugu *quartier* (neighborhood) in Man where many Jula peoples live

Kong   Dan women's version of *ge;* a women's society charged with initiating Dan women, among other things.

kɔrɔ   elder

kpɛɛ   dry

kwiiɗuwon   tradition (lit., affair, matter of ours)

lourd   (French) heavy

lökö'së   small drum, an optional element of many Ge performance ensembles

masques ye ye (French)   masks that demonstrate "new comportment" (dancing popular music rhythms, imitating American movies, etc.)

Man   city of roughly 100,000 people in western Côte d'Ivoire near the borders of Guinea and Liberia

muezzin   person who intones the call to prayer five times daily from mosques

nii   soul; spirit

Petit Gbapleu   offshoot of Gbapleu (today known as Grand Gbapleu), a Dan village which today has become completely surrounded by Man and has thus become effectively a *quartier* (neighborhood) of Man

plöwon   (lit., affair/matter of the village); tradition

sape (French)   a hip, urban lifestyle involving particular high fashion attire and a "modern" attitude

sekpe   a rattle made of a small, woven basket filled with tiny pebbles

sraman   a factory-manufactured bell attached to a *bisa;* used by Gegbadë when he is receiving a divinatory message from the *yinan*

tan wɔsi   "hot" music/dance

tanɓo ge   singing *ge*

tankë ge   dancing *ge*

tankwi (pl. *tankwinu*)   short musical interludes used to keep energy high and maintain performers' focus in between songs during Ge performances

téléphone   *bisa* used by Gegbadë to receive messages from the *yinan*

télévision   *bisa* used by Gegbadë to see into the world of sorcerers

ti-ti-din   one of the rhythms played on the drums and *gle* to manifest the sonic aspect of certain genres of *genu*

tiyin   totems—rules that must be followed; can refer both to rules that must be followed in Ge performances and to rules that members of specific families must follow (e.g., members of Jacques' family never eat weaver birds or a certain snake called *gba*)

trukë ge   genre of *ge* who specializes in comedic stories, songs, and gestures

Wè   large subgroup of Kru-speaking peoples who live along and near the Liberia/Côte d'Ivoire border

Wobé   subgroup of Wè peoples who live to the east of the Dan

wɔsi   hot—a term used to describe powerful and excellent performances of music

Yahabö   yam festival, usually held biannually in Déoulé

Yakuba   term which Ivorian Dan use to identify themselves to the outside world in certain contexts

yinan (pl. *yinannu*)   a powerful type of spirit, linguistically related to the Bamana *jinɛ* and the Arabic *jinn*

Zaouli   an extremely popular rejoicing dance mask of the Gouro peoples; also used to refer to rhythms and dance routines associated with the Zaouli mask

zigblithy   Ivorian popular music style popularized by Ernesto Djedje in the 1970s and 1980s

zii   soul; spirit

zikri   the time-keeping drum used in many Ge performances; also refers to the most common of the three rhythms played on the drums and *gle* to manifest the sonic aspect of certain genres of *genu*

Zlan   God, the supreme being in the Dan religious system

zouglou   popular music style associated with student advocacy for multipartyism in early 1990s Abidjan *zu*   a role whose responsibilities include acting as a healer, diviner, mystical specialist, and sorcery combatant; related to the term "*zo*" (or "*zoo*") found in other Mande languages of the forest belt

zu ge   genre of *ge* who specializes in the work of a *zu*

zuɗe   female *zu;* leader of the Kong society

zumi (pl. *zuminu*)   male *zu*

zumiwoɗiöyɔrɔmɛn   person who transmits the words of the *zu*

NOTES

Introduction

1. Dan terms for tradition include "*kwiiduwon*" (lit., affair/matter of ours) "*plöwon*" (village affair/matter), and, most interestingly for this study, "*Gewon*" (Ge affair/matter).

2. Ge performance in this sense serves as an example of a pattern John Chernoff observed: values can be generated through music performances that "vitalize the efforts of individuals and communities as they meet the realities of new situations" (1979, 154).

3. The concept of intertextuality originated in linguistics and literary criticism, where the term was first introduced by Julia Kristeva (1986, 448) to describe the transposition of one or more systems of signs into another. Alessandro Duranti (1994), Richard Bauman and Charles Briggs (1992), and others have applied this concept to studies of oral texts in performance, adding that intertextuality involves not only the transposition of text but also the interlinkage of context. Duranti explains: "Even the apparently most homogeneous or self-contained text exhibits, at close analysis, elements that link it to other texts, with different contexts, different norms, and different voices" (1994, 5). In this study, I am extending the concept of intertextuality from the domain of text to more broadly encompass the various dimensions of Ge performance, including sound and movement.

4. Art historians who research African mask traditions often use the term "masquerade" to refer to all components of mask performance, including the complete costume, the music, and the dance. Art historians have favored this term as they have moved away from the representation of a static piece of art—the mask—and toward attempts to describe this phenomenon not as an isolated product but as a process in which the facial covering called "mask" is but one aspect. While I fully support the efforts of art historians to locate a word that, for them, approaches a comprehensive representation of mask performance, I have chosen not to use this word. Nigerian ethnomusicologist Meki Nzewi (1994) dislikes the use of "masquerade" to describe African mask performance because he believes this term carries with it the connotation of masquerade balls and Halloween. The only time I observed the use of the French version of this term, "*mascarade,*" was in a newspaper editorial blasting the profanation of sacred mask traditions (Zio 1997).

5. Anthropologist Ichiro Majima writes that the Dan have no word that translates as "mask" (1997, 241) This could well be the case in other Dan dialects (Majima worked among Dan in the Danane region), but my consultants did use the term "*gewëdë*" to refer to the mask worn by a *ge,* which supports their assertion that *ge* should not be translated as "mask."

6. Other Africanist ethnographers have deliberately chosen styles and forms that mirror the content they are trying to represent. Margaret Drewal emulates the nonlinear, multilayered forms of Yoruba rituals in the writing of *Yoruba Ritual* (1992). Michael Jackson had similar goals in mind in writing his ethnographic novel *Barawa* (1986). By adopting Kuranko narrative style, Jackson grounds his narrative in a sense of place rather than of any one person. In *In the Time of Cannibals,* David Coplan writes "My narrative is deliberately constructed to resemble the 'concatenated' incrementation of a Sesotho *sefela*" (1994, xix). Ruth Stone makes use of the common *kpelle* metaphor of a path in the organization of her multimedia publication, "Gbarbea Funeral" (Stone 2000).

7. The use in Dan and French of "outside" to qualitatively describe a *ge*'s state brings to mind Ruth Stone's description of Kpelle reckoning of their musical performances. "Kpelle performance places considerable stress on qualitatively distinguishing music by

reference to space," Stone writes. "Actions occur in three-dimensional space and sounds occur 'under,' 'above,' 'outside,' and 'inside' (1988, x).

8. Bamanankan (or Bambara) and Jula, a trade language spoken widely in Côte d'Ivoire, are mutually intelligible.

9. Although the kolas demanded of me were consistently far larger than they are for most Dan, in general I do not view the exchange of the kolas in my research simply as some kind of reverse exploitation. There were, however, times when *ge* performers did take this practice beyond the limits of acceptability, demanding outrageous sums of money not just from me but also from Jacques. Gba Daouda, using strong language, complains about this problem in his thesis, inferring that consultants sometimes attempted to take advantage of the cultural expectation of the kola to rake in extraordinary profits (Gba 1984).

10. The Objectivist perspective was thought to enable access to universal knowledge because of the "shareable, abstract, and general nature of concepts" (Johnson 1987, xxii). It follows logically that the Objectivist-based sciences have assumed that their intellectual history represents "successive theories that progress ever and ever closer to *the* correct description of reality" (xii). Objectivist science has sought not *a* correct description, and not of *a* reality, but the single correct description of a universal reality "disembodied" (xxii) from human experience.

11. I am not suggesting, however, that I have not acted as interpreter in writing this ethnography; I mediate at every step of the way, including the selection of quotations and their translation. I do not deny my role as mediator between the reader and the people about whom I am writing or the responsibility that creating a text from ethnographic experience entails.

12. Barber's compelling edited collection *Readings in African Popular Culture* (1997a) explores expressive forms that, according to Barber, problematize the categories of tradition and modernity and can be better labeled "popular culture." I certainly do not disagree, but I am doing something different with this book by focusing on the perspectives not of academics but of Dan people themselves about these terms.

13. My thinking about categories follows Jackson, who, drawing on Piaget, describes categorizing, or "structuring," of experience thus: "Structures . . . are to be regarded as simply one horizon of experience, one mode of human activity, tied to particular ends, serving particular purposes, and having particular consequences. Structuring is an ongoing, open-ended activity, not the completed product of activity which, in fetishized form, can be said to predetermine activity from without or within" (1996, 25).

14. It is no accident that Thompson developed these ideas when he did, as ethnomusicology and folklore both were undergoing similar transformations. During the past three decades, ethnomusicologists have expanded their lenses beyond the study of music sound to see the ways that music exists as part of the larger cultural picture of human actors. As ethnomusicologists have put into action Alan Merriam's call to study music in culture (1964), and later music *as* culture (1977), they have freed music sound from the isolation of Western notation and Western notions about music, and, one could say, have begun to look at music as a verb, in action. Likewise, performance theorists have expanded beyond the study of texts to include texts and their enactment (see, for example, Bauman 1977). As ethnographers of the arts have begun studying events—as opposed to the arts as products or objects—the frame of analysis has widened considerably beyond the first note or first utterance of a story to include things such as rehearsals, the negotiation and organization of events, and what people say about their music (see Stone 1982 and Fabian 1990, among others).

15. Scholars of West African Islam offer insights into the complexity of the negotiation of identities. Robert Launay writes that individual Jula in Korhogo, Côte d'Ivoire, conceive of themselves in a variety of ways, expressing multiple social, economic, and religious identities within their neighborhoods, between their neighborhoods and the larger town of Korhogo, between and among other localities in the region, and on the national and global levels (1992, 131). Furthermore, Launay shows that the Jula define themselves not just in opposition to others in their present but also with reference to their own pasts

(46). Launay's multidimensional model shows that various identities—local, national, global, gender, familial, religious, and others—can exist independently of one another and can coexist simultaneously within single individuals (25).

I find it helpful to visualize what I imagine Launay to describe. I imagine a hologram to represent each individual in which each potential expression of identity is represented by its own fuzzy-boundaried image. Depending on the angle of view (which would correspond with different situations in the individual's life), certain of these images would appear at certain moments. Tilt the hologram a bit, and the images representing familial and religious identity might come into view, for instance. All of these identities coexist, but only certain combinations might find expression at specific moments. And a performer's consciousness of these various identities may shift from performance to performance or moment to moment within a single performance.

In a single Ge performance, for example, a performer may be expressing and generating multiple identities and may be more conscious of one or another of these identities at specific moments. Meanwhile, simultaneously, audience members may be experiencing their own combinations of identities. People thus attribute multiple meanings to single performances. And this process only expands and complicates in the pluralistic setting of late twentieth-century Côte d'Ivoire.

16. Kisliuk articulates well the need to emphasize ethnographic field experience as an epistemological grounding of ethnographic writing (1998, 12–13). Lawless's *Holy Women, Wholly Women* features extensive first-person narratives of the women whose lives she studied. In a similar vein, Dan sociologist Mamadou Koble Kamara published a monograph set in the village of his birth that consists almost exclusively of short first-person narratives about specific peoples' experiences surrounding Ge performance events (1992).

17. Other Africanists have experimented with ethnographic structure and style in efforts to better represent their subjects of study. See, for example, Michael Jackson's *Barawa* (1986), Margaret Drewal's *Yoruba Ritual* (1992), and David Coplan's *In the Time of Cannibals* (1994).

1. On the Road to Man

1. The term "*gedëmɛn*" describes all male participants, from the singers and drummers to those elders who may not appear to be participating in performances in any active way but in fact are doing so simply by virtue of their presence. Each sacred house is run by elder *gedëmɛn,* who are in charge of determining when a *ge* may perform and who watch over Ge performances to be sure things are being done in a proper manner.

2. My use of the phrase "negotiated sense of time" follows Ruth Stone's nuanced interpretation of time in Kpelle epic performance (1988, 86; see also Stone 1985).

3. Théodore equates spiritual and physical filth; they are one and the same thing. A person can be "clean" (in a spiritual sense), but his or her shoes will still be dirty. So shoes must be kept away when Gegbadë is in the process of exorcising, or purifying, a person or place.

4. In many African music performance contexts, nearly everyone present participates in some way, there often being no clear distinction between audience members and performers. Yet a distinction can be drawn between those highly skilled musicians who lead the performance and others who participate in less central ways. Koetting (1992) uses the term "performing nucleus" to describe the core group of musicians who are at the center of a performance and lead others present.

5. The *gekia* has many responsibilities, which vary from *ge* to *ge.* Generally, the *gekia* shadows the dancing *ge,* watching over the *ge*'s clothing, the mask, and all other aspects of the *ge*'s outfit. If any problem arises—for example, if a strip of *gbuŋ* (ankle bells) is falling off or if the leather strips which hang from the *ge*'s hat or waist become twisted—the *gekia* immediately acts to rectify the problem. He helps guide the *ge* around in the often-crowded performance spaces. He dances alongside the *ge,* collecting gifts of money and acting as an intermediary between the *ge* and the crowd. For a *ge* who speaks, the *gekia* will repeat his words after each phrase in a loud clear voice to be sure everyone

has heard. For a highly sacred *ge* such as Gegbadë, several *gekianu* are necessary, each of whom have specific tasks. The *gekia* holds a sacred flywhisk in his right hand, a symbol of authority.

6. The Bété are a Kru-speaking ethnic group whose homeland is in southwest Côte d'Ivoire.

7. The familial base of Ge is somewhat analogous to the *nyamakala* of northern Mande peoples (see Johnson and Sisɔkɔ 1992 [1986] and McNaughton 1993 [1988]). Specific social needs are met by certain families' *genu,* and these *genu* are passed down hereditarily from older to younger men within the family. Like all things Ge, though, change occurs. Occasionally, as people move around, *genu* are brought with them and sacred houses either move, are created anew, or merge. Oulai Théodore, whose family has moved extensively around western Côte d'Ivoire, settled in his current home in Grand Gbapleu only in the 1980s. Upon his arrival, Théodore relocated his sacred house. More recently, Lambert Celestin, originally from Déoulé, merged his family's sacred house with that of Théodore, which added another *zu ge* and a rejoicing *ge* to the already powerful sacred house. In Man and Abidjan, people often create extensions of sacred huts back in their home villages in small utility buildings or rooms of houses that are restricted to noninitiates.

8. I am not permitted to share the specific techniques used for voice alteration, as this is one of those aspects of Ge performance that my consultants deemed too secret and sacred to be publicized.

9. As I later considered the way Gegbadë directed the event, I thought of Ruth Stone's discussion of segmentation in Kpelle performance. Stone writes, "The Kpelle delight in segmenting performance into discrete little units that are also part of a larger fabric" (1988, 66).

10. My consultants frequently described "whites," or "Americans," as being "sorcerers" because of their technology. Everything from airplanes to my camcorder was cited as evidence of "*la sorcellerie des américains.*" Jacques explained to me that this was a metaphorical use of the term "sorcery"—that people use this term whenever a human accomplishes something extraordinary, that seems to surpass the level of human ability. Since this viewpoint is so common, I find the use of metaphors such as "*télévision*" fascinating—this is a direct comparison of a powerful object used in Ge performance with another that originated in the U.S. that serves a similar function: to see into another world. Geschiere (1997) found similar views regarding technology in Cameroon.

11. Many Ivorian women wear an extra cloth wrap, called a *pagne,* around the waist, which they use for multiple purposes in different contexts—carrying babies on their backs, keeping stashes of coin change, and so forth. Adams writes that Wè women similarly throw down cloths to create pathways for mask performers to walk on (1986, 48).

12. Also present at many Ge performances are elders from other families who also have sacred houses and *genu.* The presence of these elder *gedëmɛn* aids the *ge* who is performing. There is strength in numbers: the greater the number of *gedëmɛn* the stronger the presence of Ge and thus the greater the protection from negative spiritual attacks and the greater the power for the performing *ge* to accomplish his goals.

2. Coexistence, Cooperation, and Conflict in the City of Eighteen Mountains

1. Beginning in the 1980s, the Ivorian government also began adopting the image of the mask as a symbol of national identity (see Steiner 1994, 93–99). The appropriation of masks by the national government for such purposes is further explored in Chapters 3 and 7.

2. *Madrasa* schools are Islamic schools found in many parts of Africa which blend aspects of Western pedagogical techniques, and sometimes even secular education, with traditional Koranic school education. In Côte d'Ivoire, *madrasas* developed in parallel with the French-styled state-run education system (LeBlanc 1998; see also Brenner 1993, 6–7).

3. Etta Donner writes that in the 1930s when she was in the Dan region she found

many villages in which sizeable populations of other ethnic groups lived (1977 [1939], 136). We thus know that many Dan villages have been multiethnic for some time. My consultants' oral histories suggested that their villages have been home to other ethnic populations for generations.

4. For a detailed discussion of Dan women's roles and the idea of ownership of women in Dan life, see Fischer 1964.

5. This designation, "Jula," is rather complex. The word "*jula*" means "trader" in northern Mande languages such as Jula, Bamanankan (Bambara), and Maninkakan (Malinké). Generally speaking, all immigrants, many of them merchants, from the savanna and Sahel who have settled in central and southern Côte d'Ivoire are identified by others as "Jula." A small percentage of them actually come from the Jula ethnic region in north-central Côte d'Ivoire and southern Burkina Faso, but many belong to other ethnic groups. Yet in part due to their dress (generally *bubus* associated with Islam), they are automatically associated with Islam and the north and are called "Jula." To further complicate the matter, even converts to Islam who are from the forest region sometimes are identified by others as "Jula." This is true of many Dan Muslims in Man. For excellent discussions of the complexities of "Jula" identity in Côte d'Ivoire, see Launay 1982 and 1992. Simply put, when discussing the hundreds of thousands of various northern peoples of myriad nationalities and ethnicities living in southern Côte d'Ivoire, northerner = Jula = Muslim.

6. I am not suggesting that in precolonial times Ge performances were uniformly interpreted by a homogeneous Dan populace. I am merely pointing to the extent to which multiple viewpoints and perspectives existed in the 1990s due to the increasing diversification and pluralization of Man.

7. Many scholars note that the colonial period wrought dramatic changes in Africa. However, too many ethnographies have treated the period of European colonization as the sole distinctive before/after point in African history. Kasfir comments on this problem in studies of African art: "There are innumerable befores and afters in this [African] history, and to select the eve of European colonialism as the unbridgeable chasm between traditional, authentic art and an aftermath polluted by foreign contact is arbitrary in the extreme" (1992, 43).

8. "Pleu" in the Man dialect of Dan means "home of" or "village." The names of many villages in the Dan region end with "pleu" and begin with the family name of the village founders, such as Gba and Gbé. Gbapleu and Gbépleu thus translate as "Gba's village" and "Gbé's village," respectively.

9. The locations of many Dan villages changed at least once during the colonial era. Historically, Dan villages tended to be small and scattered on mountaintops, in part for reasons of security. Colonial government officials forced the relocation of these villages, ostensibly in order to improve their accessibility for electrification, schools, and other services (though increasing control of the population was surely also a motivation). Many Dan villages in the 1990s were actually comprised of several older resettled villages combined into single villages in new locations along roads.

10. The *dozo* phenomenon is fascinating. In cities and large towns throughout Côte d'Ivoire, *dozow* have established themselves as security forces, alternatives to the federal police. *Dozow* work in traditional uniforms—leather outfits and hats, often covered with protective amulets from the wilderness—and with the same traditional weapons they use in hunting game in the savanna. Many Ivorians regard *dozo* as a fearless, physically and mystically powerful group who are much more effective than ordinary police, many of whom are overweight and are more concerned with collecting bribes than with providing security. The growing presence of *dozow* is the cause of much controversy in Côte d'Ivoire, as the federal government views them as an armed and potentially dangerous force that is not under their control. For a thorough study of the contemporary *dozo* society in Côte d'Ivoire, see Joseph Hellweg's dissertation (2001).

11. The logging industry and the mining industry (of iron ore and other minerals), with bases in the mountains around Man, involve foreign investment and workers. Most of these people do not live in Man itself, though they do pass through now and then.

12. I am uncomfortable asserting causal, logical, pragmatic explanations alone for

peoples' decisions to convert to a religion. Many individuals, of course, attribute their religious identity to faith, to feeling a calling, to feeling *at home* in a particular religious persuasion, opinions that should not be overlooked.

13. The West African Wahhabi movement is a contemporary outgrowth of the puritanical Muslim reform movement founded by Muhammad ibn ᶜAbd al-Wahhab in eighteenth century Arabia (Denny 1987, 134).

3. "When a rooster goes for a walk, he does not forget his house"

1. Gnassene's opinion here is reminiscent of a comment an elder Dogon man made to Walter van Beek: "[Dogon] religion is a means for the old men to get meat" (van Beek and Blakely 1994, 11). This is suggestive of the idea that some use religion to legitimate and enact power over others and to benefit themselves.

2. The youth in each Dan village or *quartier* elect a Président des jeunes, or youth president, to act as an advisor to local youth activities.

3. Each Dan family has a totem or totems—animals that cannot be eaten or harmed by members of the family.

4. Previous studies cite dreams as the means through which *ge* reveal their wish to manifest in a concrete form to carvers (Johnson 1987, 3; Himmelheber 1965, 82). *Genu,* who otherwise are in a metaphysical form in the spiritual realm called *geɓɔ,* reveal in dreams the specific physical form they desire—the mask, the clothing, and even performative aspects such as music and dance. Very few of my consultants would discuss this; most simply stated that *ge* "have always been." Consultants in Déoulé did confirm that during the time of their earliest ancestors, dreams were how *ge* made their wish to manifest known. But unlike in some other studies, not a single one of my consultants stated that this process is continuing today. I did not study with carvers, so I cannot guess what they would have said about the issue. Aimé's story, however, was a variation of this process, though in this case an ancestor herself, not a *ge,* communicated the message, and it did not involve a new *ge* but a dormant one.

5. Edward Lifschitz writes that generally in West Africa entertainment masks are increasing, while more highly sacred masks, which usually have only an aural manifestation, are on the wane. The increase in entertainment *genu* in the Man region confirms his findings. However, it is not true that Ge performance has become purely entertainment; all *genu* are by definition sacred, and some highly sacred *genu* such as Gegbadë maintain relevance.

6. I generally prefer to use James Koetting's Time Unit Box System (TUBS) to transcribe Dan rhythms because it minimizes the superimposition of Western rhythmic concepts onto them (see Chapter 6 for a full discussion of this issue). However, conventional Western notation can better represent the polymetric relationship between *zaouli* and *zikri* transcribed in Figure 3.3. TUBS assumes a single lowest common denominator, a single smallest pulse, which is represented by a box; these boxes are layered over one another to show relationships between parts. As Figure 3.3 shows, in Western music theory terms, *zaouli* and *zikri* are in simple and compound meters, respectively, and thus there is no lowest common denominator, or single smallest pulse shared between the parts. The way these two parts do align is in the repeating strong pulses of quarter note duration in the *zaouli* part and dotted eighth note duration in the *zikri* pattern.

7. Jean-Claude's comments echo those of one of John Chernoff's drumming teachers, Ibrahim Abdulai: "When we imitate you, it won't be the same as you are playing" (Chernoff 1979, 63).

8. Hannerz, drawing on Drummond (1980), Fabian (1978), and others, argues for extending the notion of creolization from linguistics to models of culture. He writes, "Creole cultures like creole languages are those which draw in some way on two or more historical sources, often originally widely different" (Hannerz 1997 [1987], 15). Such a model, Hannerz asserts, is better suited to descriptions of culture in postcolonial societies, in which older cultural models stressing homogeneity and essential coherence seem outmoded and limited.

9. Barber and Waterman (1995) assert that both the Yoruba popular-music form *fuji*

and the older Yoruba oral poetic form *oriki* feature selective appropriation and incorporation of disparate materials. Yet they contrast the two forms on the grounds that while both forms feature references to or incorporations of other indigenous Yoruba oral forms, only *fuji* features the appropriation of materials from beyond the performers' geographical locale (references to Japan, England, the United States, etc.). Likewise, Barber elsewhere contrasts *oriki* poetry, whose performers regularly incorporate other traditional oral genres, and African popular-theater and musical forms, in which artists incorporate "innovations introduced in, and emblematic of, the colonial and post-independence eras" (1997b, xii). Gedro performance transcends this contrast, as performers incorporate materials from both popular and traditional sources, from mass media and local indigenous Dan forms. In this sense, then, Gedro performance bears the most resemblance to popular expressive forms such as *fuji* and popular theater. And yet performers themselves call Ge a traditional form. Gedro performance thus supports Barber's argument that traditional and popular arts in Africa are not bounded categories but fields "whose edges are indeterminate" (1987, 19).

4. What Is Ge?

1. Certain aspects of Gueu Gbe's theory of Ge, in particular his ideas about Ge's historical origin, differ from the opinions of most of my other primary consultants.

2. I use the term "metaphor" here with anthropologist Michael Jackson in mind. Jackson writes that metaphor is not just a means of "saying something 'in terms of' or 'by way of' something else" (1989, 142). Metaphor is thus not, as is often argued, a way of talking around something but rather a way of getting at what something really is. "Metaphor reveals, not the 'thisness of that,' but rather that 'this is that' " (ibid.). It is this kind of understanding of the concept of Ge that I gleaned from Gueu Gbe.

3. Georges Courrèges (1989) writes about "The Trilogy of Mask" which consists of *masque homme, masque objet,* and *masque institution.* This begins to approach my consultants' ideas about Ge in that it includes the idea of the system, the theories, and the social organization (the "institution") inherent in this word. Yet I do not find his "Trilogy" idea a perfect match with what I learned about Ge: absent is the idea of a spirit and overly emphasized is the object of the "mask," which is not even a necessary aspect of Ge. Many *genu* manifest among humans without a "mask." Still, Courrèges's notion of "Trilogy" underscores Gueu Gbe's argument that "*masque*" is a misleading and inaccurate translation of "Ge."

4. The idea that Ge is beyond rational understanding and description is echoed by a Dan person interviewed by Dan researcher Gbongue (1984): "The Mask itself is indefinable because of its immensity. We are all a sign of its infinity" (in Gba Daouda 1984, 10).

5. Most important to this description of Ge are Gueu Gbe Alphonse, Goueu Tia Jean-Claude, Oulai Théodore, Gba Ernest and, of course, Biemi Gba Jacques. Additional and very valuable contributions came from many others as well.

6. In using the term "religion," I am following the definition of Joachim Wach: "Religion involves relation to a numinous or sacred reality, and . . . it expresses this relation in three ways: the theoretical, the practical, and the sociological. Religions are characterized by the simultaneous presence of ideas and stories about the numinous, practices such as meditations, ritual, or prayer, and the presence of groups of individuals who join to share their experiences of the sacred" (1944, 29).

7. I am much indebted to my friend John Lindamood for helping me to steer clear of the pitfalls of extremist deconstructionism in my research.

8. Roger Janelli and Dawnhee Yim Janelli's *Ancestor Worship and Korean Society* (1982) offers an excellent model of a study of a group religious practice which does not essentialize but recognizes individual agency by representing multiple viewpoints on aspects of ancestor worship beliefs and practices.

9. Consultants regularly made reference to a metaphysical dimension when discussing spiritual matters with me. This dimension, *geɓɔ,* they translated variously into French as *monde astral* (astral world), *domain mystique* (mystical domain or realm), *monde spirituel* (spiritual world), *monde divin* (divine world) and *l'au dela* (the beyond).

10. Dan names of the various spiritual energies are problematic. Many previous ethnographies present terms which differ from what I encountered in the field. Probably this is partially due to regional differences. The majority of the previous research on the Dan has been conducted among the southern Dan (Gio) of Liberia. Himmelheber (1965) offers an assortment of terms: "*dy*"—a fundamental spiritual essence which takes corporal form in nature (e.g., trees), masks, fetishes, and people (75); "*zu*"—an immortal spirit manifest in humans (77); and "*nii*"—a mortal spiritual presence which is the basis of personality that dies when a human dies (84). Fischer (1978, 18), Fischer with Himmelheber (1984, 6), and Johnson (1987, 3) all use the term "*du*" (perhaps what Himmelheber had earlier termed "*dy*"?) to describe an animating essence; Fischer and Himmelheber stated that this same term is sometimes called *zu*. Zemp's findings (1971, 162ff), based on research conducted in Côte d'Ivoire, most closely match mine. Zemp states that "*zii*" and "*ni*" are interchangeable terms that mean "soul," something found not just in humans but in other animals and natural phenomena as well. Zemp calls "*di*" a "vague spiritual force" which can be either negative or positive.

Although Gueu Gbe Alphonse argues that "*nii*" is actually a Maninka word, it was the term most commonly used by my consultants to refer to the souls of earthly things, so I use it here.

11. Gueu Gbe emphasized that all prayer for Dan people is directed toward Zlan. As he said, "If you pray through a fetish, and it works, you do not say, 'Thanks, fetish,' you say 'Thanks, God.' " But someone praying directly to God does not negate the existence of the intermediaries. To explain this, he offered an analogy: "A Catholic could pray alone, and not talk to Mary or Jesus, but directly to God. But that does not mean that Mary and Jesus are not between him and God" (Geue Gbe 1997g).

12. Himmelheber states that fetishes are not intermediaries but rather have power in and of themselves (1965, 82). Since he does not offer a Dan term for "fetish," I cannot say for sure, but he could be referring to what my consultants called "*duga*"—sorcery fetishes that are not used to mediate between Zlan and people but rather are created by negative sorcerers (*duyaami*) to attack other people. *Duga* are contrasted to *ge6ɔga,* which are power objects or fetishes used to communicate with spiritual powers in the metaphysical dimension *ge6ɔ.*

13. These terms differ from much previous literature, the majority of which is based on research in the southern and western Dan regions. See, for example, Majima 1997 (243) for a list of very different terms and different translations of similar terms that is based on his research with Dan in the Danané region.

14. Dian's short size, and the fact that they are associated with the deep forest, might explain why Dan sometimes refer to them in French as "*pygmée*" (pygmies).

15. Majima (1997) writes of a type of mask among the southern Dan that manifests solely in sound which is also called *dian.* Whether there is any connection between this mask and the spirit of which my consultants spoke is not known and is worthy of future exploration.

16. Gueu Gbe's conception of *yinan* actually differs somewhat from that of most of my other consultants. He does not consider *yinannu* to be spirits who enforce their will upon people. Rather, he views *yinan* as a source for human agents to use. He complained that too many people today attribute all mysterious, unexplainable things to *yinan* and Allah, which to him is an imported Maninka idea. Gueu Gbe favors what he considers a Dan emphasis on free will—human agents choosing to make use of various spiritual options at their disposal—as opposed to a kind of fatalism he associates with the Maninka and Islam.

17. Synonymous with "*bɛman*" is "*diömɛn.*" I use "*bɛman*" here as it was the term most frequently employed by consultants. Gueu Gbe preferred "*diömɛn*" to "*bɛman*" because he argued that the latter is of Maninka (probably Mau) origin. This may well be the case, since many northern Mande words are now very common in Dan.

18. Majima's work (1997) serves as a recent example of the differences evident across the Dan region regarding spiritual concepts and terms. Majima writes that the southern Dan in the Danané vicinity have a spiritual association that governs Dan society called Gɔ. While this society, as described by Majima, bears resemblance to Ge as described to

me by my consultants, it differs in some respects as well. Majima states that the mask society and Gɔ are two different institutions, though they have an ambiguous relationship to one another (281). Additionally, masks who perform corporeally Majima calls *glöö,* which he translates as *"génie"* or *"spirit"* (243).

19. Of all previous studies, Gba Daouda's most closely matches mine in terms of categorization of *genu.* This is not surprising, since Gba grew up in Petit Gbapleu, one of my primary research sites, and conducted research both there and in Déoulé, another of my field locations, in relatively recent times (his theses were published in 1982 and 1984). Still, differences arise, some of which might simply be due to the fact that Gba uses very few Dan terms in his writings, aside from proper names of specific *genu.*

20. I am basing the details of the distinction between dressed and undressed on what I learned from my consultants, a distinction that differs somewhat from what Zemp (1993 [1969]) and others have described. Zemp asserted that undressed masks are "sound masks created solely by their voices" (2). My consultants confirmed that such "acoustic" *genu* exist. However, for them, the category of undressed *ge* also includes those *genu* who do have a visual manifestation but one that only initiates are permitted to see. Note also that Gba Daouda chooses different French names for these categories: *masques de jour,* or day masks, and *masques de nuit,* or night masks (1982, 57ff).

21. The type of *ge* my consultants (some of whom are Gba Daouda's close relatives) called *gundïöge* Gba Daouda calls *gounli gue.* The differences are in part because Gba uses French orthography ("ou" instead of "u") but also perhaps because he bases much of his study not on his home of Petit Gbapleu but on the Goh-speaking town of Déoulé. The Goh language is a mixture of Dan and Toura.

22. This Jesus Christ Superstar analogy was suggested to me by Nicole Kousaleos. What she was getting at with this analogy is the idea of popular religion and Gedro's relatively broad appeal, especially to youth.

23. Monni Adams (1986) reports that French-speaking Wè peoples (neighbors of the Dan) use the phrase "the mask of the women" to refer to a dance in which women wear an elaborate headdress and leaf skirt similar to Wè male masqueraders.

24. I cannot confirm whether or not the *gegɔn* from Libreville is a genuinely new *ge* or is a reformulation of an older *ge.*

25. The root of the word *zu ge,* "*zu,*" is sometimes called "*zo*" in other sources. Schwab, who studied a number of ethnic groups in the Liberian hinterland, mentions a "doctor of medicine" called a "*zo*" (1947, 374ff), though he does not specify exactly in which language(s) he found the word. Fischer and Himmelheber write that "*zo*" describes anyone with exceptional spiritual powers (1984, 99). Fischer and Himmelheber also state that "*zo*" is the name for masquerader (or, in the parlance of my consultants, the one who "accompanies" the *ge*). For my consultants, *zu* does not describe just anyone who accompanies a *ge* but rather refers to the specific role of healer. "*Zo*" is a linguistic root also found among Mande speakers of the forest belt to refer to certain ritual spiritual specialists. For example, Monts writes of the *zoo-ɓa*—the leader of the female Sande society among the Vai (1984, 326).

26. The concept of *du* has been defined somewhat differently in previous literature than my consultants defined it. Previous literature sometimes attributes to *du* qualities that my consultants attributed to *yinan* or *nii/zii.* Many have described *du* as the animating force in Dan life. Himmelheber, who spelled the term "*dy,*" called it the "fundamental spiritual essence" that takes corporeal form in masks, fetishes, trees, and people (1965, 75). Likewise, Fischer states that "the Dan believe all living creatures (people, animals and spirits) to be the manifestation of power particles (or spirit-souls) named *dü*" (1978, 18). Fischer and Himmelheber unsurprisingly follow this same definition (1984, 6ff) as does Johnson (1987, 3). Tabmen offers a hint of something more similar to what I encountered, using the term *du* to describe both good and bad witchcraft: "Korgbin du" is an evil witch, while "Gordu" is peaceful version of the same who must prove he has the spiritual power to withstand attacks by the former (1971, 6). Zemp's (1971, 162ff) description more closely matches what I learned. Zemp calls "*di*" an "indefinite spiritual force" which has both good and bad forms. Persons beneficial to society (excellent musicians, wearers of important masks) could possess good *di,*

while a person with *diyaa* is a sorcerer (*dimɛ*). Zemp asserts that for the northern Dan, though, *du* is inherently considered to be bad (164). Again, There could be many explanations for the variety of opinions here, including geographic variation and change over time.

27. Concepts similar to *du* are found in other parts of Africa. The central African Pende have a concept called *wanga*, which is "crudely translated as sorcery." *Wanga*, which can be benign or evil, is the ability to manipulate the material and spirit world for personal advantage, or "the power to make things happen" (Strother 1998, 12).

28. Like Strother (1998), my use of the term "power" draws on Arens and Karp, who argue that power in Africa must refer both to the acts of the powerful and the *idea* of power, or the capacity to make things happen. Power, then, is more than what power does, "power is how power means" (Arens and Karp 1989, xv).

29. The role of music in manifesting Ge recalls Paul Stoller's discussion of music in Songhay spirit possession. Stoller writes, "For the Songhay, the 'cries' of the *godji* are the voices of the ancestors, socially healing voices that create the auditory context needed for spirit possession" (1996, 180–181).

30. Dale Olsen writes of a similar belief among the Warao of Venezuela: "Warao shamans themselves say that there is no spirit possession in Warao shamanism, only transformation and oneness between mortal and immortal." The shaman is not possessed by a spirit, but is transformed into the spirit; the shaman's voice then becomes the voice of the spirit (1996, 162).

31. Peter Weil has written about gender issues among the Mandinka of The Gambia. He writes that in the town of Wuli, two gendered power sources are counterposed: *nyama*, which is associated with the village and originates in Allah, is generally thought to be in direct conflict with the power of women, or *sengko*, which lives in the forest. The power of *sengko* must be controlled in masked rituals that transform it into a positive force for society (1988, 153). I have encountered no formalized Dan name for women's power, but Gueu Gbe's comments on the subject were certainly reminiscent of what Weil encountered in The Gambia.

32. John Chernoff observes in his research on music in Ghana that music performance, as a moment of personal display, is "an occasion to see people, usually at their best" (1979, 167). Chernoff asserts, as do my consultants, that dancing or drumming in an excellent manner can be an ethical matter in African societies, and thus the performative display of excellence is highly valued (1979, 40).

33. Initiation is just one ritual that now often occurs during school vacations. Some harvest rituals have been moved to accommodate nationally determined school schedules, which are based not on agricultural time but on Gregorian calendar time. Arnoldi describes the same process taking place among the Bamana of Mali (1995, 107ff). Some Bamana events continue to be linked with seasonal patterns, while others have adjusted to school vacation schedules.

34. The timing of initiation for each individual Dan varies. Generally, a family (extended family in the American sense of the word) will wait until a) there is a sizeable group of children who are within the acceptable age range (roughly between 4 and 13) and b) they have enough money for the extensive and expensive ordeal, which involves paying for and throwing huge fêtes at the beginning and end of the process. Jacques, at 12 years of age, was the eldest of his group and thus played an especially important role, that of the *kɔrɔ*, or leader of his initiated group, a role he will continue to play vis-à-vis those with whom he was initiated throughout life.

35. I have decided to keep the name of Jacques' father's home village anonymous because of the ill feelings surrounding this situation. For all intents and purposes, Biélé is the Biemi family's adopted home village. Jacques' mother's father, who was the chief of the village until his death in 1999, also has blood ties to Jacques' father. So his transfer of allegiance to Biélé was logical in more ways than one. This situation, while unusual, is not unprecedented. It is more unusual since the Biemi family no longer actually lives in the Man region. But Dan history is full of stories of "big men" such as Jacques' father leaving their home settlements to go and found new settlements or join previously existing ones (Johnson 1986, 1). Mobility is not new among the Dan.

5. Manifesting Ge in Song

1. At this performance and several others I observed, the Petit Gbapleu group replaced the more standard *gle* (a hollow gourd encased by a string net threaded with seeds or snake bones) with the *sekpe* (a woven basket rattle filled with tiny pebbles).

2. "*6o*" translates literally as "to pick" or "to gather"; "*kë*" is "to do." As Jean-Claude once stressed to me, "When a Dan says one word to you, he must tell you that that one word has several meanings" (Goueu 1997g). My experience with the language confirms that even more so than in English, single words can have multiple meanings according to the context in which they are used.

3. My consultants generally translated "*tan*" into French as "dance." In so doing, they were referring to the entire performance—sound and movement alike.

4. I use the male gendered pronoun here and throughout deliberately when referring to *ge,* because all *genu* save one, the Kong, or *ge* of the women's society, are male, according to all of my consultants.

5. Ben-Amos has been criticized on the grounds that the very idea of an "ethnic genre" which would reflect a group's worldview presumes homogeneity. This criticism is well founded in that, too often, ethnographers have assumed that systems of genres apply uniformly to entire ethnic groups. Critiques of the idea of "tribal styles" are now commonplace, as ethnographers have turned from attempts to represent large groups and toward recognizing individual agency. Despite my agreement with this contemporary academic paradigm, based on my research I cannot accept the argument that "if genre, then homogeneity." Could not individual members of an initiated society such as Ge, based on their shared experience, both in initiation and in experience over time, share a notion of genres? I am not arguing that my consultants share ideas uniformly in an unquestioning or unchallenged way; as this chapter continues, I will in fact present examples of people challenging genre boundaries. Still, the fact that each individual in a group does not share precisely the same ideas about genres of *getan,* or even of *ge* itself, does not preclude such a system's existence.

6. Throughout this chapter, I refer to individual *getan* texts by their first line, which is my own etic manner of naming songs for the purposes of this book. In my experience, Ge performers do not name individual songs, though they do associate songs with their texts and their melodic refrains.

7. *Ge* + *a* (possessive—short for *6a*) + *tan6o* (to sing) + *mɛn* (person) = "Ge's singer." "*Tan6omɛn*" itself is a general term for "singer."

8. As historians of the region have noted, the Dan migrated from the savanna region in northern Côte d'Ivoire and Guinea to their present location beginning in the sixteenth century (Person 1961, 47–54; see Chapter 2).

9. The Mau term that equates with *ge* is "*nyanwe,*" but I will use *ge* in this discussion to avoid confusion.

10. The proper name of this *ge* is Tougbi, which translates as "tough ears." Someone with tough ears is considered to be a ruffian, or a tough guy—someone to watch out for. I call him Zaclo throughout the text here, though, because that is how he is generally addressed in public.

11. Singing in parallel thirds is common for Dan (Goh) peoples who live in Déoulé. This contrasts with the parallel fourths favored by most Dan (Yakuba).

12. *Zouglou* is a genre of popular music associated with university students in Abidjan and, in particular, with the student uprisings that led to multipartyism in the early 1990s.

13. Petit Gbapleu actually did win the 1997 Gebia final, but on a technicality; their *ge* had in fact been unable to catch the majority of the other team's human racers.

14. Master drummers use several signals to indicate for the group to stop the song. Examples include *Ka dɔ* (You [plural] stop); *Ka dɔ kwung 6ë* (You [plural] wait at first/listen/be quiet); and *Kwa dɔ kwung 6ë* (Let's wait at first/listen/be quiet).

15. Note here that "*tankë,*" defined earlier as "to dance," makes up part of the word "*tankëmɛn,*" which in this context means "chorus." This is further evidence of the polyvalence (from an English-language perspective) of *tan.*

16. It is possible for people to initiate songs during manifestations of many but not all *genu* who sing. At performances of night *genu* called *gbɛnge,* for example, only the *ge* may sing; people merely observe and listen.

17. *Zu genu* generally do not attack people physically; they do so "mystically" by using the energy known as *du* (Oulai 1997b).

6. Drums as Instruments of Social and Religious Action

1. As the subtitle of his book suggests, John Chernoff explores the relationship between aesthetics and social action in *African Music and African Sensibility: Aesthetics and Social Action in African Musical Idioms.* Chernoff's discussions of the interconnectedness of aesthetics and ethics, and in particular the role of music in building a context for social action (see 1979, 161), are relevant to the present discussion of drumming in Ge performance.

2. The names of both the *zikri* and *lökö'së* are onomatopoeic, for the sound of the two rhythms most commonly played on each of the instruments. The name of the *ɓaanë-yakwade,* on the other hand, describes the instrument: small ["children"] drums (*ɓaanë*) placed (*ya*) together (*kwa;* the "*de*" is an emphatic).

3. A fourth rhythm, *ti-bi-li,* is typically used only in performances of racing *genu* (*biansëge*).

4. In many African societies, human qualities and names are attributed to instruments or parts of instruments. For example, among the Kpelle, lower strings of a zither are called the voice of the mother while higher strings are called the voices of children (Stone 1986). The names of two of these instruments follow a similar pattern—the principal drum, that played by the master drummer—is the mother drum (*ɓaade*). The central, largest drum of the *ɓaanëyakwade* is also called the mother (*de*), while the smaller drums are called children (*në*).

5. I have chosen to transcribe *getan* rhythms using the Time Unit Box System. The system, developed by James Koetting to represent Ashanti rhythms (1970), offers certain advantages in transcribing interlocking and polyrhythmic West African rhythms. Each box represents the smallest unit of time in any individual pattern of the interlocking whole. Empty boxes represent rests. This system emphasizes the idea of repeating patterns and, by visually layering them, their relationships to one another. The transactional relationship between patterns is central to Dan and many other West African rhythmic systems (Stone 1985). The Time Unit Box System shows these rhythmic relationships without imposing onto them the time signatures and measures of standard Western notation. I began using Time Unit Box System transcriptions in the field, using the mnemonic syllables Jean-Claude had taught me, to help me memorize the relationships of the patterns in each rhythm. When I shared these transcriptions with Jean-Claude, he was able to follow them easily and agreed that they accurately represented what he had taught me. One disadvantage of the Time Unit Box System is that it does not represent pitch. Since, however, the gourd rattle *gle* is not pitched, and the pitch of the drums is highly variable, representing anything other than relative pitches would be appropriate only for a transcription of a single performance, not for the general description I am attempting here.

6. A flam is produced when a drummer strikes a drum *almost,* but not quite, simultaneously, resulting in two distinct but nearly inseparable sounds.

7. I do not, however, wish to overstate this point. As Sue Tuohy reminded me, North American musicians also sometimes describe sound by using multilayered metaphors. I have often heard American musicians use the term "dark," for example, to describe qualities of timbre, pitch, and *feeling.* My point is that these metaphors are not necessarily cross-cultural.

8. I find an intriguing parallel in Zoë Strother's description of Pende mask performance. Pende masked dancers wear ankle rattles which add a much-desired percussive texture to Pende mask performance, much like the *gbuŋ* worn by some *genu.* Interestingly, Strother writes that rattles which produce a "lower tone" are "judged appropriate for more ominous masks" (1998, 48). I find, then, in both Dan and Pende mask performance, an association of lower-pitched instruments with more powerful masks. While this

may be a coincidence, it is suggestive of a possible avenue for future comparative research. Do other African ethnic groups have similar spiritual/musical associations?

7. Gedro at Gueheva

1. When discussing Gueheva, I will use the term "mask" more frequently than "Ge," since at this event there were so many masks of other ethnic groups.

8. Gegbadë in Yokoboué

1. Because of the gravity of this situation, in this chapter I use pseudonyms for the names of all members of the family who hired the *ge,* as per their request.

2. See Fisiy (1998) for an interesting parallel discussion of the development and prosecution of anti-sorcery laws in Cameroon.

3. The concept of sorcery is extremely problematic in terms of cross-cultural translation. Yet I have chosen to use this term here because it is the best translation of the word used by Ivorians to identify these ambiguous mystical forces that plague their lives (see Ciekawy and Geschiere 1998, 1–3).

4. Cyprian F. Fisiy writes of sorcery in Cameroon that "the less fortunate kin members are believed to attack the more affluent members because the latter have either failed to redistribute their wealth or have been unfair in the way they share with their relations" (1998, 146).

5. Legally, Ivorians are required to get authorization to hire someone to deal with a sorcery crime, but people can and do ignore this law. In such cases, they use traditional means to deal with the problem (which vary regionally) and decide upon punishments locally, without reporting to or involving the federal government.

6. As Ciekawy and Geschiere write, accusations of sorcery "primarily target persons from within the family" throughout Africa. That Edomtchi chose the occasion of the funeral to pursue the alleged perpetrators is not uncommon, then, as healers commonly try to assemble the family before starting a cure (1998, 4–5).

7. On numerous occasions, I was permitted to enter sacred houses despite the fact that I was never formally initiated. Perhaps the performers who were my closest consultants considered me to be a semi-initiate. It could have been that, like Jacques, the performers viewed my field research itself as a kind of initiation.

8. I find "fetish" a loaded term, and yet I used it in my field notes (and thus in this chapter) because it was the term used by my consultants to refer to power objects used by sorcerers.

9. Ivorians who are central to an important ritual often have special clothing made for them. For example, Jacques, as part of the wedding party he had missed, had, along with the rest of the party, purchased a shirt made of the commemorative cloth chosen for that occasion. At this funeral, Edomtchi and the rest of the immediate family had done the same.

9. Pathways of Communication and Transformation

1. Leslie Sharp argues that spirit possession in Madagascar works in *opposition* to national hegemonic power (1999, 13). Although Gedro and Gegbadë performances certainly do assert local power, these assertions of power are less in opposition to than in collaboration with agents of state political power.

REFERENCES

Abu-Lughod, Lila
1993. *Writing Women's Worlds: Bedouin Stories.* Berkeley: University of California Press.
Adams, Monni
1986. "Women and Masks among the Western Wè of Ivory Coast." *African Arts* 19, no. 2 (February): 46–55.
Aggrey, A.
1981. *Codes Penal: Codes et Lois de Côte d'Ivoire.* Abidjan: Juris-Editions.
Amso Edomtchi
1997. Interview with the author, Abidjan, Côte d'Ivoire, October 23 (DR97C68).
Appadurai, Arjun and Carol A. Breckenridge
1988. "Why Public Culture?" *Public Culture Bulletin* 1, no. 1: 5–9.
Arens, W. and Ivan Karp
1989. "Introduction." In *The Creativity of Power: Cosmology and Action in African Societies,* ed. William W. Arens and Ivan Karp, pp. xi–xxix. Washington, D.C. and London: Smithsonian Institution Press.
Arnoldi, Mary Jo
1995. *Playing with Time: Art and Performance in Central Mali.* Bloomington and Indianapolis: Indiana University Press.
Avorgbedor, Daniel Kodzo
1986. "Modes of Musical Continuity among the Anlo Ewe of Accra: A Study in Urban Ethnomusicology." Ph.D. dissertation, Indiana University.
Baba, Tiémoko Sébastien, Déli Tiémoko Jacob, Margrit Boli, and Eva Flik
1994. *=Danwo Seedhe 'Wo Po-Kɔ: Syllabaire Dan "Gwɛtaawo.* Abidjan: Société Internationale de Linguistique.
Babiracki, Carol M.
1997. "What's the Difference? Reflections on Gender and Research in Village India." In *Shadows in the Field: New Perspectives for Fieldwork in Ethnomusicology,* ed. Gregory F. Barz and Timothy J. Cooley, pp. 121–138. New York and Oxford: Oxford University Press.
Bakan, Michael B.
1998. "Walking Warriors: Battles of Culture and Ideology in the Balinese Gamelan Beleganjur World." *Ethnomusicology* 42, no. 3: 441–484.
Bakoyoko Adama
1997. Interview with the author, Man (Petit Gbapleu), Côte d'Ivoire, October 15 (DR97C75).
Barber, Karin
1987. "Popular Arts in Africa." *African Studies Review* 30, no. 3: 1–78.
1997a. "Introduction." In *Readings in African Popular Culture,* ed. Karin Barber, pp. 1–12. Bloomington: Indiana University Press.
1997b. "Introduction." In Karin Barber, John Collins, and Alain Ricard, *West African Popular Theatre,* pp. vii–xix. Bloomington and Oxford: Indiana University Press and James Currey.
Barber, Karin and Christopher Waterman
1995. "Traversing the Global and the Local: Fuji Music and Praise Poetry in the Production of Contemporary Yoruba Popular Culture." In *Worlds Apart: Modernity through the Prism of the Local,* ed. Daniel Miller, pp. 240–262. London: Routledge.

Barz, Gregory F.
    1997. "Confronting the Field(Note) in and out of the Field: Music, Voices, Text, and
    Experiences in Dialogue." In *Shadows in the Field: New Perspectives for Fieldwork
    in Ethnomusicology,* ed. Gregory F. Barz and Timothy J. Cooley, pp. 45–62. New
    York and Oxford: Oxford University Press.
Bauman, Richard
    1971. "Differential Identity and the Social Base of Folklore." *Journal of American Folk-
    lore* 84: 31–41.
    1977. *Verbal Art as Performance.* Prospect Heights, Ill.: Waveland Press.
Bauman, Richard and Charles Briggs
    1992. "Genre, Intertextuality and Social Power." *Journal of Linguistic Anthropology* 2,
    no. 2: 131–172.
Behrend, Heike and Ute Luig, ed.
    1999. *Spirit Possession: Modernity and Power in Africa.* Madison: University of Wis-
    consin Press.
Ben-Amos, Dan
    1976. "Analytical Categories and Ethnic Genres." In *Folklore Genres,* ed. Dan Ben-
    Amos, pp. 215–242. Austin: University of Texas Press.
Benoit, Camille
    1931. *Histoire Militaire de l'Afrique Occidentale Française.* Paris: Imprimerie nation-
    ale.
Berger, Harris M.
    1997. "The Practice of Perception: Multi-functionality and Time in the Musical Expe-
    riences of a Heavy Metal Drummer." *Ethnomusicology* 41, no. 5: 464–488.
Berliner, Paul
    1978. *The Soul of Mbira: Music and Traditions of the Shona People of Zimbabwe.*
    Chicago and London: University of Chicago Press.
Biemi Gba Jacques
    1997a. Interview with the author, recorded in Field Note Book #3, 1997.
    1997b Interview with the author, Man, Côte d'Ivoire, February 19 (DR97D20).
    1997c. Interview with the author, Abidjan, Côte d'Ivoire, October 25 (DR97C76-7).
    1997d. Interview with the author, Abidjan, Côte d'Ivoire, October 28 (DR97C78).
Biemi Gba Jacques and Goueu Tia Jean-Claude
    1997a. Interview with the author, Man, Côte d'Ivoire, June 9 (DR97C15).
    1997b. Interview with the author, Man, Côte d'Ivoire, July 19 (DR97C39).
Biemi Gba Jacques, Goueu Tia Jean-Claude, Gba Daniel, and Oulai(?) Mamadou
    1997. Interview with the author, Man, Côte d'Ivoire, May 4 (DR97C11).
Blacking, John
    1967. *Venda Children's Songs: A Study in Ethnomusicological Analysis.* Johannesburg:
    Witwatersrand University Press.
Bleu, Tiemoko
    1997. Interview with the author, Man, Côte d'Ivoire, September 4 (DR97C58).
Bravmann, Rene A.
    1974. *Islam and Tribal Art in West Africa.* Cambridge: Cambridge University Press.
    1983. "Ramadan—Islamic Holy Days and African Sensibility." In *African Islam,*
    pp. 61–69. Washington, D.C.: Smithsonian Institution.
Brenner, Louis
    1993. "Introduction: Muslim Representations of Unity and Difference in the African
    Discourse." In *Muslim Identity and Social Change in Sub-Saharan Africa,* ed. Louis
    Brenner, pp. 1–20. Bloomington: Indiana University Press.
Cercle de Haut-Cavally
    1914. "Rapport politique, administratif et economique, fevrier 1914." Archives Nation-
    ales de Côte d'Ivoire, number XVII-40-7 IEE53.
Cercle Militaire du Haut-Cavally
    1911. "Rapport spécial militaire établi par le chef de Bataillon Bordeaux, de l'Infanterie
    Coloniale, commandant le Détachement du 4e Regiment de Tirailleurs Sénégalais et

le Cercle Militaire du Haut-Cavally, 31 Jan. 1911." Archives Nationales de Côte d'Ivoire, number XVII-40-7 IEE53.

Charry, Eric
1996. "A Guide to the Jembe." *Percussive Notes* 34, no. 2 (April): 66–72.
2000. *Mande Music: Traditional and Modern Music of the Maninka and Mandinka of West Africa.* Chicago: University of Chicago Press.

Chernoff, John Miller
1979. *African Rhythm and African Sensibility: Aesthetics and Social Action in African Musical Idioms.* Chicago and London: University of Chicago Press.

Ciekawy, Diane and Peter Geschiere
1998. "Containing Witchcraft: Conflicting Scenarios in Postcolonial Africa." *African Studies Review* 41, no. 3: 1–14.

Clifford, James and George Marcus, eds.
1986. *Writing Culture: The Poetics and Politics of Ethnography.* Berkeley: University of California Press.

Collins, John and Paul Richards
1982. "Popular Music in West Africa: Suggestions for an Interpretive Framework." In *Popular Music Perspectives,* vol. 1, ed. David Horn and Philip Tagg, pp. 111–141. Göteborg and Exeter: International Association for the Study of Popular Music.

Colonie de la Côte d'Ivoire, Cercle de Man
1922a. "Rapport politique. 31 decembre 1922." Archives Nationales de Côte d'Ivoire, number X-2-52, IEE80.
1922b. "Rapport Trimestriel, Third Trimestre 1922." Archives Nationales de Côte d'Ivoire, number X-2-53, IEE80.
1923. "Rapport politique, administratif et economique. Rapport Trimestriel, fourth trimestre, 1923." Archives Nationales de Côte d'Ivoire, number X-2-53, IEE80 (2).
1924. "Rapport Trimestriel, First Trimestre 1924." Archives Nationales de Côte d'Ivoire, number X-2-53, IEE80 (2).
1944. Rapport Mensuel, November 1944." Archives Nationales de Côte d'Ivoire, number XVII-40-7, IEE53.

Comaroff, Jean and John Comaroff
1993. "Introduction." In *Modernity and Its Malcontents: Ritual and Power in Postcolonial Africa,* ed. Jean Comaroff and John Comaroff, pp. xi–xxxvii. Chicago and London: University of Chicago Press.

Conrad, David C. and Barbara E. Frank
1995. "Introduction. Nyamakalaya: Contradiction and Ambiguity in Mande Society." In *Status and Identity in West Africa: Nyamakalaw of Mande,* ed. David C. Conrad and Barbara E. Frank, pp. 1–23. Bloomington: Indiana University Press.

Coplan, David B.
1994. *In the Time of Cannibals: The Word Music of South Africa's Basotho Migrants.* Chicago and London: University of Chicago Press.

Courrèges, Georges
1989. *Masques et Danses de Côte d'Ivoire.* Paris: Editions "L'Instant Durable" France.

Crapanzano, Vincent
1980. *Tuhami: Portrait of a Moroccan.* Chicago: University of Chicago Press.

Denny, Frederick M.
1987. *Islam and the Muslim Community.* San Francisco: Harper & Row.

Diawara, Mamadou
1997. "Mande Oral Popular Culture Revisited by the Electronic Media." In *Readings in African Popular Culture,* ed. Karin Barber, pp. 40–48. Bloomington and Oxford: Indiana University Press and James Currey.

Donner, Etta
1977 [1939]. *Hinterland Liberia.* London and Glasgow: Blackie & Son.

Drummond, Lee
1980. "The Cultural Continuum: A Theory of Inter-systems." *Man* 15: 352–374.

Drewal, Henry John and Margaret Thompson Drewal
  1983. *Gelede: Art and Female Power among the Yoruba.* Bloomington: Indiana University Press.
Drewal, Margaret Thompson
  1992. *Yoruba Ritual: Performers, Play, Agency.* Bloomington: Indiana University Press.
Duranti, Alessandro
  1994. *From Grammar to Politics: Linguistic Anthropology in a Western Samoan Village.* Berkeley: University of California Press.
Eades, J. S.
  1980. *The Yoruba Today.* Cambridge: Cambridge University Press.
El Dabh, Halim and Frank Proschan
  1979. "Les Traditions du Masque et de la Marionette dans la Republique de la Guinée." Subventionné par le Smithsonian Institution Foreign Currency Program, le Smithsonian Institution Folklife Program et par Puppeteers of America.
Erlmann, Veit
  1996. *Nightsong: Performance, Power, and Practice in South Africa.* Chicago and London: University of Chicago Press.
Fabian, Johannes
  1978. "Popular Culture in Africa: Findings and Conjectures." *Africa* 48: 315–334.
  1990. *Power and Performance: Ethnographic Explorations through Proverbial Wisdom and Theater in Shaba, Zaire.* Madison: University of Wisconsin Press.
Fischer, Eberhard
  1964. "Die Bezeichnung der Rollen im Socialsystem der Westlichen Dan." *Zeitschrift für Morphologie und Anthropologie* 60, no. 2: 242–255.
  1978. "Dan Forest Spirits." *African Arts* 11, no. 2: 16–23, 94.
Fischer, Eberhard and Hans Himmelheber
  1984. *The Arts of the Dan in West Africa.* Zurich: Museum Rietberg.
Fischer, Eberhard and Lorenz Homberger
  1986. *Masks in Guro Culture, Ivory Coast.* Zurich: Museum Rietberg, and New York: The Center for African Art.
Fisher, Humphrey J.
  1973. "Conversion Reconsidered: Some Historical Aspects of Religious Conversion in Black Africa." *Africa* 43, no. 1: 27–40.
Fisiy, Cyprian F.
  1998. "Containing Occult Practices: Witchcraft Trials in Cameroon." *African Studies Review* 41, no. 3: 143–164.
Friedson, Steven
  1996. *Dancing Prophets: Musical Experience in Tumbuka Healing.* Chicago and London: University of Chicago Press.
Gadamer, Hans Georg
  1975. *Truth and Method.* New York: Seabury Press.
Gba Daouda
  1982. "Les Masques Chez Les Dan." Master's thesis, Université National de Côte d'Ivoire.
  1984. "Les Masques Chez Les Dan: Fonctions Educatives." Memoire de Diplôme d'Etudes Approfondies, Université National de Côte d'Ivoire.
Gba Ernest
  1997a. Singing lesson with the author, Man, Côte d'Ivoire, August 21 (DR97C48).
  1997b. Singing lesson with the author, Man, Côte d'Ivoire, September 1 (DR97C49).
  1997c. Singing lesson with the author, Man, Côte d'Ivoire, September 24 (DR97C49).
  1997d. Singing lesson with the author, Man, Côte d'Ivoire, September 30 (DR97C49).
  1997e. Singing lesson with the author, Man, Côte d'Ivoire, October 7 (DR97C73).
  1997f. Singing lesson with the author, Man, Côte d'Ivoire, October 13 (DR97C73).
  1997g. Interview with the author, Man, Côte d'Ivoire, October 13 (DR97C73-4).
Gba Gama
  1997. Interview with the author, Man, Côte d'Ivoire, April 13 (DR97C10).

Gbage group, including group leader Sahi Emile
   1997. Interview with the author, Biélé, Côte d'Ivoire, July 14.
Gbongue
   1984. "La Phobie des Masques Chez les Dan: Approche Psycho-Sociale Clinique."
      Master's thesis, Université National de Côte d'Ivoire.
Gbongue, Felix
   1997. Interview with the author, Déoulé, Côte d'Ivoire, August 29 (DR97C53).
Geschiere, Peter
   1997 [1995]. *The Modernity of Witchcraft: Politics and the Occult in Postcolonial Africa.*
      Charlottesville and London: University Press of Virginia.
Glassie, Henry
   1975. *All Silver and No Brass: An Irish Christmas Mumming.* Philadelphia: University
      of Pennsylvania Press.
   1982. *Passing the Time in Ballymenone: Culture and History of an Ulster Community.*
      Philadelphia: University of Pennsylvania Press.
   1995. "Tradition." *Journal of American Folklore* 108, no. 430: 395–412.
Gnassene Mamadou Cherif
   1997. Interview with the author, Man (Petit Gbapleu), Côte d'Ivoire, October 12
      (DR97C70).
Gorer, Geoffrey
   1962 [1935]. *Africa Dances: A Book about West African Negroes.* New York: Norton.
Gottlieb, Alma
   1989. "Witches, Kings and the Sacrifice of Identity; or, The Power of Paradox and the
      Paradox of Power among the Beng of Ivory Coast." In *Creativity of Power: Cosmol-
      ogy and Action in African Societies,* ed. W. Arens and Ivan Karp, pp. 245–272. Wash-
      ington, D.C.: Smithsonian Institution Press.
Gottlieb, Alma and Philip Graham
   1993. *Parallel Worlds: An Anthropologist and a Writer Encounter Africa.* New York:
      Crown Publishers.
Goueu Tia Jean-Claude
   1997a. Drum lesson with the author, Man, Côte d'Ivoire, June 7 (DR97C15).
   1997b. Drum lesson with the author, Man, Côte d'Ivoire, June 9 (DR97D15).
   1997c. Drum lesson with the author, Man Côte d'Ivoire, June 26 (DR97C31).
   1997d. Drum lesson with the author, Man, Côte d'Ivoire, July 19 (DR97C39).
   1997e. Interview with the author, Man, Côte d'Ivoire, July 5 (DR97C35).
   1997f. Interview with the author, Man, Côte d'Ivoire, July 17 (DR97C38).
   1997g. Interview with the author, Man, Côte d'Ivoire, July 22 (DR97C41).
   1997h. Interview with the author, Man, Côte d'Ivoire, July 25 (DR97C60).
   1997i. Interview with the author, Man, Côte d'Ivoire, September 15 (DR97C60).
Goueu Tia Jean-Claude and members of the Gedro group
   1997. Interview with the author, Man, Côte d'Ivoire, June 26 (DR97C29). Group in-
      cluded Djomande Martine, Gba Gama, Gba Mathieu, Goueu Tia Jean-Claude, Louan
      Dominique, and Semlen Aimé.
Green, Katherine Lee
   1984. "The Foundation of Kong: A Study in Dyula and Sonongui Ethnic Identity." Ph.D.
      dissertation, Indiana University, Bloomington.
Grindal, Bruce
   1973. "Islamic Affiliations and Urban Adaptation." *Africa* 43: 333–346.
Gue Tin
   1997. Interview with the author, Biélé, Côte d'Ivoire, July 20 (DR97C26).
Gueu Gbe Gonga Alphonse
   1997a. Interview with the author, Man, Côte d'Ivoire, February 14 (DR97C4).
   1997b. Interview with the author, Man, Côte d'Ivoire, March 14 (DR97C8).
   1997c. Interview with the author, Man, Côte d'Ivoire, May 7 (DR97C12).
   1997d. Interview with the author, Man, Côte d'Ivoire, May 14 (DR97C12).
   1997e. Interview with the author, Man, Côte d'Ivoire, May 22 (DR97C16).

1997f. Interview with the author, Man, Côte d'Ivoire, August 18 (DR97C44).

1997g. Interview with the author, Man, Côte d'Ivoire, October 1 (DR97C67).

1997h. Interview with the author, Man, Côte d'Ivoire, October 14 (DR97C73).

Gyekye, Kwame

1977. *Tradition and Modernity: Philosophical Reflections on the African Experience.* New York and Oxford: Oxford University Press.

Hannerz, Ulf

1997 [1987]. "The World in Creolization." In *Readings in African Popular Culture,* ed. Karin Barber, pp. 12–18. Bloomington and Oxford: Indiana University Press and James Currey.

Harding, Frances

1990. "Performance as Political Action: The Use of Dramatisation in the Formulation of Tiv Ethnic and National Consciousness." In *Self-Assertion and Brokerage: Early Cultural Nationalism in West Africa.* Birmingham: Center of West African Studies, University of Birmingham.

Harley, George W.

1950. *Masks as Agents of Social Control in Northeast Liberia.* Cambridge, Mass.: Papers of the Peabody Museum of American Archaeology and Ethnology, Harvard University, vol. XXXII (2).

Hellweg, Joseph R.

2001. "The Mande Hunters' Movement of Côte d'Ivoire: Ritual, Ethics, and Performance in the Transformation of Civil Society, 1990–1997." Ph.D. dissertation, University of Virginia.

Herskovitz, Melville

1966 [1945]. "Problem, Method and Theory in Afroamerican Studies." In *The New World Negro.* Bloomington and Indianapolis: Indiana University Press.

Himmelheber, Hans

1965. "Le Système De La Religion des Dan." In *Rencontres Internationales de Bouaké: Les Religions Africaines Traditionelles,* pp. 75–96. Paris: Editions du Seuil.

Holsoe, Svend E. and Joseph J. Lauer

1976. "Who Are the Kran/Guéré and the Gio/Yacouba? Ethnic Identification along the Liberia/Ivory Coast Border." *African Studies Review* 19, no. 1 (April): 139–149.

Imperato, Pascal James

1980. "Bambara and Malinke Ton Masquerades." *African Arts* 13, no. 4: 47–55, 82–85, 87.

Jackson, Michael

1982. *Allegories of the Wilderness: Ethics and Ambiguity in Kuranko Narratives.* Bloomington: Indiana University Press.

1986. *Barawa and the Ways Birds Fly in the Sky.* Washington, D.C.: Smithsonian Institution Press.

1989. *Paths toward a Clearing: Radical Empiricism and Ethnographic Inquiry.* Bloomington and Indianapolis: Indiana University Press.

1996. "Introduction: Phenomenology, Radical Empiricism, and Anthropological Critique." In *Things As They Are: New Directions in Phenomenological Anthropology,* ed. Michael Jackson, pp. 1–50. Bloomington and Indianapolis: Indiana University Press.

Janelli, Roger L. and Dawnhee Yim Janelli

1982. *Ancestor Worship and Korean Society.* Stanford, Calif: Stanford University Press.

Johnson, Barbara C.

1986. *Four Dan Sculptors: Continuity and Change.* San Francisco: The Fine Arts Museums of San Francisco.

Johnson, Mark

1987. *The Body in the Mind: The Bodily Basis of Meaning, Imagination, and Reason.* Chicago and London: University of Chicago Press.

Johnson, John William and Fa-Digi Sisɔkɔ

1992 [1986]. *The Epic of Son-Jara: A West African Tradition.* Bloomington and Indianapolis: Indiana University Press.

Kaba, Lansine
1972. "Evolution of Islam in West Africa: The Wahhabi Movement and Its Contribution to Political Development 1945–1958." Ph.D. dissertation, Northwestern University.

Kamara, Mamadou Koble
1992. *Les Fonctions du Masque dans la Société Dan de Sipilou.* Zurich: Museum Rietberg.

Kasfir, Sidney
1988. "Introduction: Masquerading as a Cultural System." In *West African Masks and Cultural Systems,* ed. Sidney L. Kasfir, pp. 1–16. Tervuren: Musée Royale de L'Afrique Centrale.
1992. "African Art and Authenticity." *African Arts* 25, no. 2: 40–53, 96.
1994. "Samburu Souvenirs: Representations of a Land in Amber." Unpublished essay, distributed at Indiana University lecture.

Kassia Noël
1994. Interview with the author, Man, Côte d'Ivoire, July 28 (DR94C5).

Kisliuk, Michelle
1997. "(Un)doing Fieldwork: Sharing Songs, Sharing Lives." In *Shadows in the Field: New Perspectives for Fieldwork in Ethnomusicology,* ed. Gregory F. Barz and Timothy J. Cooley, pp. 23–44. New York and Oxford: Oxford University Press.
1998. *Seize the Dance! BaAka Musical Life and the Ethnography of Performance.* New York and Oxford: Oxford University Press.

Koetting, James
1970. "Analysis and Notation of West African Drum Ensemble Music." *Selected Reports, Institute of Ethnomusicology, UCLA* 1, no. 3: 115–146.
1992. "Africa/Ghana." In *Worlds of Music: An Introduction to the Music of the World's Peoples,* 2nd ed., ed. Jeff Todd Titon, pp. 67–105. New York: Schirmer Books.

Kpan Gbeu Antoine
1997. Interview with the author, Man (Petit Gbapleu), Côte d'Ivoire, October 7 (DR97C71).

Kristeva, Julia
1986. "The Bounded Text." In *Contemporary Literary Criticism,* ed. R. C. Davis, pp. 448–466. New York: Longman.

Launay, Robert
1982. *Traders without Trade: Responses to Change in Two Dyula Communities.* Cambridge: Cambridge University Press.
1992. *Beyond the Stream: Islam and Society in a West African Town.* Berkeley: University of California Press.

Lawless, Elaine J.
1993. *Holy Women, Wholly Women: Sharing Ministries of Wholeness through Life Stories and Reciprocal Ethnography.* Philadelphia: University of Pennsylvania Press.

LeBlanc, Marie N.
1998. "The Production of Islamic Identities through Knowledge Claims in Bouake, Côte d'Ivoire." Paper presented at the Forty-first Annual Meeting of the African Studies Association, Chicago, Ill.

Lien Sati Yvonne et al.
1997. Interview with the author, Man (Petit Gbapleu), Côte d'Ivoire, September 18 (DR97C62-3). Additional interviewees: Zou Singa Lea, Zou Monle Brigitte, Gba Gueu Ibene, Gba Logine Mirielle, Gba Goman Odette, Tiemoko Christine, and Oulai Manle Yvette.

Lifschitz, Edward
1988. "Hearing Is Believing: Acoustic Masks and Spirit Manifestation." In *West African Masks and Cultural Systems,* ed. Sidney L. Kasfir, pp. 221–230. Tervuren: Musée Royale de L'Afrique Centrale.

Loua Philippe
1997. Interview with the author, Man, Côte d'Ivoire, October 8 (DR97C71).

Loucou, Jean-Noël
    1984. *Histoire de la Côte d'Ivoire*. Tome 1: *La Formation des Peuples*. Abidjan: CEDA.
Majima, Ichiro
    1997. "Voix de masque sans visage: 'Maania' chez les Dan du Danané-Sud (Côte
    d'Ivoire)." In *Cultures Sonores d'Afrique*, pp. 237–307. Publié sous la direction de
    Kawada Junzo, Institut de Recherches sur les Langues et Cultures d'Asie et d'Afrique,
    Tokyo.
Mameri Tia Thomas
    1997. Interview with the author, Man, Côte d'Ivoire, March 9 (DR97C7).
Mameri Tia Thomas and Yoro Victor
    1994. Interview with the author, Déoulé, Côte d'Ivoire, August 1 (DR94C6).
Manning, Patrick
    1988. *Francophone Sub-Saharan Africa, 1880–1985*. Cambridge: Cambridge Univer-
    sity Press.
Manuel, Peter
    1993. *Cassette Culture: Popular Music and Technology in North India*. Chicago and
    London: University of Chicago Press.
Mark, Peter
    1992. *The Wild Bull and the Sacred Forest: Form, Meaning, and Change in Senegambian
    Initiation Masks*. Cambridge: Cambridge University Press.
McClusky, Pamela
    1987. *African Art: From Crocodiles to Convertibles in the Collection of the Seattle Art
    Museum*. Seattle: Seattle Art Museum.
McNaughton, Patrick R.
    1979. *Secret Sculpture of Komo: Art and Power in Bamana (Bambara) Initiation So-
    cieties*. Working Papers in the Traditional Arts, no. 4. Philadelphia: ISHI.
    1993 [1988]. *The Mande Blacksmiths: Knowledge, Power, and Art in West Africa*.
    Bloomington and Indianapolis: Indiana University Press.
    1993. "Theoretical Angst and the Myth of the Descriptive." *African Arts* 26, no. 4: 14–
    23, 82–84, 88.
    1998. "Aesthetics and Form Reconsidered." Paper presented at the Fourth International
    Conference on Mande Studies, Serrekunda, The Gambia, June 12–19, 1998.
Merriam, Alan P.
    1964. *The Anthropology of Music*. Evanston, Ill.: Northwestern University Press.
    1977. "Definitions of 'Comparative Musicology' and 'Ethnomusicology': An Historical-
    Theoretical Perspective." *Ethnomusicology* 21, no. 2: 189–204.
Mli Bakayoko, Boulaman
    1997a. Interview with the author, Petit Gbombelo (Biélé), Côte d'Ivoire, September 19
    (DR97C64).
    1997b. Interview with the author, Petit Gbombelo (Biélé), Côte d'Ivoire, October 5
    (DR97C69).
Monts, Lester P.
    1980. "Music in Vai Society: An Ethnomusicological Study of a Liberian Ethnic Group."
    Ph.D. Dissertation, University of Minnesota.
    1984. "Conflict, Accommodation, and Transformation: The Effect of Islam on Music
    of the Vai Secret Societies." *Cahiers d'Etudes Africaines* 24, no. 3: 321–42.
    1998. "Islam in Liberia." In *Africa: The Garland Encyclopedia of World Music*, vol. 1,
    ed. Ruth M. Stone, pp. 327–349. New York and London: Garland Publishing.
Nunley, John W.
    1987. *Moving with the Face of the Devil: Art and Politics in Urban West Africa*. Urbana:
    University of Illinois Press.
Nzewi, Meki
    1994. Lecture delivered for conference "New Directions: The West African Voice in
    Ethnomusicology," at the University of Michigan.
Okri, Ben
    1991. *The Famished Road*. London: Vintage Press.

Olsen, Dale A.
1996. *Music of the Warao of Venezuela: Song People of the Rain Forest.* Gainesville: University Press of Florida.

Oulai Théodore
1997a. Interview with the author, Man, Côte d'Ivoire, July 16 (DR97C37).
1997b. Interview with the author, Man, Côte d'Ivoire, August 20 (DR97C45).

Peek, Philip M.
1991. "Introduction." In *African Divination Systems: Ways of Knowing,* ed. Philip M. Peek, pp. 1–23. Bloomington: Indiana University Press.

Person, Yves
1961. "Les Kissi et Leurs Statuettes de Pierre." *Bulletin de IFAN* 23: 1–59.
1982. "Islam et décolonisation en Côte d'Ivoire." *Le Mois en Afrique,* no. 198–199 (mai-juin).
1990. *Cartes Historiques de l'Afrique Manding, Fin du 19ᵉ Siècle.* Paris: Centre de Recherches Africaines.

Piot, Charles
1999. *Remotely Global: Village Modernity in West Africa.* Chicago and London: University of Chicago Press.

Reed, Daniel B.
1993. "The Innovator and the Primitives: George Herzog in Historical Perspective." *Folklore Forum* 26, no. 1–2: 69–92.
1996. "Tradition in Transformation: The 1993 Celebration of Martin Luther King, Jr. Day in Bloomington, Indiana." *Midwestern Folklore* 22, no. 1: 25–33.
1999. "Masks, Music and Meaning: Ge Performance among the Dan of Côte d'Ivoire." Ph.D. dissertation, Indiana University.
2001. "Pop Goes the Sacred: Dan Mask Performance and Popular Culture in Postcolonial Côte d'Ivoire." *Africa Today* 48, no. 3: 67–86.

Reed, Daniel B. with Gloria Gibson, Alan Burdette, et al.
2002. *Music and Culture of West Africa: The Straus Expedition.* CD-ROM. Bloomington: Indiana University Press.

République de Côte d'Ivoire, Ministère du Plan.
1970(?) Etude Générale de la Région de Man, 4. Etude Sociologique et Demographique, par M. Alluson.

Rice, Timothy
1997. "Toward a Mediation of Field Methods and Field Experience in Ethnomusicology." In *Shadows in the Field: New Perspectives for Fieldwork in Ethnomusicology,* ed. Gregory F. Barz and Timothy J. Cooley, pp. 101–120. New York and Oxford: Oxford University Press.

Roseman, Marina
1991. *Healing Sounds of the Malaysian Rainforest: Temiar Music and Medicine.* Berkeley: University of California Press.

Sanneh, Lamin
1994. "Translatability in Islam and in Christianity in Africa: A Thematic Approach." In *Religion in Africa: Experience and Expression,* ed. Thomas D. Blakely, Walter E. A. van Beek, and Dennis L. Thomson, pp. 22–45. London and Portsmouth, N.H.: James Currey and Heinemann.

Schwab, George
1947. *Tribes of the Liberian Hinterland.* Edited, with additional material by George W. Harley. Cambridge, Mass.: Papers of the Peabody Museum of American Archaeology and Ethnology, Harvard University, vol. XXXI.

Semlen Aimé et al.
1997. Interview with the author, Man, Côte d'Ivoire, June 26 (DR97C29).

Sharp, Leslie A.
1999. "The Power of Possession in Northwest Madagascar." In *Spirit Possession: Modernity and Power in Africa,* ed. Heike Behrend and Ute Luig, pp. 3–19. Madison: University of Wisconsin Press.

Shuman, Amy
   1993. "Gender and Genre." In *Feminist Theory and the Study of Folklore,* pp. 71–89. Urbana and Chicago: University of Illinois Press.
Siegmann, William C. with Cynthia E. Schmidt
   1977. *Rock of the Ancestors: ŋamôa kɔni.* Suakoko, Liberia: Cuttington University College.
Speed, Clark K.
   1998. "I Have Knocked You Down with Power: Recursive Processes of Secrecy (Dissolution) Landoge (Lokko) of Northern Sierra Leone." Paper presented at the Forty-first Annual Meeting of the African Studies Association, October 29–November 1, Chicago, Ill.
Spindel, Carol
   1989. *In the Shadow of the Sacred Grove.* New York: Vintage Books.
Steiner, Christopher B.
   1994. *African Art in Transit.* Cambridge and New York: Cambridge University Press.
Stoller, Paul
   1989. *Fusion of the Worlds: An Ethnography of Possession among the Songhay of Niger.* Chicago and London: University of Chicago Press.
   1996. "Sounds and Things: Pulsations of Power in Songhay." In *The Performance of Healing,* ed. Carol Laderman and Marina Roseman, pp. 165–184. New York and London: Routledge.
Stoller, Paul and Cheryl Olkes
   1987. *In Sorcery's Shadow: A Memoir of Apprenticeship among the Songhay of Niger.* Chicago and London: University of Chicago Press.
Stone, Ruth M.
   1982. *Let the Inside Be Sweet: The Interpretation of Music Event among the Kpelle of Liberia.* Bloomington and Indianapolis: Indiana University Press.
   1985. "In Search of Time in African Music." *Music Theory Spectrum* 7: 139–148.
   1986. "African Music Performed." In *Africa,* 2nd ed., ed. Phyllis M. Martin and Patrick O'Meara, pp. 257–272. Bloomington: Indiana University Press.
   1988. *Dried Millet Breaking: Time, Words, and Song in the Woi Epic of the Kpelle.* Bloomington: Indiana University Press.
   1998. "African Music in a Constellation of Arts." In *Africa: The Garland Encyclopedia of World Music,* vol. 1, ed. Ruth M. Stone, pp. 7–12. New York and London: Garland Publishing.
   2000. "Gbarbea Funeral." In *Five Windows into Africa,* ed. Patrick McNaughton, et al. CD-ROM. Bloomington: Indiana University Press.
Stone, Ruth M. and Verlon L. Stone
   1981. "Event, Feedback, and Analysis: Research Media in the Study of Music Events." *Ethnomusicology* 25: 215–225.
Strother, Z. S.
   1995. "Invention and Reinvention in the Traditional Arts." *African Arts* 28, no. 2: 24–33, 90.
   1998. *Inventing Masks: Agency and History in the Art of the Central Pende.* Chicago and London: University of Chicago Press.
Tabmen, George W. W.
   1971. "Gor and Gle: Ancient Structure of Government in the Dan (Gio) Tribe." Mimeograph, Monrovia Liberia.
Thompson, Robert F.
   1974. *African Art in Motion: Icon and Act.* Berkeley: University of California Press.
Tia Sao, Gnassene Mamadou Cherif, and Vahan Etienn
   1997. Interview with the author, Man (Petit Gbapleu), Côte d'Ivoire, August 20 (DR97C47).
Tonkin, Elisabeth
   1988. "Cunning Mysteries." In *West African Masks and Cultural Systems,* ed. Sidney Kasfir. Tervuren: Musée Royale de L'Afrique Centrale.

Tuohy, Sue
1988. "Imagining the Chinese Tradition: The Case of Hua'er Songs, Festivals, and Scholarship." Ph.D. Dissertation, Indiana University.

Turino, Thomas
1993. *Moving Away from Silence: Music of the Peruvian Altiplano and the Experience of Urban Migration.* Chicago and London: University of Chicago Press.
2000. *Nationalists, Cosmopolitans, and Popular Music in Zimbabwe.* Chicago: University of Chicago Press.

van Beek, Walter E. A. and Thomas D. Blakely
1994. "Introduction." In *Religion in Africa: Experience and Expression,* ed. Thomas D. Blakely, Walter E. A. van Beek, and Dennis L. Thomson, pp. 1–20. London and Portsmouth, N.H.: James Currey and Heinemann.

Vandenhoute, P. J.
1948. *Classification Stylistique du Masque Dan et Guéré de la Côte d'Ivoire Occidentale (A.O.F.).* Leiden: E. J. Brill.
1989 [1952]. *Poro and Mask: A Few Comments on Masks as Agents of Social Control by G. W. Harley.* Gent: State University of Ghent, Department of Ethnic Art.

Village of Déoulé
1988. "Fête des Ignames (Yahabö) à Déoulé du 30 mars au 04 avril 1988." Published by the village of Déoulé, Côte d'Ivoire.

Wach, Joachim
1944. *Sociology of Religion.* Chicago: University of Chicago Press.

Waterman, Christopher A.
1990a. *Juju: A Social History of an African Popular Music.* Chicago: University of Chicago Press.
1990b. " 'Our Tradition is a Very Modern Tradition': Popular Music and the Construction of a Pan-Yoruba Identity." *Ethnomusicology* 34, no. 3: 367–379.
1995. "Fuji Music Video and the Production of Celebrity in Contemporary Yoruba Society." Lecture at Indiana University, November 8.

Weil, Peter
1988. "Fighting Fire with Fire: The Mandinka *Sengko* Mask." In *West African Masks and Cultural Systems,* ed. Sidney L. Kasfir, pp. 151–194. Tervuren: Musée Royale de L'Afrique Centrale.

Wondji, Christophe
1983. "Chanson et Culture Populaire en Côte d'Ivoire." *Kasa Bya Kasa* 4.

Wooten, Stephen
2000a. "Antelope Headdresses and Champion Farmers: Negotiating Meaning and Identity through the Bamana Ciwara Complex." *African Arts* 33, no. 2: 19–33, 89–90.
2000b. "Traditionally Modern: Toward an Understanding of the Ciwara Complex in a Contemporary Context." Paper presented at the Forty-third Annual Meeting of the African Studies Association, November 17, Nashville, Tenn.

Yacoob, May
1987. "Ahmadiyya and Urbanization: Easing the Integration of Rural Women in Abidjan." In *Rural and Urban Islam in West Africa,* ed. Nehemia Levtzion and Humphrey J. Fisher. Boulder, Colo.: Rennier Publishers.

Zaclo group
1997. Interview with the author, Déoulé, Côte d'Ivoire, August 28 (DR97C50). Principal interviewees: Gogueu Ze, Gueu Pascale, Gogueu Pacome, Siamade David, Mahoua Auguste, and Gbonegue Felix.

Zemp, Hugo
1964. "Musiciens Autochtones et Griots Malinké chez les Dan de Côte d'Ivoire." *Cahiers d'Etudes Africaines* 24, no. 6: 370–382.
1965. "Eine esoterische Überlieferung über den Ursprung der maskierten Stelzentänzer bei den Dan (Elfenbeinküste)." In *Festschrift Alfred Bühler,* ed. Carl M. Schmitz, pp. 451–466. Basel: Pharos Verlag.

1971. *Musique Dan: La Musique dans la Pensée et la Vie Sociale d'une Société Afri-caine.* Paris: Cahiers de l'Homme.

1993 [1969]. Liner notes to *Masques Dan.* Paris: Ocora OCR 52.

Zinsou, Jean-Vincent

1976. "L'Expansion des Missions Catholiques en Côte d'Ivoire Coloniale: Des Origines au Milieu du XXe Siècle." *Godo Goyo* 2 (July): 47–78.

Zio Moussa

1997. "Masque et Mascarade." Editorial in *Fraternité-Matin,* 8 avril, p. 5.

Zogueu Anatole and Ve Kafine

1997. Interview with the author, Déoulé, Côte d'Ivoire, August 29 (DR97C51-2).

INDEX

Page numbers in italics refer to illustrations.

Abidjan, Côte d'Ivoire, 38, 39, 161
Adams, Monni, 184n11, 189n23
Adépo Yapo, 5, 31
agency. *See* identity; representation
Amso Edomtchi, xviii–xix, 157–70, 172,
    193n1(2)
ancestors (*bɛmannu*): blessings for, 80; fluidity
    of the ancestral realm, 92–93; forms of, 74–
    75, 188n17; *genu* relation to, 55, 75, 82, 84,
    111–12; sacrifices made by, 74
Appadurai, Arjun, 35
Arens, William W., 190n28
Arnoldi, Mary Jo, 190n33
Avorgbedor, Daniel, 34–35

Bamana peoples, 64, 182n8, 190n33
Barber, Karin, 11, 34, 64–65, 182n12, 186–
    87n9
Bassa peoples, 36
Bauman, Richard, 107, 181n3
Bedie, Henri Konan, 56, 58, 79, 110
Ben-Amos, Dan, 106, 191n5
bɛmannu. See ancestors
biansëge (racing *ge*), 119–20, 123, 192n3
Biélé, Côte d'Ivoire, 42, 43, 94, 95–96, 105,
    115
Biemi Gba Jacques: on ancestor sacrifices, 74;
    biography of, xvii, 190n35; on Dan gender
    relations, 94–95; on Dan initiation, 94–98,
    172; on Dan religious views, 43, 53, 99–100;
    on the function of the *dɔɔga*, 135; on Ge
    musical genres, 105–106; as research consul-
    tant, 5–6, 9, 160, 161–62, 171; role in Ge
    performance, *5;* on the visual aspect of Ge
    performance, 89
Blakely, Thomas D., 70–71
Bleu Tiemoko, 74
Bravmann, Rene A., 42
Breckenridge, Carol A., 35
Briggs, Charles, 107, 181n3
ɓaaɗe (master drum), 20, 121–23, 131–33,
    191n14, 192n4
ɓaanëyakwade (accompanying drum): construc-
    tion of, 131–33; origin of term, 192n2,
    192n4; rhythmic patterns for, 136–41, *137,
    138, 140,* 142–43
ɓɔɗɛ (sacred gifts), 74

Charry, Eric, 64
Chernoff, John, 181n2, 190n32, 192n1

Christianity: Christian views of Ge, 155, 157–
    59, 169; Dan acceptance of, 44–45, 97–100;
    treatment in Ge performance, 28, 111–12,
    166
Ciekawy, Diane, 193n6
circumcision (*gbannë*), 33, 81, 93–94
colonialism, 37–39, 185n7, 185n9
Comaroff, Jean, 13
Comaroff, John, 13
commemoration, 193n9
community, 11–12, 70, 109–10
context, 28, 62, 112–15
Coplan, David, 183n17
Côte d'Ivoire: civil war, ix; colonial period, 37–
    39, 185nn7,9; Danané region, 188–89n18;
    government and service sector, 35; map of,
    xxii; mask as national symbol, 55–56, 150,
    184n1; sorcery laws, 157–59, 193nn2,5;
    Touba region, 18–19, 37
Courrèges, Georges, 187n3
creolization, 2–3, 11, 64–66, 186n8

Dan peoples: alternative names for, xiii–xiv;
    cosmopolitan qualities of, 32–33, 184–85n3;
    Danané region subgroup, 188–89n18; Ge as
    essence of, 93; gender relations of, 33, 90–
    91, 94–95, 125, 190n31; personal name
    forms of, xiii; "pleu" component of place
    names, 185n8; political life, 34, 47; religious
    affiliations of, 41–44, 49–53; rural vs. urban
    life, 32–34; settlement/mobility patterns of,
    36–40, 185n9, 190n35, 191n8
dance: *ɓaagen* (drum's feet), 145–46; by Geg-
    badë, 26; intertextuality in, 2, 28–29, 55, 56–
    57, 60–62; *kë* word root, 104, 191n2; use of
    popular movements, 57; *zaouli,* 61–63, 155.
    See also getan (*ge* music and dance); *tankë
    ge*
death. *See* ancestors (*bɛmannu*); funerals
Déoulé, Côte d'Ivoire: communal qualities of,
    151; ethnicity in, 116; languages used in,
    189n21; Mameri compound manifestation,
    87–88; religious groups in, 96–97; singing
    style in, 191n11; Yam Festival, 91, 110, 113,
    118
dɛɓo ge (consultation *ge*), 82
dɛn ge (initiation *ge*), 33, 81
di-pi-tin rhythm, 131, 135, 138, *138,* 140–42,
    141, 142
Dida peoples, 38, 158, 164–65

Daniel B. Reed is Director of the Archives of Traditional Music and Assistant Professor of Folklore and Ethnomusicology at Indiana University, Bloomington. He is co-author (with Gloria J. Gibson) of *Music and Culture in West Africa: The Straus Expedition* (a CD-ROM).

A Web site featuring excerpts of audio and video field recordings and additional photographs relevant to this text can be found at http://iupress.indiana.edu/reed/.